THIS PERVASIVE DAY
The Potential and Perils of Pervasive Computing

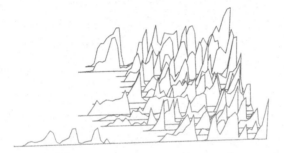

THIS PERVASIVE DAY

The Potential and Perils of Pervasive Computing

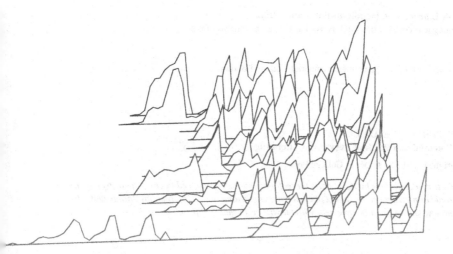

Edited by

Jeremy Pitt

Imperial College London, UK

Imperial College Press

ICP

Published by

Imperial College Press
57 Shelton Street
Covent Garden
London WC2H 9HE

Distributed by

World Scientific Publishing Co. Pte. Ltd.
5 Toh Tuck Link, Singapore 596224
USA office: 27 Warren Street, Suite 401-402, Hackensack, NJ 07601
UK office: 57 Shelton Street, Covent Garden, London WC2H 9HE

British Library Cataloguing-in-Publication Data
A catalogue record for this book is available from the British Library.

Cover design by Julia Schaumeier, Imperial College London.

THIS PERVASIVE DAY
The Potential and Perils of Pervasive Computing

ISBN-13 978-1-84816-748-3
ISBN-10 1-84816-748-2

Printed by FuIsland Offset Printing (S) Pte Ltd Singapore

Preface

Christ, Marx, Wood, and Wei
Led us to this perfect day.
Marx, Wood, Wei, and Christ;
All but Wei were sacrificed.
Wood, Wei, Christ, and Marx
Gave us lovely schools and parks.
Wei, Christ, Marx, and Wood,
Made us humble, made us good.

–child's rhyme for bouncing a ball

THIS PERFECT DAY, P. 5

How It All Began
The dry story: In 2008, The European Union's Future and Emerging Technologies (FET) programme launched a proactive research initiative into *Pervasive Adaptation*. One of the projects funded under that initiative was the Coordination Action *Panorama*. One of the partners in that Coordination Action was Imperial College London. One of the responsibilities of that partner was to lead the workpackage on Public Dissemination, to bring the emerging technology of pervasive and adaptive computing to the attention of a wider audience, in particular EU citizens. One of the deliverables of that workpackage was a 'popular science' book, exploring and explaining those pervasive computing technologies.

This is that book.

How It (Really) All Began
The personal story: My mother gave me her copy of Ira Levin's 1970 novel *This Perfect Day* to read. She also lent it to my brother. It became some-

v

thing of a family book, and the original copy something of a bone of contention, though I have conceded the argument since I started looking after,
in perpetuity, Mr Haldane's First Edition. (As an aside, with the exception
of the one following, all quotations, section and chapter epigraphs are taken
from this 1970 hardback first edition: Ira Levin, 1970, *This Perfect Day*.
New York: Random House.)

This Perfect Day is, by Wikipedia's description, a 'heroic science fiction
novel of a technocratic utopia'; or, by the description on the back cover of
the 1971 paperback edition (New York: Fawcett Crest):

> *Tomorrow's world is a place where computers rule, where
> monthly treatments keep people docile, where sex is pro-
> grammed weekly, and where death occurs at the age of sixty-
> two in the interest of efficiency ...*
>
> This Perfect Day *is the story of a citizen of the future
> in conflict with a world of nightmare ...*
>
> (This Perfect Day, back cover)

Now read on, as they say. (Don't read any more of the wiki page, it contains
spoilers. One thing we have tried to do in this book, although there are
hints, is to *not* give anything away.)

Anyway, the novel had a profound influence on me, as it does on most
people who read it, and I have re-read it many times. The social questions
it raises are timeless, and at its heart there is a rather good story, very
well told. The content and the themes stayed with me ever since, even
after many years as a computing and information technology professional,
until the *Panorama* Coordination Action gave me the opportunity to do
something I'd been thinking about for a very long time: to work on a book
that evaluated the advances in computing technology and the society in
which we live against the fictional description of the computer antihero and
the utopian society described in the novel. In particular, I had in mind a
book that explored the potential of the remarkable advances in computing
since the novel was written, and the ways in which it can be used, either
to make life wonderful, or to make life unbearable.

This is *that* book ...

Dramatis Personae, 'Glossary'

You do *not* need to have read the novel to appreciate the important informative message of this book (although, if you have not read it, you have
deprived yourself of one of life's small joys; but the novel was re-printed in

2010 and you don't have to continue depriving yourself any more).

While the most pertinent features of the 'technocratic utopia' are described in Chapter 1, along with an analysis of the computing and communication technology used to implement 'the place where computers rule', the following 'glossary' is enough to familiarise the reader with the terms of reference of the novel:

Li RM35M4419 ('Chip'): the main protagonist of the novel.

Anna SG38P2823 ('Lilac'): the love interest.

King, Snowflake, Dover, Papa Jan, Julia: other minor characters.

Uni, UniComp: the 'bad guy', the omnipotent, omniscient computer in charge of all personal and social decision-making.

Family, The: everyone on the planet belongs to one big family.

Adviser: personal counsellor and confessional; everybody has one.

Telecomp, comptroller: portable computer, used by advisers to connect wirelessly to UniComp, uses keyboard or voice input.

Classification: the job description that people are assigned to. Adviser is an example of a classification. Chip is a geneticist.

Treatment: a cocktail of chemotherapeutic drugs administered monthly.

Nameber: Each family member has a name, of which there are four for boys (Li, Jesus, Karl, Bob) and four for girls (Anna, Mary, Peace, Yin), and an alphanumeric string (e.g. SG38P2823), making a nameber.

Bracelet: worn by each member of The Family, with their nameber inscribed on it.

Scanner: ubiquitous sensor device for requesting permission to access resources, locations, etc. by touching the scanner with the bracelet.

Coveralls: identical, unisex, functional clothing with only minor variations (e.g. a red cross for medical staff).

Totalcakes, cokes: identical (Mc)food consumed at every meal.

Sounds marvellous, doesn't it? Now look out of the window. No bracelets around wrists, but mobile phones clamped to ears, recording GPS data continuously, without, until recently, our knowledge (thanks, Steve). No scanners, but if you have the (mis)fortune to live in London, CCTV cameras everywhere. Access control through radio-frequency identification (RFID) tags embedded in identity cards for travel, work, and so on. A wander around my neighbourhood reveals some restaurants without yellow arches, so there is some variation in the food still. It also reveals several yellow signs saying 'Did you see this murder?', so in London, at least, we're still cheerfully stabbing each other, implying we're not one big happy family either ... Well, you get the point. You can compare the novel's vision and your own experience, and see which is a feature of our world and which is not. This is what this book aims to do, but with the computer technology, by evaluating that technology in its socio-technical context, in the novel and in reality.

Summary

I have six fond hopes for this book. Firstly, that the interested reader will find the contributed chapters as interesting, informative, engaging, insightful and – yes – as provocative as I did. Imagine yourself in a great socio-technological bazaar and, for a few hours or more, marvel and potter as I did, and I'm sure you'll confirm there is something of surpassing interest in every chapter.

Secondly, I hope that anyone who has *not* read *This Perfect Day* and, having read our book, afterwards reads the novel and gets as much enjoyment out of it as I did (indeed I envy you the pleasures to come). Thirdly, that anyone who has *already* read *This Perfect Day* and, having read our book, will remember what a stunning literary achievement that novel was, and how well it has withstood the test of time. Fourthly, having at least read our book, that technologists and computer engineers take social responsibility for their inventions and designs; that policy-makers use evidence-based policy-making when using technology to formulate solutions to social problems; and that citizens everywhere put pressure on scientists and politicians to behave this way. It can be a perfect day, but let's make sure that it is on *our* terms.

Fifthly, I'd like to think that, if he read this book, Ira Levin would approve. And finally, I hope my mum likes it. It is a small way of saying 'thank you' for the kindness of giving me the novel to read in the first place, and much much more besides.

Jeremy Pitt
London, December 2011

Acknowledgements

"Thanks. Thanks very much. Thank Julia too."

THIS PERFECT DAY, P. 237

Authors' Acknowledgements

Ricardo Chavarriaga and José del R. Millán — This work has been supported by the EU Future and Emerging Technologies (FET) project 'OPPORTUNITY: Activity and Context Recognition with Opportunistic Sensor Configurations' (FP7- 225938).

Gualtiero Colombo *et al.* — This research was funded by SOCIALNETS grant 217141, an EC-FP7 Future Emerging Technologies project funded under the Pervasive Adaptation proactive initiative.

Simon Dobson — This research was supported under the FP7 ICT Future Enabling Technologies programme of the European Commission under grant agreement No 256873 (SAPERE).

Joan Farrer — For debate and tenacity, many thanks to Angela Finn, PhD student, Queensland University of Technology, Brisbane, Australia; and for vision and generosity, many thanks to Catherine Harper, Head of School, University of Brighton, UK.

Alois Ferscha — This work was supported by the FP7 ICT Future Enabling Technologies programme of the European Commission under grant agreement No 256873 (SAPERE), and by the FFG Research Studios Austria programme under grant agreement No 818652 'Pervasive Display Systems' (DISPLAYS).

Janis Jefferies — Many thanks to Professor Barbara Layne and her wonderful team at Hexagram, Concordia University, Montreal. http://subtela.hexagram.ca/.

Katina Michael and M.G. Michael — Particular thanks to the case study interviewees: Gary Retherford (United States) and Serafin Vilaplana (Spain).

Paul Mitcheson — This work was partially supported by the Engineering and Physical Sciences Research Council (EPSRC), under grant number EP/G070180/1, 'Next Generation Energy-Harvesting Electronics: Holistic Approach', website: www.holistic.ecs.soton.ac.uk.

Nikola Šerbedžija — Many of the ideas and results presented in this chapter have been developed under the REFLECT project (project number FP7-215893; http://reflect.pst.ifi.lmu.de/), funded by the European Commission within the 7th Framework Programme, Pervasive Adaptation proactive initiative. The author acknowledges numerous constructive discussions with other members of the reflect team who contributed in the development of the concepts described here.

Jenny Tillotson — Special thanks to Marc Rolland for introducing me to science fiction and inspiring my science fashion story.

Ken Wahren — Thanks to Yoge Patel, Phill Smith and Ian Cowling at Blue Bear Systems Research Ltd., and the Royal Commission for the Exhibition of 1851 Industrial Fellowship, for the opportunity to study for a PhD at Imperial College London.

Editor's Acknowledgements

I would like to thank Lance Sucharov (Commissioning Editor) and Tasha D'Cruz (Assistant Editor) at Imperial College Press, for their support for this project; in particular, thanks to Tasha for her patience, indulgence and good sense as it lurched towards the finishing line and I got picky about photos.

Special thanks is due to Ben Paechter, Emma Hart, Jennifer Willies, Callum Egan and Ingi Helgason at Edinburgh Napier University, the coordinating partner of the *Panorama* Coordination Action. I'm very grateful to Ben for inviting me to join the *Panorama* consortium and giving me this opportunity, Emma for managing the project so effectively, Callum for the excellent website and other design work, and Ingi for shouldering the Showcase load when the editing got really stressful, but I'm especially grateful to Jennifer, whose remarkable contextualising and coordination skills led us to, well, about as perfect a project as you're likely to get.

I apologise to Jennifer who was occasionally forced to play 'bad cop' to my 'spineless cop' when the chapter deadlines loomed, and I'm deeply appreciative of the efforts of all the contributing authors who responded to the challenge with enthusiasm, great humour and excellent content, and without whom this book would be literally nothing.

Sound programme management is essential to achieving good research outcomes and for this *Panorama* had the good fortune to have Wide Hougenhout, of the FP7 FET Unit, as its Project Officer, and many thanks to him, the FET Unit, and the Project Reviewers, whose encouragement and positive feedback was especially helpful.

I'd also like to thank the participants and contributors at the authors' workshops in London and Berlin, in particular Hugo Carr, Pedro Costa, David Sanderson and Julia Schaumeier for their helpful participation in the volcano-affected Writers' Workshop in London.

Finally, there is an outstanding debt of gratitude for the editorial assistance of Julia, who received insufficient confectionery reward in return for her LaTeX expertise, chapter commentaries, and a contribution way beyond what could reasonably be expected to the editing and typesetting. Quite probably, without her attention to detail and slightly disturbing but nevertheless encyclopaedic knowledge of the Imperial College Style Guide, Tasha would still be waiting for the book and I would be single-handedly keeping the chemotherapists in gainful employment. Needless to say, the responsibility for any remaining errors in the text are hers. I mean mine.

Contents

3. Brain–Computer Interfaces   37

Ricardo Chavarriaga and José del R. Millán

4. live scent | ɘvil stench   53

Jenny Tillotson

5. Reflective Computing – Naturally Artificial   69

Nikola Šerbedžija

Chapter 1

Introduction: This Pervasive Day

Jeremy Pitt

Imperial College London

> *"It must be true," Lilac said. "It's the final logical end of Wood's and Wei's thinking. Control everyone's life and you eventually get around to controlling everyone's death."*

THIS PERFECT DAY, P. 116

1.1 Levin's Legacy

The genre of science fiction, as an extrapolation into the future, is often rooted in the fears of its present. In the Western Bloc during the Cold War in the 1970s, these fears included nuclear holocaust, communist hegemony, and technophobia, in particular chemistry, genetics and information technology.

This Perfect Day, a science fiction novel by Ira Levin (1970), imagined a (supposedly) utopian global society governed by a single computer called UniComp (in a comput-opoly?, a comput-archy?). Similar to other science fiction novels, this particular vision avoided apocalyptic nuclear conflict, but touched a number of socio-technical nerves, or possibly aspirations, of the time, including the following concerns: the potential of computers or robots to be 'smarter' or 'better' than people; manned planetary exploration and settlement; planned economies producing social, political and cultural conformity; the use of chemicals to control individual emotion, contentment, wellbeing, and even death; uniformity of food production and consumption; genetic manipulation; and that the Chinese 'win'.

Of these seven concerns, writing in 1969–70 at the start of the US Apollo space programme, and despite the achievements of the space shuttle flight and unmanned planetary probes, only the manned exploration of the solar system seems hardly to have advanced in 40 years.

With respect to the final five concerns, one might argue that it is the victory of the market economy, combined with the rise of multi-national corporations and the pressure of globalisation, that is suppressing individualism at personal, communal and national levels. Furthermore, the scale of consumption of anti-depressants, painkillers and other chemically-engineered products of 'big pharma' has created a society that is increasingly dependent on drugs, with corresponding increases in health and social problems. Similarly, the global industrialisation of the food chain, the prevalence of processed food, and the ubiquitous brand recognition achieved by certain soft drinks and fast food suppliers, have gone some considerable distance to homogenising food production and consumption. This is not always a force for good – consider the rise of obesity in affluent countries and the still unequal distribution of food in the supposed 'third world'. In connection with this, genetically-modified food has created a debate concerning its potential benefits (disease and pest resistance, as well as tolerance to extreme conditions, leading to increased food production) as opposed to the environmental impact and long-term health effects, and the interaction of the law of intellectual property rights and the food chain. This debate has ensued, and is ongoing, even before the arguments over the potential impact of full genome sequencing have been fully explored, discussed and understood. Finally, the geopolitical significance and increasing economic ascendency of China is a necessary factor to consider in any economic or diplomatic policy debate.

Therefore, it is not only of academic interest whether or not the social, political and/or environmental developments of the last 40 years render Levin's vision of a futuristic society plausible or even desirable; but it is also reasonable, timely and important to have a debate about the *impact* of globalisation, industrialisation, pharmaceuticals, genetics and technology on the trajectory of the society in which we actually live, as it relates to the society described in the novel.

The primary target of *this* book is to address the first of these concerns: the potential impact of information and communications technology on society, up to and including the rule and direction of humanity by a computer. There are two questions to consider. The first question is: is it feasible? Would it be possible to build and program a computer to fulfil the functionality attributed to it in Levin's book? This is the ostensible purpose of this introductory chapter. The second question is deeper. It asks that even if it were feasible to build such a computer, the society it rules is not inevitable or unavoidable; so what, then, is the potential for – and perils of – the necessary computing and communications technology for actual human society as we experience it in 2011, from a social, legal, ethical, political and/or economic viewpoint?

We will address these questions in the following order. To begin with, we will review the essential aspects of the society in *This Perfect Day*. Then, we will address the first question, and examine the computer and communications technology as it is represented by the antihero of *This Perfect Day*, the UniComp computer, in comparison to the advances made since the book was written. Finally, we will set up the second question, by considering the potential and perils of *This Pervasive Day*, and then hand over to the contributors to provide the answer, or an answer, to this question in their chapters.

1.2 This Perfect Day

In *This Perfect Day*, Ira Levin described a quasi-utopian society of completely contented people. There are no nations, everyone is one 'Family'. There are no individuals, and there are just eight names, four for boys and four for girls, and any other identification is by a nine-character alphanumeric 'nameber'. Choosing is frowned upon as an act of selfishness. Everyone looks the same, male and female, and everyone enjoys a communal living, with enough to satisfy the lower levels of Maslow's hierarchy of needs (Maslow, 1943), for example: physiological, there are set sleep hours; everyone has a boyfriend or a girlfriend, with whom they have sex once a week, on Saturday nights; and there are 'totalcakes' to eat and 'cokes' to drink at communal meals; clothing, everyone wears 'coveralls', which are almost completely identical; security, in terms of personal safety (no wars and no crime – indeed, 'hate' and 'fight' are swear words in this society), and no need to make 'selfish' (i.e. personal) decisions; employment, everyone has a job (a 'classification'), to which they are assigned and which they all profess to enjoy; health, not just doctors but they also have counsellors, called 'advisers'; and love, forgiveness and belonging, from their friends, immediate family, and the simple fact that they belong to just the one 'Family'.

For this basic level of satisfaction, the members of the Family have to 'Thank Uni'; the ritual dialogue of exchange is not 'thank you' – 'you're welcome', but 'thank you' – 'thank Uni'. UniComp (or just Uni) is a super-computer which controls almost every aspect of everyone's life: who gets assigned to which job, who gets to travel where, who gets access to which resources. Interaction with UniComp is either through scanners, against which people place bracelets displaying their namebers, or by using wire-less computers called 'telecomps' (or 'comptrollers'). It turns out, of course, that Uni is controlling more than just this: it decides who lives and who dies (people die of 'old age' at 62, more or less), and suppresses the higher end of Maslow's needs, in particular self-esteem and self-actualisation. This control is effected by the ruthless administration of chemotherapeutic drugs in regular 'treatments' which vastly diminish the 'human' capacity to think, feel, create, criticise or indeed act as anything much other than sheep, or cogs in the machine.

So far, just another science fiction dystopia, but it is also one of the finest in its genre and it compares favourably with *Nineteen Eighty-Four* (Orwell, 1949) and *Brave New World* (Huxley, 1932). It is part social commentary, part action thriller and part simple romance, with any number of twists. However, the advantage of science fiction as a genre is that it can not only be used to tell a good story, but also that *alternative* societies and cultures can be portrayed via the futuristic conceit, usually as a metaphor for exploring concerns of *present* societies. So, there was a strong element of Cold War concerns about the suppression of individuality, sexuality and culture, and the compulsion for passivity, conformity and compliance in Levin's quasi-utopian society. For this reason, males and females were presented as physically identical, men and women wore the same unisex clothing (i.e. the 'coveralls'), and there were only eight names, and so on. Furthermore, passivity was culturally pre-determined by the use of language (i.e. 'fight' and 'hate' were swear words, while certain other four letter 'f-words' were entirely acceptable), and recreative sex was entirely open but reduced to once-a-week functional and perfunctory Saturday night routine. All this was reinforced through rote education, chemical treatment and advisory supervision.

Forty years later, these same concerns remain at the heart of sexual, racial, cultural and generational discrimination and diversity within societies, along with the uneasy tension between the individual and the state across almost all societies, and the growing concern of how people and cultures themselves are almost being 're-defined' by ubiquitous computing, continuous visual stimulation and entertainment. Using hindsight, we must remember that the purpose of Levin's book was to engage in a satirical social commentary and a critique of contemporary issues; he wasn't concerned with actually trying to predict the future. So when, in the next section, we compare the computer science, information technology and interaction affordances of UniComp to the state of the art at the time of this volume (2011), it is not to evaluate if the fiction turned out to be right or wrong, but to see where we are now, and to expose how the technology relates to the social issues raised by Levin.

1.3   UniComp, Revisited

The main protagonist of the novel, Chip, is taken on a visit to Uni:

> *The voice of the elevator spoke in his ears, telling him, while the lights showed him, how UniComp received from its round-the-world relay belt the microwave impulses of all the uncountable scanners and telecomps and telecontrolled devices; how it evaluated the impulses and sent back its answering impulses to the relay belt and the sources of inquiry.*
>
> *Yes, he was excited.   Was anything quicker, more clever, more everywhere than Uni?*
>
> (This Perfect Day, pp. 24–25)

As we stressed above, the objective of this section is not to critique or evaluate the science and technology behind UniComp. Instead, we will first consider the basic issue of the feasibility of constructing such a computer, its peripherals and the necessary communications network. Then we will review advances in human–computer interaction, the computing infrastructure, and the potential functionality of such a system. This review will reveal that the technology has advanced much further than Levin could possibly have imagined.

1.3.1 *Construction*

Considering the time of publication (1970), and in relation to the quotation
at the start of this section, the following landmarks in the history of computer networking are worth noting. In the 1950s, long distance telephone
calls within the United States were usually carried by microwave radio relay
links. The Internet timeline indicates that by 1970 there were five nodes
in the ArpaNet (the forerunner of the Internet) and that the first packet
radio network, AlohaNet, was in use in 1970. Only in 1972 were the two
networks joined together. Wireless LAN protocols, for example Bluetooth,
use microwaves in the 24GHz band, while Metropolitan Area Networks,
for example WiMAX, use the 2–11GHz range. In December 2008, it was
reckoned that there were 4 billion mobile phones worldwide; the number of
embedded microprocessors, by any definition of the term, is literally 'un-
countable'. Google (not the only search engine) responds to a minimum of
10,000 searches a second and, while response times are dependent on many
factors, it is not often a problem.[1]

Although Levin was unable to predict either the invention of fibreoptics
or the proliferation of the microprocessor, the global networking infrastructure and response times of the book are safely achievable today. In his
fictional world, Levin is necessarily terse about the genesis and evolution of
his perfect society, and the computer which controls it. The text hints at a
time when there were five computers, one for each continent, and measures
time from 'unification', when all five computers were replaced by a single
computer, i.e. UniComp. The brief description of the machine room described Uni as occupying two levels, each of 1,240 'mammoth steel blocks'.

In the 'real' world, Google operates a warehouse-sized computer (server
farm) in a building which offers approximately 100,000 square feet of data
centre space. Depending on the type of servers and applications, a typically-
sized rack can contain between 10 and 80 computing nodes, and between
20 and 60 racks can be aggregated into a power distribution unit. With a
footprint of approximately 11 square feet, 100,000 square feet of floor-space
is sufficient to contain about 10,000 racks, and so about 2,500 such units.
If each of Uni's 'mammoth steel blocks' equated to a power distribution
unit, then on a rough approximation we can conclude that it is physically
possible to build a UniComp-sized computer.

---

[1]Ironically, while researching this chapter, I searched Google for 'google response times
and the page returned 'Results 1–10 of ... (1.32 times the velocity of a laden swallow).'
Search was conducted on an April 1st (All Fools' Day).

However, given the energy requirement for running a data centre which normally presents a 50% energy overhead for cooling, one of the main physical problems of a warehouse-sized computer is the power provisioning (Uni is given a nuclear reactor or two as its source). Levin does mention refrigeration – the fictional computer required near-zero temperatures for superconductivity, a theoretically fast way of circuit switching but not yet used in any real commercial computer – but this does make the decision to situate Uni *under* a mountain not, perhaps, such a smart idea.

Nevertheless, superficially, the basic construction of Uni – wireless access devices, global internet, central supercomputer – was a reasonable extrapolation of the technology of the time, and the basic properties of speed and capacity (in terms of bandwidth, numbers of connected devices, raw computing power) have been met by contemporary technology. In the rest of this section, we address, in turn, the issues of interactivity, functionality and infrastructure, with respect to the other properties of 'more everywhere' and 'more clever'. Moreover, we consider how, if we had built Uni, we could interact with it.

1.3.2 *Interaction*

The book mentions the following three forms of human–computer interaction (HCI), or data input. Firstly, each person wears a bracelet with his or her nameber. They have to hold the bracelet to a scanner which flashes green for 'yes' or red for 'no' for any decision. This could be access to a building or a room within it, boarding a plane, having a toy, making a phone call (all examples from the novel) and so on. Secondly, the advisers – but no-one else – have portable wireless devices (i.e. 'telecomps'), which use keyboards (with 'a dozen black keys') to enter data. There is a reference to voice-input telecomps replacing key-input ones, as a sign of technical progress made in six or seven years. Thirdly, there is one instance where a member speaks another's nameber into a phone in order to call him.

Considering each of these in turn, the bracelet/scanner combination seems plausible. The state of the art in optical character recognition (OCR) technology is such that, in principle, it should not be hard to 'read' the nine character identifier of the nameber, irrespective of the angle at which it was presented (given control over font, size, etc.). In fact, the limitation here was to not consider the possibilities of miniaturisation and the instrumentation of the bracelet itself. If it was necessary to implement such a scheme in 2011, radio-frequency identification (RFID) tags, embedded in the bracelet itself, would be used. Then some form of access control system, as often used in city transit systems, could be implemented. The advantage is that the RFID tag on the bracelet can be used to store data, and then localised processing (i.e. located in the scanner, or a 'nearby' computer) could decide yes/no, rather than needing to consult a single central computer directly over every decision (although, as with Oyster Cards in the London transit system, the scanner (card-reader) intermittently updates a central database).

On the other hand, the ideas that the keyboard or microphone are the sole input mechanism for the computational devices, with text and speech as the only signalling systems used for communicating information, and the restricted use of wireless devices to a segment of the population (nowadays, people carry multiple micro-processors with them), are extremely limited. This of course turns out to be far from what is actually possible, for example using scent, emotions, gesture recognition, facial recognition and even neural activity (brain signals).

1.3.3 *Functionality*

As indicated above, one 'scary' aspect of the book, for a 1970s US and West European audience, preyed on the Cold War-generated fear of a soviet-style planned economy and surveillance society taken to an extreme. Thus, UniComp made every decision, in particular job assignments: for example, as a teenager, Chip is told by his adviser, on discovering that Chip is thinking about his own 'classification':

> *You've been given hundreds of tests since your first day of school, and UniComp's been fed the results of every last one of them. You've had hundreds of adviser meetings, and UniComp knows about those too. It knows what jobs have to be done and who there is to do them. It knows everything. Now who's going to make the better, more efficient, classification, you or UniComp?*
>
> (This Perfect Day, p. 42)

Traditional computing models store data and retrospectively analyse it. In 2009, IBM proposed a new computing model, called stream computing, which analyses data in real-time, to provide what is called *perpetual analytics*. IBM describe the technology as 'using computers to rapidly analyse multiple streams of diverse, unstructured and incompatible data sources in real time, enabling very fast, accurate and insightful decisions'. It is not therefore unreasonable to suppose that the combination of both retrospective and stream analysis could provide the planning and logistical functions ascribed to Uni.

In another case, Chip is denied a toy because previously he had been 'teasing a scanner'. The iCars exhibition (Pitt and Bhusate, 2010) uses a sensor-saturated environment to infer high-level behaviours from patterns of 'low-level' actions and signals to affect usage policies of interactive exhibits. These policies include a formal expression of permissions, namely who is allowed to do what to which object; so, in one sense, this functionality already exists. More generally, other functions could be implemented, although, as mentioned previously, the computing model would more likely use distributed computing techniques rather than centralised ones.

Therefore, what could not have been foreseen, but should not be underestimated, are the following three developments. Firstly, stream computing, which makes 'real-time' event recognition possible, and there are algorithms which add semantics to events, so that we can move from event recognition to complex event or situation recognition. Secondly, cloud computing, which makes shared computing resources available 'on demand', but means that 'your' data, once stored on your own hard drive, is now stored on someone else's hard drive – and, crucially, owned by them. Thirdly, ubiquitous computing, which creates electronically-saturated physical environments. The convergence of stream, cloud and ubiquitous computing provides an apparent single point of access for all an individual's computing needs at the time and place of demand. However, from the software engineering perspective, the hardest part of converging ubiquitous, stream and cloud computing, and of ensuring service interoperability, security, maintainability, availability and other non-functional requirements, is the job of the systems architect, i.e. the limiting factor is human design capability and ingenuity, not the software or hardware.

Despite the missed opportunities of ubiquitous computing described in the book, and the fact that service delivery is given better by the cloud computing paradigm than the mainframe or client-server paradigms, the real issue in delivering functionality is not so much the physical engineering but the abstract systems architecture and the computer science behind service interoperability. These are the essential foundations for using the full, rich range of signals described above to develop an entirely new sociotechnical functionality in healthcare, transport, education, sustainability, and social networking.

1.3.4 *Infrastructure*

The key point of the previous discussion is that the minimal, 'traditional' style of interaction described in the book could be achieved: indeed, it is actually possible to go well beyond it with current technology. Furthermore, the functions supported by UniComp could be implemented, and it is possible to deliver analytics and logistics, health and education, on a local and a global scale, in short and long-term time-scales.

In addition, there are various other aspects of *infrastructure*, in particular communication *channels*, which were not anticipated in the book. This includes firstly that advances in camera technology, image processing and data storage have made possible surveillance and identification techniques, using biometrics, of a far more sophisticated capability. Secondly, it includes microprocessor miniaturisation, which, coupled with advances in surgical techniques, has made it possible to implant microchips in the human body. This same miniaturisation has made possible sensors and sensor networks which differ in scale, form and measurement from simple optical scanners. Thirdly, at the other end of the scale, satellite technology, timing and the portability of devices has made tracking an individual's location potentially continuous and highly accurate. However, given the number of devices in operation, there is a fundamental issue in keeping everything powered.

The consequence of this is that human–computer interaction is no longer just a conscious action, but a continuous activity and even possibly unintended – what Alois Ferscha (Chapter 2) calls *implicit interaction*. If the sensors are embedded in your clothing (wearable computing, where clothing, shoes or jewellery provide the interface), or implanted under the skin (such that the *body* is the interface), then there is no switching off, or even opting out. The logical extrapolation of this is that an individual is never off-line, can be uniquely identified, and, if the Internet 'never forgets', there are severe repercussions for the social and cognitive function of memory. Furthermore, there is no necessary requirement for the telecomps not to have a motor system of their own or for the scanners to be static, as advances in robotics have made both interactive mobile terminals (i.e. robots) and mobile surveillance by UAVs, or Unmanned Aerial Vehicles, possible. However, there is a requirement to supply enough power to keep all these new channels open (wearables, implants, robots and UAVs) for communicating signals.

1.4   This Pervasive Day

1.4.1   *Summary*

There are three main conclusions to be drawn from comparison of real computing with the fictional UniComp. Firstly, like all the best science fiction writing, the essential technological basis was accurate for its time, and predictive in its future. It has withstood the test of time and there is nothing far-fetched in the novel concerning the information technology (the starships and 'antigrav gear', as it turns out, remain science fiction). Secondly, in point of fact, there is no reason to suppose that we could not build UniComp today. Thirdly, in point of fact, there is no reason to suppose that we have not *already* built UniComp ...

It is this last point that is the motivation for this book. It is crystal clear that we do *not* understand, appreciate or have fully thought through the social, legal, economic and political implications of the technologies that we are developing and deploying. For example, the convergence of data mining techniques, social networking, location-based tracking and advanced biometrics are all conspiring to have a profound impact on 'the thumb generation' and their understanding of the social construct of 'privacy'. Yet there can be no doubt that it was the proliferation of instant messages through social networking sites that exposed and collapsed the super-injunction (which precludes mentioning that there is even an injunction) in the Trafigura case (Leigh, 2009), which in turn shed light on some of the murkier aspects of UK libel law and political lobbying (see also Colombo *et al.*, Chapter 7). Equally, as Morozov (2011) warns, it is delusional to suppose that social networking is an unstoppable force inevitably advancing democratic ideals and civil liberties, and that autocratic governments can use these methods equally effectively for their own political purposes. Indeed, the message is not lost either on supposedly democratic governments that political control can be achieved by saturation surveillance and superficial entertainment. Hence, one might argue, the proliferation of CCTV in the UK and the infiltration of undercover agents into peaceful and legitimate protest groups on the one hand; cheap beer and easy porn for the boys, salacious gossip and soap operas for the girls on the other; and pseudo-participation Strictly/X-Factor 'reality' TV trash for all.

So there are forces for good as well as gauntlets to be run: the potential and perils of pervasive computing. This book aims to expose (at least some of) them, using *This Perfect Day* as a backdrop to the discussion.

1.4.2   *Chapter overviews*

The structure of this book is as follows. It starts with the idea that ubiquitous or pervasive computing is a reality, that the slogans 'interface as territory' and 'the disappearing computer' have materialised. There is no longer a box, a user, and an interface between them. The environment is the interface, and the user is in the environment; and so the user can also be the interface. It then looks at new signals that can be transmitted through the interface, what new functionality can be created from processing these signals, and the new communication channels that the user-as-interface paradigm provides. The new signals considered are electrical activity in the brain, scent and emotions; the new functions are healthcare, sustainability, and social networking; and the new channels are wearable computing, implants, robots, UAVs. We open with the new model of interaction, and close with the general problem of keeping all the channels powered up.

In more detail, Alois Ferscha (Chapter 2) introduces and discusses this notion of implicit interaction. Human–computer interaction with UniComp was based on conventional forms. This included keyboards for data entry, scanners for access control, and so on. However, the real prospect of pervasive computing means that it is not just what you do that is significant, it is also what you don't do that is potentially significant. While implicit interaction is required to support speculative computation and other forms of pro-active behaviour, there are other implications for how information can be used, at different levels of complexity.

Electroencephalography (EEG), the measurement of electrical activity within the brain, has a number of diagnostic applications. More recently, the measurement and processing of these signals has been proposed for identifying cognitive processes, and so can be leveraged as the basis for *brain–computer interfaces*. Originally intended to support users with impaired physical or cognitive function, Ricardo Chavarriaga and José Millán (Chapter 3) describe the state of the art and consider some applications for *assistive living*.

In *This Perfect Day*, there are no cosmetics (everyone looks the same anyway), and supposedly no artificial fragrances like perfume or after-shave. However, scent has been shown to have a profound effect on mood, physiology and psychological states. Jenny Tillotson (Chapter 4) explains the use of the olfactory system and devices in human–computer interaction, and explores the concept of *scents-on-a-chip*, an invisible nanochip in a future society whose bi-directional functionality allows it to release mood-altering fragrances and sniff the surrounding atmosphere. These sensing devices are already small enough to be embedded in smart sensory clothing, jewellery or other fashion items.

Chemotherapeutic drugs were used in the novel to suppress extreme emotions. The aim of *affective computing* is, on the other hand, to use physiological signals to infer those emotional states. The idea of what Nikola Šerbedžija (Chapter 5) calls *reflective computing* is to use those emotions to adapt the computational environment to the user in an instinctive, unobtrusive and non-explicit manner. On the one hand, this can make future control systems that are friendly, personalised and responsive to the needs of an individual user, but on the other hand there are questions of control, trust and privacy with respect to the ownership of user-generated environment data that need to be addressed.

As part of this user-generated environment data, the recording of physiological signals can be of significant benefit in healthcare applications, as discussed by Simon Dobson and Aaron Quigley (Chapter 6). However, as mentioned above, in the novel characters die at the age of 62, more or less, ostensibly because of old age, in reality for reasons of efficiency, population control and resource management. Clearly the Hippocratic Oath (essentially 'do no harm') was not preserved in the medical profession of Levin's novel. However, a more general aspect of the Hippocratic Oath, that of patient confidentiality ('All that may come to my knowledge in the exercise of my profession or in daily commerce with men, which ought not to be spread abroad, I will keep secret and never reveal.'), is more pertinent to today's society. Indeed, verifying that personal, implicitly-generated data remains private (in some sense) is a common concern in both healthcare and reflective applications.

Pervasive healthcare applications can also be founded on the idea of a mutual support network based on social networking. Levin took the idea of the 'nuclear family' to its logical extremes: from the two-adult two-children family unit at one end, to the entire Family at the other, and nothing in between. However, what we have actually seen is the convergence of Pinker's observation about the evolution of language (Pinker, 1994) in order to satisfy a need to gossip, with global networking instant messaging. This has had its upside, as indicated above through the Internet enabling the *fifth estate* (Dutton, 2009), as well as it downside (cyberbullying, grooming, etc.). Walter Colombo *et al.* (Chapter 7) consider the prospects and outcomes for forming social groups and sharing information inside and outside groups.

Social networking has a profound effect on people's knowledge, opinions and behaviour. Understanding the processes of information diffusion, opinion formation and compliance pervasion in social networks is important in getting people to change that knowledge, and those opinions and behaviours, for example in relation to social movements like climate change, fair trade or sustainability. In *This Perfect Day*, members were expected not to be selfish and use resources wisely. The exponent of this was the coveralls, a functional garment that eschewed fashion and had marginal variations (some medics are described as having coveralls with a red cross on them). Joan Farrer (Chapter 8) reviews a number of ways in which fashion and textiles, in conjunction with mobile and pervasive technologies, can be used to promote the sustainability agenda and stimulate people's engagement with the sustainability issue.

Wearable computing is also a theme of the first chapter in the collection on 'new channels'. Janis Jefferies (Chapter 9) asks the question: could the society of *This Perfect Day* be seen as an 'ideal' world, free of sexism and multi-cultural conflict, if only by the simple expediency of imposing mono-sexual and mono-cultural identities? Or is there a better way of accommodating cultural diversity without accompanying division? These issues are explored in the context of generational shift, fashion, culture and, of course, pervasive computing.

From the idea of clothing-as-interface, Katina Michael and M.G. Michael (Chapter 10) consider the idea of body-as-interface, using microchip implants. With reference to *This Perfect Day*, effectively this technology could have replaced the bracelet and nameber for access control, as well as opening up 'opportunities' for tracking and surveillance. Like scent, implants too can be bi-directional, and if implanted in a nerve can be used to transmit the sensations of the implantee to a base station as well as cause artificial sensation. This chapter looks at the controversy surrounding implant technology, catalogues its commercial development, describes two recent trials using this technology, records people's reaction to them, and considers some of the socio-ethical implications.

We step outside the body again for the next chapter, which considers robotics as a channel for communication. The point is that there is no absolute requirement for scanners to be fixed; once they get moving, there is no requirement for them only to have sensors for perception. We can add actuators, displays, and intelligence – and we have a robot. Serge Kernbach (Chapter 11) considers the future of *human–robot interaction* and the people's expectations of robotics.

In Chapter 12, the idea of a robot (or a mobile scanner) is extended to the UAV. This is not considered in *This Perfect Day*, but was almost anticipated by another science fiction author, Robert Sheckley. In his short story *Watchbird* (Sheckley, 1967), he describes a UAV (the eponymous watchbird) which is able to detect the brain signal characteristic of prospective murder. The watchbirds also have a learning algorithm and can communicate with each other, but unfortunately they 'learn' wrongly and start classifying other signals as signs of incipient murder. Since they are also equipped with an electroshock stun gun, they start zapping people for swatting flies, chopping vegetables, and so on. Chaos ensues; so a stronger, more powerful UAV is launched, which is designed to hunt the watchbirds. These in turn learn to hunt other things. Chaos ensues ...

Ken Wahren surveys the state of the art in UAV and considers the socio-political and socio-technical implications in the transfer of military technology to civilian applications.

Sheckley does mention in his short story the recharging apparatus for the watchbirds. In *This Perfect Day*, one of the characters ('Dover') does have a micro-telecomp, which he keeps in a matchbox, though how he powered it is not mentioned. The requirement to provide power to so many micro-processors is an increasingly pressing problem. Paul Mitcheson (Chapter 13) concludes the book with a survey of *energy harvesting* techniques for mobile devices and sensor networks, and the power required to achieve what is described in the book: control over the weather system.

1.4.3 *Final remarks*

We are living in a time when the human body is not just a sensor and processor of data through its five senses and cognitive capability, but has become a generator of data just by virtue of being situated in a sensor-saturated environment. That data can be integrated with millions of (indeed, up to 7 billion) data streams and processed by systems far better suited to that activity than the human brain. The result: someone knows you, perhaps even better than you know yourself.

This data – in fact enough clean data – is clearly important for commercial, social and political reasons. However, the ownership of this data remains an open question. It is evident that as we advance into the unexplored territory of socio-technical pervasive computing, we need to harness security models based on trust and forgiveness, privacy models based on understanding information sensitivity, receiver, and usage (Adams and Sasse,

1999), usability models, and the idea of *design contractualism* (Reynolds and Picard, 2004). The idea of design contractualism is that any design decisions on security, privacy, etc. should be grounded within an appropriate model and on a mutual agreement, or 'social contract'. System designers have to make moral or ethical judgements and then encode them in their design; there are in fact many examples of this already, e.g. copyleft, ACM code of conduct, TRUSTe and so on. In the unlikely event that system designers will all accept their share of social responsibility, the question is whether enough users will vote with their feet in the forthcoming world of pervasive services, and use the services of those designers that do.

There is one final question that is not considered further than here. The characters in the book anthropomorphise UniComp, begging the artificial intelligence questions about UniComp – is UniComp intelligent? is UniComp conscious? and so on. There is an answer (of sorts) to these issues in the novel, but – no more spoilers – it is left as an exercise for the reader to find it. A more detailed discussion of this issue is reserved for another book. For now, we put the metaphysical questions aside and address the fundamental issue:

> *What kind of socio-technical, physical and*
> *political world do we wish to inhabit?*

You decide ...

Chapter 2

Implicit Interaction

Alois Ferscha

University of Linz

"And then what?" King said. "What do we do when we're twenty or thirty strong? Claim a group visit and blow Uni to pieces?"
"The idea has occurred to me," Chip said.

THIS PERFECT DAY, P. 59

2.1 Introduction

The 'nightmare' scenario of Ira Levin's *This Perfect Day* imagines a world run by a computer. The technological reality is somewhat different: the world *is* the computer. The computer and the user are no longer separate physical entities, with the user on the outside and the computer behind an interface. With pervasive computing, the user is drawn into the interface; and opting out ... isn't an option.

Research in pervasive and ubiquitous computing has developed a vision where the 'computer' is no longer associated with the concept of a single device or a network of devices, but rather the entirety of situated services originating in a digital world, which are perceived through the physical world. It is expected that services with explicit user input and output will be replaced by a computing landscape, sensing the physical world via a huge

variety of sensors and controlling it via a plethora of actuators. The nature
and appearance of computing devices will change in order to be hidden in
the fabric of everyday life, invisibly networked, and omnipresent. Applications and services will have to be greatly based on the notions of context
and knowledge, and will have to cope with highly dynamic environments
and changing resources. 'Context' refers to any information describing the
situation of an entity, like a person, a thing or a place. Interaction with such
computing landscapes will presumably be more implicit, at the periphery
of human attention, rather than explicit, i.e. at the focus of attention. In
this chapter we will give an overview of the emerging issues of interaction in
pervasive computing environments. After computing devices pervade into
objects of everyday life, computers will be 'invisible', but physical interfaces will be 'omnipresent'. It will contrast implicit and explicit interaction
approaches at the frontiers of pervasive, integrated, and thus 'hidden', technology. Perceived invisibility and the invisibility of technology will spawn
the interaction design space challenge, and help identify strategies for embedding interaction into everyday objects and environments, into literally
every 'thing'.

2.2   The Environment is the Interface

Computer science appears nowadays to be challenged (and driven) by
technological progress and quantitative growth. Among the technological
progress challenges are: advances in sub-micron and system-on-a-chip designs; novel communication technologies; microelectromechanical systems;
nano-technology; and materials sciences. The vast pervasion of global networks over the past years, the growing availability of wireless communication technologies in the wide, local and personal area, and the evolving
ubiquitous use of mobile and embedded information and communication
technologies are examples for challenges posed by quantitative growth. We
perceive a shift from the 'one person with one computer' paradigm, which is
based on explicit man–machine interaction, towards a ubiquitous and pervasive computing landscape, in which implicit interaction and cooperation
is the primary mode of computer supported activity.

This change – popularly referred to as *pervasive computing* – poses serious challenges to the conceptual architectures of computing, and to related
engineering disciplines in computer science. Historically, pervasive computing has its roots in ideas first coined by the term *ubiquitous computing*.

Mark Weiser's central statement in his seminal paper (Weiser, 1991) in *Scientific American* in 1991 was:

> *The most profound technologies are those that disappear.*
> *They weave themselves into the fabric of everyday life until*
> *they are indistinguishable from it.*

Furthermore, his conjecture, that:

> *we are trying to conceive a new way of thinking about com-*
> *puters in the world, one that takes into account the natural*
> *human environment and allows the computers themselves*
> *to vanish into the background.*

has fertilised the embedding of ubiquitous computing technology into a physical environment, which responds to people's needs and actions.

Most of the services delivered through such a 'technology-rich' environment are services adapted to context; particularly to the person, the time and the place of their use. Alongside Weiser's vision, it is expected that context-aware services will evolve, enabled by wirelessly ad hoc networked, mobile, autonomous, special purpose computing devices (i.e. 'information appliances'), providing largely invisible support for tasks performed by users. It is expected that services with *explicit user input* will be replaced by a computing landscape sensing the physical world via a huge variety of sensors, and controlling it via a manifold of actuators in such a way that it becomes merged with the virtual world. We refer to this interaction principle as *implicit interaction*, since input to such a system does not necessarily need to be given explicitly or attentively. Applications and services will have to be greatly based on the notion of context and knowledge, will have to cope with highly dynamic environments and changing resources, and will thus need to evolve towards a more *implicit* and *proactive interaction* with users.

A second historical vision impacting the evolution of pervasive computing claimed for an intuitive, unobtrusive and distraction-free interaction with technology-rich environments. In an attempt to bring interaction 'back to the real world' after an era of keyboard and screen interaction, computers started to be understood as secondary artefacts, embedded and operating in the background, whereas the set of all physical objects present in the environment started to be understood as the primary artefacts, the 'interface'. Instead of interacting with digital data via keyboard and screen, physical

interaction with digital data, i.e. interaction by manipulating physical artefacts via 'graspable' or 'tangible' interfaces, was proposed. Inspired by the
early approaches of coupling abstract data entities with everyday physical objects and surfaces like Bishop's Marble Answering Machine, Jeremi-
jenko's Live Wire and Wellner's Digital Desk, tangible interface research
has evolved, and so physical artefacts are considered as both representa-
tions and controls for digital information. A physical object thus represents
information, while at the same time acts as a control for directly manipulating that information or underlying associations. With this seamless
integration of representation and control into a physical artefact, input
and output devices fall together. Placed meaningfully, such artefacts can
exploit physical affordances suggesting and guiding user actions, while not
compromising existing artefact use and habits of the user. Recent examples
for 'embodied interaction', where input and output are fused into physical
object manipulation, include architecture and landscape design and analysis, as well as object shape modelling interfaces using brick-like blocks or
triangular tiles.

Although the first attempts of the ubiquitous and pervasive computing vision in the early 1990s fell short due to the lack of enabling hardware and software technologies, they are now, about ten years later, viable
due to technological progress and quantitative growth. Pervasive computing initiatives and projects have emerged at major universities worldwide,
and national and international research funding authorities (IST Future
and Emerging Technologies programme of the EU, DARPA, NSF, etc.)
have accelerated the efforts of a rapidly growing, vibrant research community. Although initially suffering from a plethora of unspecific terms like
'Calm Computing', 'Disappearing Computer', 'Ambient Intelligence', 'Sentient Computing', 'Post-PC Computing', 'Everyday Computing', etc., the
research field is now consolidating from its foundations in distributed systems and embedded systems, and is starting to codify its scientific concerns
in technical journals, conferences, workshops and textbooks. This process,
however, is far from settled in 2011.

2.3   What is Implicit Interaction?

Technological advances, miniaturisation of embedded computing technology and wireless communication, together with the evolution of global networks like the Internet, has brought the vision of pervasive and ubiquitous
computing to life: technology seamlessly woven into the 'fabric of everyday

life'. Along with this development goes the need and challenge of interfaces supporting an intuitive, unobtrusive and distraction-free interaction with such technology-rich environments. Considering the large and ever growing number of manifold small, embedded and mobile devices, traditional styles of interaction (e.g. via a keyboard) appear hopeless. To make computing part of everyday life, the interfacing must go beyond traditional explicit interaction: pervasive computing system designs will have to – and already are – successfully attempting to revert the principle of the user being in an active and attentive role to one where technology is attentive and active. Interaction is becoming implicit.

Implicit interaction is based on two main concepts: perception and interpretation. Perception concerns gathering information about the environment and situations, usually involving (electronic) sensors. This information is generally provided implicitly to the system and displayed naturally to the user. Interpretation is the mechanism to understand the sensed data. Conceptually, perception and interpretation when combined are described as *situational context*. A system aware of its situational context does not have to be explicitly forced to act (by the user), but, by collecting and interpreting information about its environment, it can autonomously trigger actions. Input is not necessarily explicitly stated or intentionally given, but the system understands the information it collects as input. The active, driving role in the interaction is thus moved from the user to the system. Consequently, the user does not have to be attentive and responsive to a plethora of devices, but the devices – as single entities or as ensembles of cooperative entities – develop a 'sense' for the user, and act accordingly.

To make computing part of everyday life, the interface to new computing devices should go beyond traditional explicit interaction. The vision of future information appliances drawn by Schmidt (1999) motivates the need for modalities of implicit interaction:

> *we will be able to create (mobile) devices that can see, hear and feel. Based on their perception, these devices will be able to act and react according to the situational context in which they are used.*

Accordingly, the following definition has been proposed:

> *Implicit human computer interaction is an action performed by the user that is not primarily aimed to interact*

with a computerised system but which such a system un-
derstands as input.

2.3.1 *Interacting with landscapes of digital artefacts*

As we observe an increasing number of real-world objects with embedded computing capabilities, like vehicles, tools and appliances, computers,
mobile phones and portable music players (we refer to such technology-
enriched physical objects as digital artefacts, or just artefacts), the issue of
their interaction becomes a dominant issue of human–computer interaction
research. Technology integrated into everyday objects like tools and appliances, and environments like offices, homes and cars, etc. turns these artefacts into entities subject to human–artefact interaction, whenever humans
use those appliances or become active in those environments. Moreover,
built with networked embedded systems technology, they become interconnected, diverse and heterogeneous entities subject to artefact–artefact interaction, raising the challenge of an operative and semantically meaningful
interplay among each other.

One approach to address this challenge is to design and implement systems able to manage themselves in a more or less autonomic way. While
self-management stands for the ability of single digital artefact to describe
itself, to select and use adequate sensors to capture information describing its context, self-organising stands for the ability of a group of possibly
heterogeneous peers to establish a spontaneous network based on interest,
purpose or goal, and to negotiate and fulfil a group goal. A way of implementing digital artefacts is based on miniaturised stick-on embedded computing systems, integrating sensor, actuator and wireless communication
facilities. Such stick-on solutions can be attached to or built into everyday
objects, and executing software stacks that implement self-organisation in
a totally distributed style. Interaction at the application level is invoked
based on the analysis of self-describing profile data exchanged among nearby
artefacts. Self-management builds up the basis for the self-organisation of
artefact ensembles, which represents their ability to establish a spontaneous
network based on individual interest, purpose or goal, and to negotiate and
fulfil a group goal through cooperation. Research on self-managing and self-
organising systems has attracted interest from the computer science community (Herrmann *et al.*, 2005; Jelasity *et al.*, 2006; Kephart and Chess,
2003; Mamei *et al.*, 2006; Di M. Serugendo *et al.*, 2003).

2.3.2   *Context awareness*

Context awareness refers to the ability of the system to recognise and lo-
calise objects as well as people and their intentions. The context of an
application is understood as *'any information that can be used to characterise the situation of an entity'*, an entity being *'a person, place or object
that is considered relevant to the interaction between a user and an application, including the user and applications themselves'*. A key architecture
design principle for context-aware applications is to decouple mechanisms
for collecting context information and its interpretation, from the provision
and exploitation of this information to build and run context-aware applications. Sensing context must happen in an application-independent way,
and context representation must be generic for all possible applications.

Technology trends in the domains of sensors and actuators, processing
devices, embedded systems and wireless communication have fertilised the
evolution of software architectures for building context-aware systems, see
Fig. 2.1 (Ferscha *et al.*, 2006). Usually, the addition of a world model
representing a set of objects and their state in the physical (or 'real') world
is suggested, with mechanisms to sense, track, manipulate and trigger the
real-world objects from within the world model. People living in the real
world, acting, perceiving and interacting with objects in their environment
are represented in the world model by 'virtual objects' or 'proxies'. Proxies
of people, things and places are linked to each other in the virtual world,
such that this 'linkage' is highly correlated with the 'linkage' of physical
people, things and places in the real world. A context-aware application
then monitors the state and activity of the real-world objects via a set
of sensors, coordinates the proxies according to the rules embodied in the
application, and notifies, triggers or modifies the physical world objects via
a set of actuators. We shall in future be concerned with the issue to what
extent context information can act as the trigger for actions that are either
a direct consequence of intentional or implicit user input.

Understanding implicit interaction as a result of processing context
within digital artefacts autonomously, and triggering appropriate actions
accordingly, encourages the study of digital artefacts with respect to two
important properties: autonomy and context-awareness. As artefacts are,
by nature, distributed throughout physical space, obvious considerations
for implicit interaction are their inherent spatial properties – in particular their position, direction and shape – as well as spatial relationships
among them. Awareness about spatial relationships among distributed en-

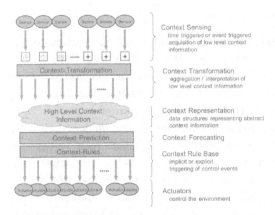

Fig. 2.1   Framework architecture for context-aware systems.

tities is considered to be valuable for self-organising systems (Zambonelli and Mamei, 2004), and most of the known phenomena of self-organisation and self-adaptation in nature are actually phenomena of self-organisation in space.

The ability to describe itself is an important aspect of an autonomous digital artefact, which allows for expressing all kinds of context information. The use of a self-description is twofold: it provides local applications with an awareness of the artefact's context, and it also serves as a basis for achieving awareness about other artefacts by exchanging the self-descriptions (see Fig. 2.2). We consider the concept of self-describing artefacts as a promising approach of implementing implicit interaction among autonomous systems, particularly with regard to an open-world assumption (i.e. interacting artefacts do not know each other in advance), where an ad hoc exchange of self-descriptions upon encountering other artefacts is required in order to get an awareness of their context. We therefore follow the approach of autonomous digital artefacts able to exchange the self-description upon becoming aware of the existence of another artefact in a direct peer-to-peer manner (Ferscha *et al.*, 2006). Further interaction can then be parameterised and contextualised considering the provided context information of the interaction counterpart. Here, our focus is specifically on the spatial context of artefacts, as well as its quantitative and qualitative representation.

Having explained *implicit interaction* as an operational principle of self-describing, self-managed, self-organising digital artefacts, we first recall es-

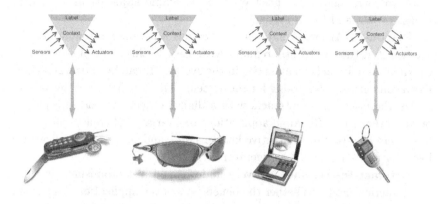

Fig. 2.2   Context-aware autonomous digital artefacts.

sential enabling technologies, including location sensing, a foundation for spatiotemporal reasoning, and sensing of velocity, orientation and general context. In the next section we look into categories of applications exploiting implicit interaction in person-to-person interaction, person-to-artefact interaction, and artefact-to-artefact interaction. The categories are defined above the type and amount of information an application uses to steer interactions, this being information on: pure *presence*, i.e. 'just being there'; *identity*, i.e. being there as a person or as an identified object; *proximity*, i.e. being in a certain area of spatial proximity of someone or something; *profile*, i.e. describing preferences, abilities, goals, etc. of someone or something; and finally *context*, i.e. any information collected via sensors that describes the situation of a person or an entity. Potential fields of application are highlighted, and an outlook into some challenging open research issues is given.

2.4   Categories of Implicit Interaction

Depending on the type and number of involved entities (person-to-person, person-to-artefact (person-to-thing), and artefact-to-artefact (thing-to-thing) and the kind of information used to trigger and steer interactions, a variety of different categories of implicit interaction appear possible.

Person-to-Person refers to the modes of interaction where technology acts on behalf of people, once a certain relation (e.g. spatial relation like 'close to each other') has been verified. Example applications are friend finder, or lost and found systems.

Person-to-Artefact interaction provides functional autonomy to the artefact, but the control still remains with user. In this mode of interaction, the digital device acts as an entity in the system. It can be a virtual object, like a software agent working for the system. The beneficiary of the system is still the user but he interacts with a digital object, instead of a person on the other side. Example applications are variants of smart spaces like intelligent classrooms, interactive kitchens etc., and smart box applications like smart cabinet, smart refrigerator etc.

Artefact-to-Artefact is a very undeveloped, yet promising, category of interaction mode. Whether the beneficiary of the application is a human user or the system itself, autonomous digital objects interact with each other to achieve certain goals. The end user does not necessarily need to be involved in the interactions among artefacts; this can happen unobtrusively in the background.

We can further categorise applications based on implicit interaction with respect to the kind and amount of information they use to trigger and steer interactions. With increasing complexity, it is possible identify the following five categories:

- **Presence:** systems exploiting information about the pure presence or absence of people or things.
- **Identity:** systems exploiting identity information about the involved interaction entities, like the ID of a person, the serial number of a product, the MAC address of a network node, etc.
- **Proximity:** systems that exploit information about the mutual spatial relationships among entities involved in the interaction, like the distance, the direction, or the topology.
- **Profile:** systems that exploit a predefined self-characterisation (self-description) of the entities involved in the interaction, including their associations, preferences, tastes, habits, goals, needs, capabilities, or even emotions.
- **Context:** systems that consider any available information that describes the situation of entities involved in the interaction.

The first consequence of interaction between things is the ability of things to record the history of their interaction. Applications based on things lacking this capability can be named as *non-memorising*, in contrast to *memorising* applications, in which things are able to record the history of their interaction. Probing further, a direct consequence of logging the interaction and contextual information may lead to more advanced *memorising and predicting* applications.

2.4.1 *Presence*

Presence of a thing perceived by another thing represents the simplest form of implicit input to a system. A thing in *interaction range* of another thing indicates presence of a sensed object in the vicinity of the sensing object (see Fig. 2.3). The sensed object, while being explored by a sensing object, may register the presence of the sensing object in its vicinity, though the exploration activity was not initiated by it. Furthermore, it is important to note that the status 'not-present' can be as useful as 'present' in many applications.

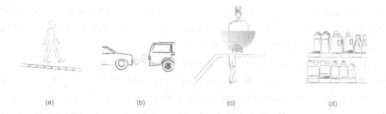

(a)   (b)   (c)   (d)

Fig. 2.3 Implicit interaction based on presence recognition. a) Automatic lighting as user walks on the path: presence sensors under the path detect the user and lights on the way start working. b) Automatic vehicle detection to help in parking: both vehicles generate alarms as they feel presence nearby. c) Work place safety system: a worker's helmet indicates that he is under a heavy load. d) A smart shelf: indicating in-stock and out-of-stock status of items on the shelf.

Some familiar technologies used for detecting presence are acoustic, electromagnetic, photoelectric, capacitive, pressure and temperature sensing. All these techniques are application oriented and specialised. For example, for acoustic sensing, the object to be sensed should have capability to generate sound waves, whereas the sensing object should be able to listen to those waves, similar to photoelectric sensing requiring light reflection and capture capability. Electromagnetic field sensing is primarily for detecting the presence of metal objects. Pressure and temperature sensing is basically connected with detecting human presence in an environment.

In addition to those specialised systems, wireless communication technologies, based on radio, provide presence sensing as a default functionality. Initial hand shaking and periodic beaconing in established protocols of Cellular Networks, Radar Systems, Bluetooth, Wireless LANs, Infrared and Ultrasound communication keep peer devices updated about their presence. Mobile ad hoc and sensor networks also implement communication protocol, which enables peer devices to know about many parameters, presence being the default.

The simplest application of presence in use today is the *automatic door*, with an emphasis on ease of access. Similarly, in smart homes, *automatic lighting* is becoming popular, which operates on the basis of instant presence (motion) detection. In the context of energy (power) saving, in an application like automatic lighting, the sensing of the non-presence of a person or an object is crucial to be able to 'switch-off', in case of absence. Similarly, *home and industrial alarm systems* gain from advanced sensing technologies. In industrial environments or logistics, an object knowing about its safety requirements can generate alerts upon the detection of the presence of hazards. The simplest example can be package safety of fragile goods: in a warehouse, this package can generate an alarm upon attempts to store another package on top of it, etc.

All these application scenarios reflect instantaneous reaction upon the detection of presence, objects as such are not memorising. With memorisation, we can imagine many application categories exploitable by industry, market places and busy areas like airports. Memorising timestamped events of detected presence, and thus declaring the epochs of absence, can help to implement more sophisticated interactions, like readiness for the anticipated occurrence of recurring events learned from the occurrence history, or the prediction of future events as a learning effect from patterns in the event history ('future awareness'). For memorisation alone, the timestamp-based presence history enables applications broadly categorised as applications concentrating on *process speed*. In an automatic production environment, a sensor knowing the process speed which couples the presence with timestamps can alter the speed of a conveyor belt or assembly line to get the optimum performance (if speed is too slow) or to avoid a process deadlock (if speed is too fast). Extending the memorisation capabilities to a whole group of individuals or objects, by, for example, counting and storing the number of objects detected to be simultaneously present, enables applications broadly categorised as *queuing* and *inventory control*. Sensing the increase or decrease of the population of objects in a queue waiting for service can help in taking alternative actions. It can be very helpful in busy areas like airports, shopping malls and during celebrations and special events. In manufacturing and logistics, knowing the relative health of a queue can initiate alternative actions, to increase performance and productivity. For inventory control, an object knowing that 'few' things are left in the shelf can raise a 'low inventory' alarm.

It is easy to extend any of the scenarios presented above into the category of memorisation and prediction. A prediction logic (based on the collected object history) embedded into an object can help to implement 'proactive' behaviour. A *smart room* can start its heating system when it senses the presence of the user. But before the room temperature is normalised, the user would have to live with default severe conditions. It would be more convenient to predict the future situation (user approaching), and to act in advance in order to accomplish the desired state in a timely due manner.

2.4.2 *Identity*

This category is defined by the fact that it is not the mere presence, but the recognised identity of a person, object, or artefact, that defines the input to the system. For implicit interaction, the quest would only be limited to things identifying other things. Applications like access control, product inventories, or road toll systems are traditional representatives of this category of applications (see Fig. 2.4).

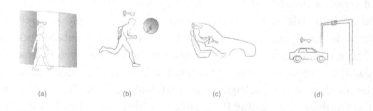

(a)　　　　　(b)　　　　　(c)　　　　　(d)

Fig. 2.4 Implicit interaction based on identity sensing. a) Access control: only an authorised user is allowed to enter a passage. b) Time management in sports: in track and field events, athletes are informed about their timing based on their identity on a mobile device. c) Personalised controls: car offers personalised settings based on the identity of the current driver. d) Automatic toll payment: car does not need to stop at the tollhouse. The identity of licensed vehicle is sensed and the amount is automatically debited from the driver's account.

Identification of a thing by another thing can be done in three ways. First, a thing can identify another thing by verifying the identity that a thing may 'have'. Examples include the identification of keys in a smart card, bar codes, visual markers and radio-frequency identification (RFID). Second, a thing can identify another thing by verifying the identity that a thing may 'possess'. Examples include verification of biometric identities like finger print detection, iris scan, human radiation detection and voice recognition. Last, a thing can identify another thing by verifying the identity that a thing may 'know'. An example is password or security code matching. The third category implies an explicit interaction, thus denying our emphasis on implicit interaction. The technologies enabling the automatic exchange and authentication of identification keys have been investigated in many technological environments, RFID being the most prominent.

As discussed above, the most common example of identity-based application is *access control*. For example, it is desirable that only employees of an office are allowed to enter an office building. It can easily be checked by a reader opening the door if the company identity of the employee matches with the identity printed on his company card. If enhanced with memorisation, the system can perform *activity monitoring* by registering the presence of a particular user in or out of the office. Activity monitoring is not restricted to human beings. In automatic production, logistics and sales, the lifecycle of the product can be monitored. If that is the case, the anticipation of a disaster can stop future disasters. Disaster prediction in a controlled environment can be achieved by logging both the activities of the personnel and events. Similarly, identifying a thing at a place that could create a hazard can immediately be remedied.

In an industrial environment, automatic *component assembly* can be achieved by applying an identification mechanism. A sub-component related to its compatible sub-component can be ensured before assembling. Similarly, in logistics, *container loading* has been a problematic task. Based on the identity of the packages, a related container can be ensured, avoiding the troubles of reloading if a problem is identified after loading or even shipment of products to the wrong destination. Extending the example, memorisation capabilities lead to the category of *production line* applications. As an example, an RFID-enabled production could operate according to the following steps. Firstly, carts containing items move along the production line for processing, where each item is associated with a tag and each carrier has writable tag. An RFID reader is mounted at each station and writes the information about the performed steps onto the tags of the carts. Secondly, readers at the end of the production line check for completeness of the production steps performed on the items. If complete, items are scanned and packed into packages. Thirdly, packages are packed into containers in a warehouse. Finally, containers are loaded onto a truck and transported. As illustrated by this example, *identity management* solutions are among the most promising approaches of implicit interaction based process automation.

2.4.3 *Spatial proximity*

In this category of applications, facts like distance, orientation, and spatial relations are automatically recognised and used to control the system. Reasoning about space in the vicinity of another thing may be based on one of the two concepts of space: quantitative space and qualitative space. *Quantitative* spatial reasoning is related with measurement of exact space metrics. *Qualitative* spatial reasoning is based on non-metric abstractions of space related to topology, distance and orientation.

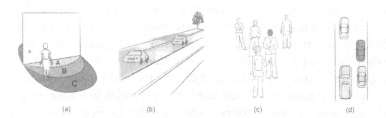

Fig. 2.5 Implicit interaction based on spatial proximity sensing. a) A public wall display: based on the proximity (nearness) of the user, the display changes appearance and contents. b) Drive-by-wire: a car adopts the right cruising speed with respect to the preceding car, or generates an alarm as it senses another car approaching too close. c) Spontaneous interaction in social settings: a user knows about other users near him. d) Driver assistance system: the car knows about its proximity and can support decision for driving.

Geographic information systems (GIS) based on global positioning technologies (e.g. GPS), are the main enabler for spatial proximity sensing, particularly concerning distance and orientation. On a smaller scale, a mobile ad hoc network, a sensor network or an RFID system may be used to estimate distance and orientation between two objects, based on relative signal strength, particularity in qualitative domain. Coupling this qualitative measure with inference, relative to a node having global coordinates, can result in quantitative measures.

Applications that build upon the spatial proximity of objects among each other include industrial production (e.g. *congestion control in production lines*), transport, logistics, storing, etc. Indication and placement can be coined as a term representing a group of applications suitable for shelves in sales environments. By detecting proximity, an item in a shelf can indicate a gap to the right, left, top or bottom of itself, taking a shelf containing books as an example. Knowing about objects in proximity has many applications in *automotive systems*, where future vehicles will behave more like intelligent agents traveling in intelligent spaces. Car-to-car interaction can guide the driver (or driver assistance system) to proceed or not, depending on traffic rules and speed. Car-to-roadside interaction can assist in finding parking slots, etc. *Large size public displays* on walls or mirrors are becoming popular in public places. Many of these displays use proximity sensing to select and control the content being displayed to the user. In many projects, the interaction is situation-based, determined by three zones of interactions (see Fig. 2.5). The closest zone is the space from which the user can touch the display to interact with the system. The second zone, outside the interaction zone, is the notification zone, where the user can be notified based on the person in front of the wall so that he/she starts thinking about interaction and may decide to proceed further to interact. The last and outermost zone is the ambient zone, which indicates the presence of a user near the wall. Different sensing technologies can help to scan these zones appropriately. Thinking about proximity sensing with the ability to memorise and predict opens application possibilities, e.g. *unmanned driving systems*, within which autonomous vehicles can safely perform any activity, like overtaking, turning, speeding up, slowing down and stopping etc.

2.4.4 Profile

Exchanging the self-descriptions of objects encoded in metadata format (e.g. XML) to induce adequate (implicit) interaction is yet another increase in the quality of spontaneous interactions. The metadata related to an object may cover material properties, object structure and general physical characteristics, whereas metadata referring to a person could indicate physiognomic properties of that person, personal preferences, likings or habits, intents, capabilities, goals or even emotions. The exchange of profiles, automatically triggered among co-located objects, and the analysis of correspondences within them, enables interactions best adapted to the individual counterparts. In person-to-person interaction, exchanged 'business profiles', for example, could help to check the level of 'compatibility' between two people. In person-to-artefact interaction, we imagine display systems that present content that 'matches' the interest of the person. And in artefact-to-artefact interaction, an application may assist in alerting about a situation in which a container with certain contents must not go with a container with incompatible contents (see Fig. 2.6).

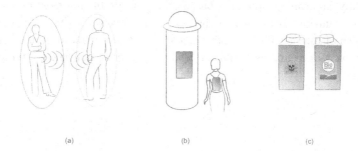

(a) (b) (c)

Fig. 2.6 Implicit interaction based on exchanged self-descriptions. a) Person-to-person: two people exchanging profiles. b) Person-to-thing: a person and a thing exchanging profiles. c) Thing-to-thing: two things exchanging profiles.

In non-memorising implementations of profile-based implicit interactions, the most common and popular examples come in the form of *intelligent* (or *smart*) *appliances*. Examples range from 'web luggage', implementing containment recognition and inventory services accessible via the Internet, 'magic wardrobes', knowing about clothes placed inside and suggesting combinations that fit together, 'smart shelves', in which goods are monitored to enhance replenishment and identify misplaced products, to 'smart medication cabinets', monitoring the medication taken by the patient while reminding, alerting, and displaying information about prescriptions, incompatibilities or recalled medicines, etc. In the memorising category, an 'autonomic product' solution appears viable, with technology support for every product to manage its own lifecycle, from production to disposal and recycling autonomously. Implicit interaction principles deployed in manufacturing and production, transport and logistics, sales, customer support and even separation and recycling, as well as at the points of handover from one lifecycle phase to another, can make product lifecycles self-managed, swift and trustworthy. In *wildlife monitoring*, the tagging of animals with sensor beacons, collecting environmental data and keeping track of their position and movement, are already common today. *Physical activity monitoring* is another potential application in this category. We can imagine wearable sensors that sense the physical activity of the user in a gym, say, and exercise machines communicating with the sensors worn by the user to provide guidelines for an optimal workout.

2.4.5 *Context*

Certainly, steering interactions based on any available information describing the situation within which the interaction occurs is the most versatile approach of implicit interaction. Basically every circumstance, as identified from sensor data analysis, can be used to trigger or constrain interactions (see Fig. 2.7).

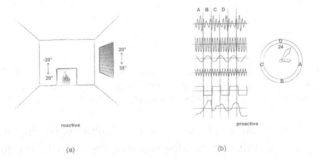

Fig. 2.7   Implicit interaction based on arbitrary information describing the situation of an entity (person, thing, artefact). a) Reactive: as the temperature outdoors changes, the heating system indoors reacts and adjusts the thermostat. b) Proactive: the system identifies recurring patterns of user activities from sensor data time series. Learning from this experience, the system estimates the user preferences and acts accordingly.

As already mentioned, a context-aware system can be designed to be reactive or proactive. We have already discussed a simple adaptive heating system in Section 2.4.1. Including context in the same example, the heating system can refine its function by knowing the number of people present in the room, or it can start the ventilation function after sensing smoke (the system does not have to generate a smoke alarm in this case). This scenario is an example of a *reactive adaptive environment*. A *proactive adaptive environment* predicts and takes a decision well before time. A variety of assisted-living examples implement services with the features of 'being ready' for the user just in time (proactive door-openers, scene lighting, warm up of coffee makers, etc.). Finally, there is a coordination aspect of implicit interaction as soon as collections, groups or ensembles of entities are concerned. We can address this with an abstract concept which we call *'Things that go Together'*. The criterion for things to belong to a group is to fulfil a certain relation that holds among all group members. There can be many types of relations between things like similarity, likeliness, compatibility, or suitability. In some sense, entities may be considered to belong to a group if they share the same context. Implicit interaction at the level of this group can then be used to implement coordinated, collective behaviour.

2.5 Outlook

Implicit interaction is based on the principle that a system does not have to be explicitly forced to act (by the user), but, by collecting and interpreting information about its environment or situation, it can autonomously trigger actions. Input is not necessarily explicitly stated or intentionally given, but the system understands the information it collects as input. The active, driving role in the interaction is thus moved from the user to the system. Consequently, the user does not have to be attentive and responsive to a plethora of devices, but the devices as single entities or as ensembles of cooperative entities develop a 'sense' for the user, and act accordingly. Implicit interaction, as well as person-to-person interaction, is also a promising approach for person-to-artefact interaction, but most of all artefact-to-artefact interaction. Particularly for the latter case, it can be seen as an operational principle of self-* digital artefacts: self-describing, self-managing and self-organising.

In this chapter we looked into categories of implicit interactions that make use of information at different levels of complexity. At the lowest level are systems that act based on the detection of the pure *presence* (or *absence*) of an entity, like a person or a thing. Given systems that can not only sense presence, but also recognise the *identity* of entities, like the identity of a person, the serial number of a tool, or the license plate number of a vehicle, more specific implicit interactions can be implemented based on that information. Space and relation of entities in (physical) space are very crucial concepts for implicit interaction. The *proximity* of an entity, i.e. the recognition of other entities in a certain area of spatial proximity of an entity, is a yet more powerful concept to steer interactions. *Profiles*, describing attributes of objects, or preferences, abilities or goals of users, allow for the design of interactions that are particularly tailored for individual entities. Finally, the tailoring of interactions to particular situations is made possible when considering the *context*, i.e. any information collected via (electronic) sensors, that describes the situation of interacting entities.

Chapter 3

Brain–Computer Interfaces

Ricardo Chavarriaga and José del R. Millán

Ecole Polytechnique Fédérale de Lausanne (EPFL)

> *"What do you think a treatment consists of?"*
> *King asked.*
> *Chip said, "Vaccines, enzymes, the contraceptive, sometimes a tranquilizer –"*
> *"Always a tranquilizer," King said. "And LPK, which minimizes aggressiveness and also minimizes joy and perception and every other fighting thing the brain is capable of."*
>
> THIS PERFECT DAY, P. 67

3.1 Introduction

The possibility of tapping into our minds has continuously fascinated science fiction authors, whether for controlling external devices using our brain waves, or for implanting, restoring or modifying our memories and thoughts. Although this type of interaction is not considered in the dystopian world of Levin's *This Perfect Day*, it has been explored by the likes of Philip K. Dick in *We Can Remember It For You Wholesale* (1969b) and William Gibson (1984), as well as movies such as *Firefox* (1982), *The Eternal Sunshine of the Spotless Mind* (2004), and *Avatar* (2009). Developments in

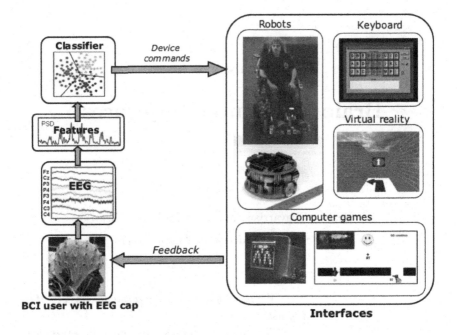

Fig. 3.1   General architecture of a BCI system.

neuroscience, signal processing and machine learning mean that it is now possible to control devices using the activity of our brains. Indeed, brain activity can be recorded and analysed in real-time, allowing their use to infer human intentions and translate them into control commands for an external device. These *brain–computer interfaces* (BCI) can currently control devices such as virtual keyboards, games, smart wheelchairs or mobile robots (Dornhege *et al.*, 2007; Millán *et al.*, 2008; Nicolelis, 2001; Wolpaw *et al.*, 2002). These interfaces rely on machine learning techniques to classify brain-generated signals into predefined patterns of activity that are associated with particular intentions (e.g. to imagine our left hand moving will correspond to moving the device towards the left).

Initially, these interfaces were conceived as a means to provide a communication and control channel for people suffering from severe motor disabilities due to traumatic lesions (for example, spinal cord injury), stroke or degenerative neuromuscular diseases like muscular dystrophies or amyotrophic lateral sclerosis (ALS) (Millán *et al.*, 2010; Wolpaw *et al.*, 2002). These disabilities are characterised by a progressive loss of muscular activity while cognitive functions may remain largely spared, allowing the potential operation of a BCI. In addition, there is an increasing interest in the possibility of it being used by a larger population (Nijholt *et al.*, 2008b); including disabilities such as autism or epilepsy. Alternatively, they also may target able-bodied subjects, including applications ranging from games (Nijholt *et al.*, 2008a) to image retrieval (Gerson *et al.*, 2006). Moreover, healthy subjects may experience *situational disabilities*: where they are not able to exercise their motor or cognitive capabilities for reasons that are not physiological or pathological. For instance, a person can be situationally deaf in a very noisy environment. Furthermore, some types of work lead to situational disabilities, as in the case of astronauts who experience motor situational disabilities during extra-vehicular activity while in space (Menon *et al.*, 2009). BCI can become a tool to overcome such limitations. In this chapter, we will mainly focus on brain–computer interfaces for users without severe disabilities. Readers interested in more information about clinical and assistive applications of BCI may refer to (Broetz *et al.*, 2010; Daly and Wolpaw, 2008; Kübler *et al.*, 2005; Millán *et al.*, 2010)

3.2   BCI Architecture: Translating Thoughts into Actions

Figure 3.1 shows the general architecture of a BCI system. It records and processes brain activity in order to extract relevant features that are then passed on to some mathematical model (e.g. statistical classifiers or neural networks). This model interprets the neural activity pattern and infers the corresponding commands to control the device. Finally, feedback about the performance of the brain-actuated device is provided to the subjects so that they can learn appropriate mental control strategies in order to achieve proper control (Millán *et al.*, 2008).

3.2.1   *Monitoring and recording brain activity*

The activity of the brain can be monitored in either an invasive or non-invasive manner (Millán and Carmena, 2010). In the former case, micro-electrodes are implanted in the subject's brain, allowing the recording of electrical activity of single neurons (Hochberg *et al.*, 2006). Alternatively, a grid of electrodes can be placed under the skull without penetrating the surface of the cortex; a technique referred to as electrocorticogram (ECoG) (Hinterberger *et al.*, 2008). These approaches require surgical implantation of measuring electrodes in the brain, thus imposing a strict eligibility criteria – involving concerns about bio-compatibility and ethical factors – to define which patients are suitable for such procedure. In contrast, non-invasive BCIs use electrical, magnetic or metabolic measures of brain activity recorded on the scalp surface, allowing their use by healthy subjects. Some non-invasive methods are based on magnetic fields, recorded through magnetoencephalography (MEG) (Mellinger *et al.*, 2007) and brain metabolic activity – reflected in changes in blood flow – observed with positron emission tomography (PET), functional magnetic resonance imaging (fMRI), and optical imaging (fNIRS) (Sitaram *et al.*, 2006; Strangman *et al.*, 2002). Unfortunately, metabolic responses are characterised by long latencies and thus less appropriate for interaction. Furthermore, with the exception of fNIRS, they require a complex setup for which no portable or affordable recording equipment is available.

For these reasons, the vast majority of non-invasive BCI systems are based on electroencephalography signals (EEG). These exploit electrical signals generated by synchronous activity of cortical neurons. This technique provides a simple way to monitor brain activity since it has a high temporal resolution, is cost-effective, portable devices are available and the set-up procedure is not too complex. However, it does not provide detailed information on the activity of single neurons or small brain areas. Moreover, it is characterised by small signal amplitudes (a few micro-volts) and noisy measurements (especially if recording outside shield rooms). An illustrative comparison of the different recording techniques is shown in Fig. 3.2.

3.2.2 *Decoding brain activity*

Recorded brain activity is decoded into corresponding commands. This process is based on supervised machine learning techniques, where a model is trained to recognise specific, pre-established mental tasks; in other words, these systems are not able to perform *mind reading* but are only capable of recognising those activities for which they are trained. In general, brain signals used to control a BCI can be categorised in two main groups: *evoked* and *spontaneous* activity[1].

Evoked activity corresponds with brain activity elicited by the perception of an exogenous stimulus. These automatic responses are, in principle,

---

[1]Note that other types of BCI categories have been proposed: distinguishing between asynchronous and synchronous BCIs (Millán *et al.*, 2008); or between passive, active and reactive BCIs (Zander and Jatzev, 2009).

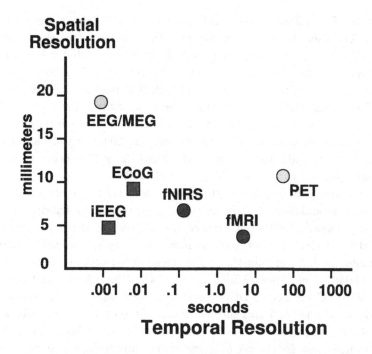

Fig. 3.2 Comparison of different recording techniques with respect to their spatial and temporal resolution. iEEG corresponds to intra-cranial EEG recordings. Invasive techniques are denoted by squares (■), while non-invasive techniques are marked by circles (●).

easier to decode from scalp EEG. However, the operation of these interfaces is time-locked to the external stimuli presentation, without allowing the user to provide commands at any other time, thus restricting their applicability. Examples of the evoked signals used by these interfaces are the steady state visual evoked potential (SSVEP) (a natural brain response to a visual stimulus) and the P300 potential (a brain response elicited by occasional, task-relevant stimuli).

Specifically, SSVEP refers to the evoked cortical activity to blinking visual stimuli of different frequencies (Allison *et al.*, 2008; Middendorf *et al.*, 2000; Müller-Putz and Pfurtscheller, 2008). The P300-based BCIs are based in the so-called 'oddball paradigms', where several types of events are sequentially presented to the patient and EEG responses to rare, relevant stimuli show a characteristic positive modulation 300 ms after the stimulus is presented (Donchin *et al.*, 2000). The most common application of this type of BCI is a communication system based on a matrix of characters in which different rows and columns get highlighted one after the other. The user should deploy her attention on the letter she wants to type; whenever the corresponding row/column is highlighted, a larger P300 component can be observed in the evoked EEG. Several variations of this protocol have been tested on ALS and locked-in patients for communication (Kübler and Birbaumer, 2008; Kübler *et al.*, 2009; Nijboer *et al.*, 2008; Sellers and Donchin, 2006), as well as in healthy subjects in applications like navigation in virtual environments (Bayliss, 2003), wheelchair control (Iturrate *et al.*, 2009; Rebsamen *et al.*, 2006), as well as other computer programs (Kübler *et al.*, 2008; Mugler *et al.*, 2008)

Alternatively, BCI systems using *spontaneous* activity rely on the user's intentional modulation of brain rhythms. They include modulation of slow cortical potentials (SCP) (Birbaumer *et al.*, 1999), or rhythms associated to predefined mental tasks, such as motor imagery (i.e. mental rehearsal of a motor action), arithmetic or language-related tasks (Babiloni *et al.*, 2000; Galán *et al.*, 2008; Millán *et al.*, 2004; Pfurtscheller and Neuper, 1994, 2001). Compared to BCIs based on evoked responses, these systems provide a more natural and suitable mean of interaction, especially when controlling dynamic devices such as a mobile robot or a wheelchair. Indeed, these signals allow for the use of *asynchronous* protocols, where the subject can provide self-paced commands to the device by voluntarily changing the mental task that she executes. However, such flexibility is often limited by the time required by the interface to reliably decode the brain activity, which usually takes around half a second (Millán *et al.*, 2008).

3.3   Applications

Unsurprisingly, most of the BCI applications that have been proposed are in the clinical domain, targeting people with severe disabilities. More recently, the use of BCI has also been proposed as a support in rehabilitation therapies after stroke or spinal cord injuries (Daly and Wolpaw, 2008), as well as in combination with assistive technologies (Millán *et al.*, 2010). Nevertheless, non-clinical applications can also be conceived, ranging from its use on hostile environments where situational disabilities may arise, such as space applications, as described above (Menon *et al.*, 2009), to entertainment and gaming applications (Nijholt *et al.*, 2008a,b).

Figure 3.3 shows the principal application lines of current BCI systems. Among the most representative examples of communication applications

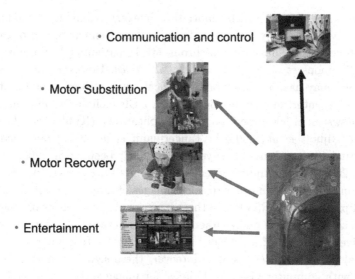

Fig. 3.3   Main applications of non-invasive BCI systems.

we can count the P300-based spellers, described in the previous section (Donchin *et al.*, 2000; Kübler and Birbaumer, 2008; Kübler *et al.*, 2009; Nijboer *et al.*, 2008; Sellers and Donchin, 2006). A recent version, termed Hexo-Spell, exploits state of the art human–computer interaction principles for improved control of the system (Williamson *et al.*, 2009). Similarly, several BCI-based web browsers have also been developed, using both evoked activity (Mugler *et al.*, 2008) and spontaneous activity (Bensch *et al.*, 2007; Karim *et al.*, 2006).

In turn, motor substitution applications include assisted mobility devices, such as robotic wheelchairs, controlled using P300 signals (Iturrate *et al.*, 2009; Rebsamen *et al.*, 2006) or spontaneous rhythm modulation (Galán *et al.*, 2008), as well as the control of tele-operated robots (Perrin *et al.*, 2010; Tonin *et al.*, 2010). Another line of research in BCIs for motor substitution relies on muscular functional electrical stimulation (FES) to restore grasping capabilities (Leeb *et al.*, 2010; Müller-Putz *et al.*, 2006, 2007; Pfurtscheller *et al.*, 2003).

The idea of using BCIs to help in the recovery of motor capabilities (e.g. for stroke patients) has also been explored. The main idea is to couple motor imagery BCI (where the subject activates the brain patterns corresponding to specific motor actions) with existing therapies based on active movement training or passive mobilisation (Millán *et al.*, 2010). This is supported by studies which report that imagery training, in combination with conventional physiotherapy, leads to improvement in the recovery of hand functions in subacute and chronic stroke patients (Braun *et al.*, 2006, 2008; Simmons *et al.*, 2008; Verbunt *et al.*, 2008). However, the real impact that BCI may have in this type of applications is still an open question.

Finally, entertainment applications for BCIs include the aforementioned web-browsers, P300-based painting applications (Kübler *et al.*, 2008), games (Nijholt *et al.*, 2008a,b; Tangermann *et al.*, 2008) and navigation of virtual environments (Lecuyer *et al.*, 2008; Leeb *et al.*, 2007; Scherer *et al.*, 2008). Furthermore, recent experiments have shown that EEG signals can be decoded in order to select images of interest during rapid serial visual presentation (RSVP). In these experiments, sequences of images are shown at a high speed and characteristic patterns are elicited when the user perceives an image of a category she is looking for (e.g. images of cars or houses) (Gerson *et al.*, 2006). Moreover, these signals can then be combined with computer vision techniques for image sorting and retrieval for the development of brain-controlled image browsers (Wang *et al.*, 2009).

3.4 Context-Aware BCI

Despite the impressive achievements attained so far, BCIs are strongly limited by their low throughput and the number of commands they can deliver. The design of context-aware interfaces has been proposed as a way to cope with these limitations (Chavarriaga and Millán, 2010a). Under this approach, the interface gathers information about the state of the device, as well as its surrounding environment, and combines it with the commands decoded from brain activity. This allows performance of complex tasks with a reduced number of mental commands (typically 2 or 3), by using these commands to signal high level instructions while smart devices take care of low-level control signals. For instance, non-invasive BCIs can be used to control an intelligent wheelchair or a tele-operated robot in realistic conditions and in real-time (Galán *et al.*, 2008; Tonin *et al.*, 2010). In these applications, BCI commands are limited to general directions of movement (i.e. move forward, turn left, turn right) that are interpreted by the device (wheelchair or robot), taking into account information of the on-board sensors in order to compute the actual control command to be executed (i.e. speed and angle of movement), so as to perform smooth trajectories and avoid obstacles. Alternative approaches in context-aware BCI robotics applications dynamically change the behaviour corresponding to a particular mental task depending on context. For instance, when controlling a mobile robot, a 'left' command emitted by the BCI would have a different meaning depending on whether or not there is a wall to that side of the robot: in the first case the robot will move along that wall while in the second case the robot will turn to the left on the spot (Millán *et al.*, 2004). In both cases, this *shared control* approach increases the robustness of the overall system, allowing it to achieve complex tasks.

Besides information about the device and the environment, the interface can also extract information about the subject's cognitive and perceptual state from the recorded brain activity. A paradigmatic example of these states is the awareness of erroneous decisions, whether these decisions are by the subject itself or by an external agent. Previously, it has been shown that it is possible to detect, in real time, error-related EEG activity on single trials and use this activity as corrective or learning signals for BCI systems (Chavarriaga and Millán, 2010b; Chavarriaga *et al.*, 2007; Ferrez and Millán, 2008). Furthermore, in the frame of semi-autonomous navigation (akin to the wheelchair experiment described above), a tele-operated robot platform has been developed, which navigates autonomously in indoor environments, using its on-board sensors, until it reaches a decision point, as it does not know the target destination. At this location, it uses visual feedback to propose one possible action to the user (see Fig. 3.4). That action is selected or discarded based on online detection of error-related EEG potentials (ErrP). During the experiments, the user remotely commands the robot while observing a video stream provided by an on-board camera, with the visual feedback superimposed on the video image (Perrin *et al.*, 2010). Experiments using both real and simulated robots show that it is possible to successfully guide the robot while providing natural brain–machine interaction that reduces the user's cognitive load, since the system behaves autonomously 80% of the time.

Alternatively, error-related EEG signals can also be used to adapt the behaviour of the interface. It is possible that similar potentials can be used to assess and improve the system's performance. A hybrid approach to human–computer interaction can be designed that uses human gestures to send commands to a computer and exploits brain activity to provide implicit feedback about the recognition of such commands (see Fig. 3.5). Using a simple computer game controlled by wearable motion sensors as a case study, it can be shown that EEG activity evoked by erroneous gesture recognition can be classified in single trials above random levels. In

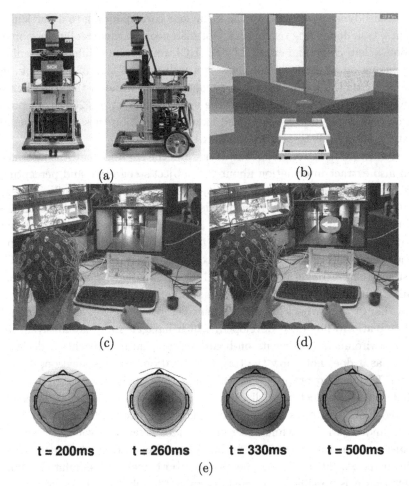

Fig. 3.4 Experimental setup for EEG error-based based navigation (Perrin *et al.*, 2010).
(a–b) Real and simulated robot used in the experiments. (c) The user observes the video
from the onboard robot camera. (d) The robot moves autonomously and wherever it
cannot take a reliable decision it proposes an action to the user using visual feedback.
(e) Error-related brain activity. The plots show the differences in the activity generated
by erroneous and correct propositions. Each topographic plot shows the activity over
the scalp (nose points up) at different times after the visual feedback. EEG levels of
activity are coded in grey scales, where negative values are shown in black and positive
in white. An increased negative activity can be seen in fronto-central areas about 250 ms
after erroneous feedback, followed by a positive peak in the same area around 330 ms.
This differential activity can be decoded using machine learning techniques to confirm
or reject the action proposed by the robot.

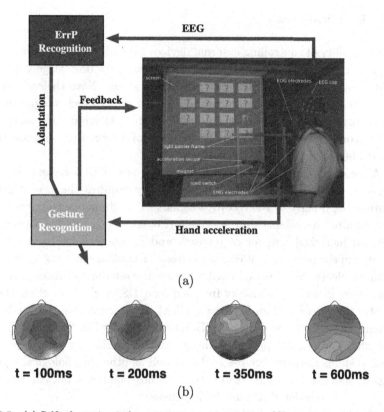

(a)

t = 100ms   t = 200ms   t = 350ms   t = 600ms

(b)

Fig. 3.5 (a) Self-adaptation in human–computer interaction (Chavarriaga *et al.*, 2010). The computer game is controlled by motion-based gesture recognition while EEG-decoded error-related activity is used for self-adaptation. (b) Topographic representation of EEG changes of activity at fronto-central electrodes (error-correct condition). As in Fig. 3.4 a negative activity can be observed around 200 ms and a positive peak at 350 ms.

this way, the gesture recognition system becomes self-aware of its own performance (Chavarriaga *et al.*, 2010; Förster *et al.*, 2010). This work also presents a simple adaptation mechanism, which uses the EEG signal to label newly acquired samples that can be used to re-calibrate the gesture recognition system in a self-supervised manner. Off-line analysis shows that this technique can significantly improve the accuracy of a user-independent gesture recognition system.

3.5 Practical Issues

The feasibility of controlling external devices through decoding brain activity, of both disabled and able-bodied people, has now been largely demonstrated by several research groups across the globe. Nevertheless, several questions remain about the acceptance and use of such technologies by potential users – especially those not suffering from severe impairments – as well as concerning the uses that can be made of information obtained from monitoring brain activity.

Among the current limitations of a wider use of BCI systems lies the fact that current EEG acquisition technology requires the use of gel to improve the quality of the recorded signals. This simple fact increases the time required for setting up the system (Popescu *et al.*, 2007). To counter that, an increased number of research and commercial efforts are being invested in the development of *dry electrodes*, as well as more ergonomic and aesthetic electrode helmets, in order to ease the setting up process. Several companies, including NeuroSky Inc (San Jose, USA) (Sullivan *et al.*, 2008), Emotiv Systems Inc (San Francisco, USA), Quasar Inc (San Diego, USA) (Sellers *et al.*, 2009) and Starlab (Barcelona, Spain) (Ruffini *et al.*, 2007), now offer commercial products aiming at the gaming sector. Typically, these systems measure brain-signals, as well as other physiological signals (e.g. muscular-related electrical activity), thus making it unclear whether they can be considered as pure BCI systems.

Another limitation of EEG-based systems comes from their sensitivity to signal contamination due to movements. In fact, muscular activation generates potentials which are several orders of magnitude higher than brain-generated signals. For this reason, neurophysiological experiments require the subject to remain still during the recording, a constraint that is not desired for actual BCI use. In order to reduce this constraint and extend the scope of operation of these techniques, special focus is now given to the development of machine learning techniques for filtering out signals that are not originated in the brain (i.e. artefacts) (Gwin *et al.*, 2010; Jung *et al.*, 2000; Makeig *et al.*, 2009; Schlögl *et al.*, 2007). Finally, more efforts should be devoted to the development of compact, easy-to-use BCI applications. Currently, most implementations are developed for research purposes, running in personal computers, with user interfaces that do not take into account user ergonomics or other human factors.

Apart from the technical aspects discussed above, an extended use of BCI systems raises a range of ethical issues to be considered (Clausen,

2009; Haselager *et al.*, 2009). One aspect concerning BCI applications of communication and control is the liability for decisions expressed through this means. In the case of severely impaired people, taking into account the possibility of errors in the brain signal decoding, can consent expressed via BCI be considered valid (Haselager *et al.*, 2009)? Similarly, who should be considered liable for the consequences of actions performed through a BCI (e.g. imagine a BCI-controlled wheelchair that runs into another person)? It has been claimed that these cases may be similar to scenarios already covered by existing ethical and legal frameworks (Tamburrini, 2009); i.e. the inability to exactly predict the behaviour of BCI-controlled devices may be comparable to the impossibility of a dog owner to fully control the behaviour of the animal, while still remaining responsible for any damage the dog may cause. Under this assumption, Tamburrini concludes that current policies may need small adjustments to accommodate for liability of BCI use.

A final aspect to discuss is the information that can be obtained from the brain activity. One example is the possibility of using brainwaves for person authentication (Marcel and Millán, 2007). Moreover, although the actual decoding of a person's thoughts is clearly beyond the capabilities of the current technology, differential brain responses to specific stimuli can provide extra information about the subject's perception of these stimuli. For example, a system termed Cortically Coupled Computer (Co3) Vision exploits neural activity to search for images of a specific target class among a large image database (Gerson *et al.*, 2006). Specifically, it identifies neural activity generated when the user perceives an image of the intended class (e.g. images of a car presented among images of other objects). Such activity is generated unconsciously in the brain and are not the result of voluntary activation or conscious modulation. For these reasons, such systems have been pointed out as making a sub-personal use of their operators (Tamburrini, 2009), since they are not required to act intentionally or even to be aware of their contribution the system. Therefore, as the debate about privacy protection in the information age keeps evolving, it is probably time to include brain-extracted information in this discussion.

The idea of exploiting unconscious information, extracted through monitoring of brain signals, has been pushed even further, as some people propose to use brain imaging techniques, in particular fMRI, as lie detectors (Farwell and Donchin, 1991; Ganguli, 2007; Harris, 2010; Langleben *et al.*, 2005; Spence, 2008). However, many doubts persist about the validity of these systems (Greely and Illes, 2007). Their reliability is yet to be demonstrated, as reported results are inconclusive and may not reflect differences across subjects or specific situations (e.g. it is not the same to tell a lie as a voluntary subject in a research study as it is when sitting on the accused bench at a trial). These doubts have not stopped some companies selling brain scan-based lie detection services, mainly to settle legal actions outside court. In a highly commented case (see e.g. Saini (2009)), a woman was convicted of murder on the basis of a brain scan in 2008, however she was released a year later, as the evidence against her was considered insufficient. Furthermore, some argue that the suitability of using these technologies in legal settings should not rely entirely on their scientific validity but should depend mainly on legal standards (Schauer, 2010). (In the context of *This Perfect Day*, one can wonder what the medics who were assessing Chip for over-treatment would do with such technological capability.)

3.6 Discussion

To summarise, over the last years the field of brain–computer interfaces has experienced an astonishingly rapid development, showing the feasibility of using brain activity to control complex devices despite existing limitations in terms of reliability and number of commands. In several applications it has been shown that enriching the interface with contextual information yields more robust interfaces.

For instance, robotic applications can gather information about the environment by using on-board sensors. This information can then be used to better interpret the user's intentions, as decoded by the BCI. This allows the user and the device to share the responsibility for control. Alternatively, EEG signals can provide information about the subject's assessment of the device performance. In particular, error related activity can be used to identify the system's erroneous decisions. This information can, in turn, be used to trigger corrective actions or to adapt the system in a self-supervised manner to improve performance over time.

Future research endeavours along these lines include the study of mechanisms to change the level of autonomy of the system depending on the context or expected reliability (e.g. giving more or less responsibility to the system depending on whether the environment is well known). Furthermore, other mental states decoded from brain activity – such as fatigue, attention or alarm – can also be included to better fit the user needs at different specific situations.

Although state of the art BCI is not yet ready to become a widely used technology, it is currently moving outside of the lab and proving its capacities in applications involving both disabled and healthy subjects. Research efforts for improving the robustness of these systems, as well as to reduce the setting up complexity, makes it probable that wearable devices will be available in the near future (Campbell *et al.*, 2010). Consequently, the possibility of a broader use of BCI systems – both in terms of applications and users – leads to new issues to be addressed, in particular regarding the reliability and content of the information extracted from the brain signals. Moreover, another aspect to be reflected upon is the impact of such use in society. On the one hand, this technology may allow for some individuals to better integrate into the society (e.g. through the use of communication devices or neuroprosthesis); while on the other hand some may be tempted to use these systems to gain information about the user state, for example to survey attention during working hours.

Chapter 4

live scent | ɘvil stench

Jenny Tillotson

University of the Arts London / Sensory Design & Technology Ltd

> *[Chip] laughed. "I decided that you worked in the gardens," he said. "You smell of flowers, do you know that? You really do."*
> *"I wear perfume," [Lilac] said.*
>
> THIS PERFECT DAY, P. 122

4.1 Introduction: A 'Live Scent' Beginning

This chapter explores pervasive computing alongside olfaction, our most primitive and powerful sense. The role of scent was minimal in *This Perfect Day*, but we cannot know if this was because, in Levin's reduction of individuals to replaceable components, it was assumed that such a distinctive characteristic as body odour could be eliminated, or because he underestimated the remarkable technological advances made (especially in recent years) in detecting and producing scent. (Or because it was a simple plot device to name the character 'Lilac', but that is another matter.) As this chapter will show, though, the use of scent and olfactory scanners could have been used to complement the administration of treatments in regulating collective behaviour (e.g. hunger and sexual appetite) and in the detection of individuals. For example, one of the characters is reported to smell of flowers (hence her nickname Lilac) because she wears 'parfum'; if UniComp had access to scent scanners then this deviant behaviour would then have been detected. On the other hand, there are also many potentially beneficial aspects of scent that will also be explored.

Science fiction has always been a fertile ground for the emerging sphere of 'Wearable Technology'. This refers to garments and headwear with built-in electronics, cameras or sensing devices and to new materials that enable functions beyond conventional ranges of applications (see Jefferies, Chapter 9). Pioneers in this field include MIT Media Lab graduates Thad Starner and Steve Mann. In the early 1990s, they envisioned computers that could be worn at any time or place, but with the power to augment human perception, multiply human mental capabilities, and have the awareness of the physical environment and incorporate this awareness in their functionality.

In 1999, a spin-off company from the MIT Media Lab Wearable Computing group was established, called Charmed Technology Inc, and went on to sell the 'CharmIT', based on Thad Starner's *Lizzy* wearable computing kit (Starner, 1993). Other conceptual products were paraded as fashion items for health and wellbeing at the 'Brave New Unwired World' catwalk show. At a later date, Microsoft Research developed *SenseCam* for memory loss. This was a ubiquitous, wearable, sensor-augmented camera, invented by Lyndsay Williams, which captured stills throughout the day and could be played back as required. Now a commercialised product called *Revue*, which has helped make lifelogging a reality, the pioneering Microsoft technology has recently been licensed to Vicon. As a powerful retrospective research tool aimed by researchers to assist people with Alzheimer's disease, this may have considerable benefits; on the other hand, some neuroscientists claim that 'forgetting' is crucial in the efficient functioning of the mind (Kuhl *et al.*, 2007). Moreover, as Mayer-Schönberger (2009) argues, forgetfulness has been an important factor in human social, cultural and psychological development, and the possibility of digital technology to record everything, coupled with an inability to delete it, could have unforeseen, and unpleasant, consequences.

This chapter explores and explains the concept of *scents-on-a-chip*; an invisible nanochip in a future society that doubles up as an olfactory sensing device, disguised in smart sensory clothing and as jewellery. The nanochip is capable of targeting timed/controlled mood-altering fragrances and 'sniffing' out the surrounding atmosphere. *Scents-on-a-chip* is part fictional and part fantasy, but it is an extension of eScent® (Manz *et al.*, 2005), an interdisciplinary design-led Wearable Technology research project. The purpose of eScent® was to develop a new liquid delivery system to dispense odours that can readily influence moods or emotional states in different situations.

The background to eScent® was inspired by *Star Trek* films and leading science fiction authors, including J.G. Ballard, Aldous Huxley, and Philip K. Dick. This has led to the creation of responsive jewellery that alters mood and improves emotional wellbeing through the evocative sense of smell. In a science fiction journal in 1993, Ballard defines fashion as 'the recognition that nature has endowed us with one skin too few, and that a fully sentient being should wear its nervous system externally' (Ballard, 1992), and in *Brave New World*, Huxley introduces a 'scent organ' that releases a spectrum of herbal scents (Huxley, 1932). The science fiction film *Minority Report* is loosely based on stories by the author Philip K. Dick, including a futuristic glove-controlled interface. Philip K. Dick also describes the notion of 'reality-in-a-can'; a mystical, sparkling metallic substance called *UBIK* (ubiquity), which is sprayed out of a can as a magical 'bubble', to stabilise a nightmare (Dick, 1969a). Further examples include the film *Star Trek: The Next Generation*, which portrayed military police with mood-enhancing clothes. In the episode *Encounter At Farpoint*, the character 'Q' and his fellow soldiers wore uniforms that had in-built olfactory 'sniffers' in their suits, so that they had the capability to change their state of mind.

Besides science fiction, this research is also inspired by key fashion designers who were asked to predict the future of the fashion industry back in 1980. Thierry Mugler, the French designer who was influenced by sci-fi, comic books and robots said that:

> *Fashion will change dramatically in the coming years. Good clothes – garments well designed and well made for the purpose of protecting the body and enhancing the personality – will prevail. Fashion will be more human, closer to the needs of the people in terms of their wellbeing, not 'well showing'.* (Khornak, 1982)

On the other hand, Karl Lagerfeld, who finds technological gadgets very attractive, although does not use them, and claims to have no human feelings before his fashion shows, said:

> *Deep changes in fashion will come with new developments in fabric technology. Will fabrics ever become computerised? Everything will be, us included. People are be-*

> *coming programmed. It is dangerous, but it is the future*
> ... (Khornak, 1982).

eScent® is an ongoing research project that sits at the cutting edge of aroma and medical work. It investigates the interface between the arts and biomedical sciences, around emerging technologies and science platforms and their applications in the domain of health, wellbeing, fragrance and fashion industries. Building on the latest developments in electro and photo active materials, miniaturisation (MEMS) and sensor technology, the aim is to create a platform exploiting the integration of design and innovative materials and technologies. The project introduces a new movement in functional, life-enhancing smart clothing and jewellery by inventing a new science of aroma delivery that takes 'scratch and sniff' to a new dimension.

eScent® is potentially life-changing; it transforms the experience of fragrance to a more intimate communication of identity by employing body sensor networks with the ancient art of perfumery. It explores the concept of implanting 'lab-on-a-chip' devices into multi-sensorial clothing and jewellery, to create new sensory systems of precisely metered fragrance delivery and release. One of the advantages of eScent® is that it could accelerate the trend away from alcohol based fragrances, introduced by the French in the 17th century, and could lead to a reduction in the carbon footprint of cosmetic products (less packaging, no bottles, smaller use of fragrance materials, less wastage, and less skin irritation caused by solvents). It will start a new trend, offering a greener, leaner image to the fragrance and wellbeing industries, and therefore appeal to the eco-minded consumer because it offers 'less for more'.

Trend analysis involves creating a highly emotional and original story; an experience reflecting a personality and an environment. The art of storytelling is at the core of the inherent skill set for any new brand wanting to connect in a meaningful, enduring way with consumers. A good story involves all the senses and should create an ambiance which is visual, tactile, intellectual but also olfactive in nature. A trend is having the finger on the pulse of fashion, entertainment and style, as well as cultural, political, ethnic, socio-economic and demographic issues. Societal pressures are causing radical changes in the fragrance industry, due to an increase in health consciousness and particularly wellbeing trends. Following on from tobacco trends and banning smoking in public, there is a new emerging trend of 'perfume-free zones' cropping up on the streets of North America, encouraging 'clean air' and open office environments. In Europe, the International Fragrance Association (IFRA), which was set up in 1973 to monitor the safety of ingredients used in the fragrance industry, has recently banned and restricted many ingredients in the field of fragrance creation, due to public outcry to allergies which, in some cases, can cause skin irritation and sensitivity (i.e. redness, blisters and itchiness).

Scents-on-a-chip is a conceptual extension of eScent®. It takes us on an imagineering journey into the future, whereby miniaturised electronic nose sensors are embedded invisibly into fashion items, in order to monitor the body and create enhanced sensory systems for protection. *Scents-on-a-chip* is inspired by advances in olfaction science and the accelerating pace of nanotechnology, combined with healthcare improvements over recent years. This chapter introduces the various benefits that the technology could offer to improve emotional wellbeing, tighten up security and guarantee survival. It achieves this in two ways. Firstly, through the notion of 'live scents', to condition sentient beings by using mood-altering scents to change behaviour (inspired by 'Q' and his military police in *Star Trek*), or communicate a message, whether it is good or bad. Secondly, through the notion of 'live sense', in order to monitor and sense its surroundings via electronic nose technology, as a channel for human–computer interaction. This chapter also argues that if the technology fell into the wrong hands and was controlled by unprincipled powers in a society like that described in *This Perfect Day*, the clothes could cause havoc to the human race with a wicked 'evil stench'.

Our sense of smell is 10,000 times more sensitive and powerful than the other senses because we simply cannot turn it off. We breathe all the time, so therefore we constantly smell our surroundings. As humans, we have the ability to distinguish 10,000 different smell molecules (odourants) in our sensory world. In prehistoric times, humans relied on what we now under-use: our sense of smell was used to 'sniff' out danger, when females were ovulating, when it was time to sow and reap, and what foods to avoid. Animals still rely on discriminating those changes. As humans, we have not lost those cognitive sensing faculties, but have learnt to rely on data presented to us in completely different ways. Vision, hearing, smell, taste, and the tactile senses serve as bridges between our brain and the external world we live in. Micro-sensors detect chemical, physical, or biomedical signals that can be processed on a computer. The miniaturisation of most sensors has already been achieved, but the electronic nose that mimics smell remains a large piece of machinery, producing 'fingerprints' for distinct odours. It consists of olfactory sensors and signal processors to detect and distinguish odours in the food and pharmaceutical industries, environmental control and dentistry.

Perfume takes us on a life-long voyage. Each scent is a unique adventure, an emotional story that we should treasure as a window to our inner world. Behind each nose that sniffs, there is a brain that thinks; the hotline plumbed into the limbic system, our emotional centre. For the nose to smell, it requires memory, attention, comparison and judgment. There is an instinctive connection between feeling and the sense of smell. This is because memory is evoked as our sense of smell records the emotions we feel at specific times or in certain situations during different life experiences. It is precisely these effects that are being used by retailers to influence product recognition and approach behaviour and therefore persuade consumers that a product is effective (for example, the smell of lemon-scented washing up liquid). Research has shown that there is a consistent relationship between smell and effect, i.e. a pleasant smell always had a positive effect and never a negative effect and vice versa (Bone and Ellen, 1999).

The art of perfumery can have a major influence over our life and the way we behave: it shows us who we can be, and it brings life to a landscape of our own personal vision, like a personal sentient 'veil' or bubble of perfumed air that reveals the inner soul. The air in this 'veil' is our reality check, our personal space which carries the senses: music, light, colour, taste, odours and perfumes (inspired by Philip K. Dick's *UBIK* reality-check bubble). Scent has the power to condition us – it alters our reality and perception of the world in order to create a new vision. The 'veil' of scent described in this chapter is an anagram of 'live' and 'evil'. It is either portrayed in a positive ('live') or negative ('evil) context, creating a 'scentient' live or evil veil around the user – depending on how *scents-on-a-chip* itself is programmed.

Computer science has the ability to recognise, process, interpret and stimulate emotions through affective computing (Picard, 1997). This is an interdisciplinary field that spans psychology and cognitive science, originally developed by Rosalind Picard at MIT to recognise interest, distress and pleasure. By embedding affective devices into smart sensory clothing and jewellery, it is possible for computers to interpret the emotional state of humans and adapt their behaviour to them, giving an appropriate response to those emotions. That response might be a carefully selective 'wellbeing' fragrance – delivered on demand – to reduce stress, stimulate the mind and improve the emotional wellbeing of the wearer.

Founded on the principles of affective computing (Picard, 1997) and building on the latest developments in electro/photo active materials, miniaturisation, lab-on-a-chip, MEMS, electronic nose technology and sensor networks, this chapter exposes different scenarios of wearable technology combined with olfactory research, and the positive outcome this might attract in the future. Topics are explored such as health and wellbeing, diagnostics, sex and procreation, fertility, entertainment, security, education, finance, military and public spaces. The chapter will conclude by suggesting a future society as described in *This Perfect Day*, which entails similar life-enhancing topics and scenarios, but in a negative light, if *scents-on-a-chip* were to be maliciously programmed to lose control and abuse mankind in an evil manner.

4.2 Health and Wellbeing

Since 1989, research in the field of 'Aromachology', funded by the Sense of Smell Institute has shown that the properties of fragrances can benefit everyone and are of particular value to people susceptible to anxiety (Jellinek, 1999). Fragrances have the power to promote a positive mood, balance the nervous system and reduce heart rate (Christensen *et al.*, 2003b). They can also help insomniacs and people who suffer from muscle stiffness, bronchitis, poor concentration, indigestion and high blood pressure (Christensen *et al.*, 2003a). The 'veil' of scent dispensed from clothing at periodic intervals throughout the day could potentially reduce obesity by suppressing appetite (Hirsch and Gomez, 1995). It could also act as an odour training mechanism to regain the sense of smell, which could be a useful tool for the elderly since our sense of smell declines from the age of 65. Fragrances are also used to assist 'reminiscence therapy', which helps the elderly fall back on lost memories from the past. Or it could be a useful tool to benefit people suffering from Alzheimer's and dementia. With a growing global elderly population and Alzheimer's expected to affect up to 65 million people by the year 2030, this would enhance quality of life, improve independence skills and the ability to communicate.

4.3 Sex and Procreation

It is well documented that every human body has an individual odour signature. The sense of smell plays an important role in mammalian reproductive biology and can ultimately have an impact on human fertility. Smell plays a vital role in mother–infant bonding. After only a few days, newborn babies are able to recognise their mother by her specific odour.

A failure to bond between mother and baby may be a factor in post natal depression, although no studies have been carried out to investigate this further. Chemical signals that send messages through the sense of smell are known as pheromones. Emitted from one animal to the other in the same species, they can cause a variety of changes in behaviour and physiology. A 'veil' of pheromones could be shared between different individuals or groups of people. Electronic nose sensors in garments could detect someone whose pheromone 'veil' profile is of interest and send them a sample of pheromones. Research has proved that male pheromones alter the mood of females by reducing tension and increasing relaxation (Preti *et al.*, 2003). Sensory clothing could emit 'modulator pheromones' from human sweat, particularly from a male partner's sweaty underarm, which contains physiologically active pheromones that have been shown to relax women (see Fig. 4.1).

Fig. 4.1   Relaxing male modulator pheromones.

4.4   Fertility

In 1971, McClintock proved that the menstrual cycles of women who spend a considerable amount of time together tend to synchronise over time (McClintock, 1971). She studied students in an all-female dormitory and found a significant increase in synchronisation in the onset of menstruation among roommates. She speculated that the cause was pheromones. In 1998, McClintock co-authored another paper in *Nature*, reporting on experiments in which cotton pads soaked in donors' armpit sweat were wiped on the upper lips of recipients. She alleged that this process changed the length of the recipients' cycles (McClintock and Stern, 1998). Conception clothes for population control could be worn and used to manipulate ovulation by emitting pheromones to change the cycle of potential mothers.

4.5 Diagnosis

Dogs have long been able to sniff out explosives, narcotics and detect diseases. Breast and lung cancers are recognised worldwide as the leading fatal cancers. Exploratory research at the Pine Street Foundation in California has shown that biochemical markers have been found in the exhaled breath of patients with early stage cancers. Canine scent detection has demonstrated that dogs can be trained to accurately distinguish the exhaled breath of cancer patients, through scent alone (McCulloch *et al.*, 2006). The embodiment of the electronic nose, integrated within the structure of a shirt collar, could emulate a dog's powerful sense of smell and potentially diagnose life-threatening diseases (see Fig. 4.2).

Fig. 4.2   DiagNOSING breast cancer.

4.6 Entertainment

Creating sensory connections between odours and musical themes in the theatre has been practised in London since the 19th century. The French perfumer Eugene Rimmel not only created scented jewellery and other artefacts, but 'perfume fountains' were incorporated into theatres to scent an entire music hall. Since the 1960s, directors in Hollywood have also been experimenting with scent in movies, for example, when 'Smell-O-Vision' was introduced at the Warner Theatre in Manhattan. In 2009, the New York Guggenheim Museum auditorium experienced an audio perfumed opera of *Green Aria* , using unfamiliar scents with surreal names: *Shiny Steel, Runaway Crunchy Green* and *Absolute Zero*. There are similarities to Aldous Huxley's scent organ in *Brave New World* (Huxley, 1932), although Huxley described a sensory sonata dispensing familiar odours:

> ... *the scent organ was playing a delightfully refreshing Herbal Capriccio – rippling arpeggios of thyme and lavender, of rosemary, basil, myrtle, tarragon ... a series of daring modulations through the spice keys – and a slow return through sandalwood, camphor, cedar and new mown hay*

Produced by Stewart Matthew and composed by Nico Muhley and Valgeir Sigurdsson, the scent opera delivered perfumed airstreams to the auditorium seats using scented microphones. The performance proved that smell can powerfully affect the perception of music, allowing the audience to focus on the interplay of sound and scent, rather than getting side-tracked by the mental associations of smells (as in Huxley's 'scent organ'). By fusing musicians with the legendary perfumer Christophe Laudamiel, an original performance was composed, which not only stimulated the mind and senses, but did not leave a lingering smell behind (a problem that occurred in air conditioning systems in previous theatres).

4.7 Security

No two people have the same personal smell. Man has been using dogs' scenting power for many years and nature has solved the problem for an age old crime-catcher. Scientists in France have perfected a technique called *odourology* which utilises scent as forensic evidence in relation to the law. This relies on police dogs to 'bottle' and identify an individual's odour signature, left lingering in the air at a crime scene (Dergay and Fiodorov, 1996). Wherever people go, they leave behind molecules of their own personal butyric acid (a component of human sweat) which will remain on anything they have touched. Sniffer dogs can identify suspects by their odour, successfully matching it to the correct odour signature. Police concluded that smell can be as effective as using fingerprints or DNA samples to link a criminal with a crime. This technique could be mimicked by wearable artificial nose sensors; clothes could mimic dogs by embedding sensors that detect, collect and store a criminal's body odour in an embedded 'smell network'. It could then be matched with the correct suspect in the olfactory equivalent of an identity 'smell' parade within the structure of the criminal's fabric (see Fig. 4.3).

Fig. 4.3 Body odour smell network.

4.8 Military

Besides pleasant smelling aromas, odours are one of the quickest ways to move people away from a situation. At the Monell Chemical Senses Centre in Philadelphia, psychologist Dr Pamela Dalton has developed a method to desensitise soldiers with odours; a tactic she uses to prepare soldiers to become accustomed to the smell of burning flesh at war. Being exposed to unpleasant and unfamiliar odours on the battlefield during periods of extreme emotional stress can later trigger problems such as flashbacks. For the US Department of Defense, Dr Dalton developed a cross-cultural chemically synthesised 'stink bomb' to deter people from restricted areas. The odour is from biological origins (faeces, sweat, urine, rotten vegetables etc.), with a stench so universally repulsive that it induces vomiting, shallow breathing and increased heart rate (Rouhi, 2002). It could also be used for crowd control.

4.9 Learning

Olfactory research has proved that sleep facilitates memory consolidation, which can maximise effectivity in learning situations. There is evidence to suggest that aromas given to a user during a learning task (for example in the classroom at school or college) can improve consolidation of the memory of that task, if that aroma is later 'pulsed' whilst the user is asleep. Functional magnetic resonance imaging has revealed significant hippocampal activation in the brain in response to odour re-exposure during the 'slow-wave sleep' period (Rasch *et al.*, 2007), see Fig. 4.4.

Fig. 4.4   Slow-wave sleep.

4.10 Finance and Consumerism

Studies in Las Vegas casinos have shown that areas surrounding casino slot-machines that had been conditioned with ambient aromas can have a radical impact on consumers' behaviour. Research has shown that money gambled in slot-machines located in an odourised area was measured and compared to those in scent-free zones. The results proved that money gambled in the aromatic surroundings was greater than the amount gambled in the scent-free zones, and when the odour concentration was increased, the amount of money spent on the slot-machines also increased (Hirsch, 2006).

For some time, aromatic messages have been injected into supermarkets to entice the consumer to buy more fresh bread, or drink more coffee in Starbucks. The domain of scent marketing is on the increase, creating

'Sensory Biotechnological' commercial opportunities in olfaction (Gilbert and Firestein, 2002). At the MIT Media Lab in 2001, a project called *Dollars & Scents* demonstrated an ambient personal finance system, which could communicate abstract information by emitting certain scents during a change in the stock market or personal shift in banking information (Kaye, 2001). As a memory jogger, scents could be embedded in clothes to remind wearers to attend to certain tasks.

4.11 Public Space and the Environment

We are living in a world where we are learning to change our lifestyle through trends, due to the fact that the legal system has made it so easy to sue someone. An example of this is the growing trend for 'clean air' and open office environments. Anti-fragrance activists are striving towards a 'fragrance-free' society in the 21st century and vigorously turning the population against the art of perfumery. In the future, we could be accused of being 'olfactive offenders' and only allowed to enjoy perfume in the seclusion of our homes. In Canada and the USA there are already 'perfume-free zones' in certain areas, particularly in university campuses. More recently, employees in Detroit have been urged to resist wearing perfumes at work, after a settlement in a federal lawsuit which claimed that a colleague's perfume made it challenging for the claimant to do her job. A way to overcome this issue could be to turn the fragrance off altogether as a user enters a 'perfume-free zone'. Components in clothing could communicate with sensory environments, or it could change the relationship between people and the environment, in order to inhibit the release of certain fragrances should an individual approach the zone.

4.12 An 'Evil Scent' Conclusion

Pervasive computing is a trend that continues to move towards increasingly ubiquitous, connected, tiny and invisible wireless computing devices. These can be either mobile or embedded in our environment (cars, tools, appliances, clothing and consumer goods), all communicating through increasingly interconnected networks. There are already 'smart' devices around us, which maintain information about our locations, the contexts in which they are being used and relevant data about users. Computing is becoming so miniaturised and naturalised within the environment that people will no longer realise that they are using them. Despite this, little progress has been made with computerised scent technology on a small or large scale.

Smells arouse fear, sadness, loss, love, disgust, longing and passion. These are all buried deep in our subconscious, waiting to come to the surface with a single sniff. Having explored olfactory research, the conclusion to this chapter will suggest what might happen if the human–computer interaction of *scents-on-a-chip* became the norm in 'smart sensory clothing', and was managed by a central computer, similar to UniComp in *This Perfect Day.*

Should this unwittingly get into the wrong hands of a future civilisation, it could be maliciously programmed to mistreat and exploit the user. An 'evil stench' scenario could see communities becoming confused or overloaded with inappropriate sensory information. This would be particularly distressing to the sensory-impaired, who already have a heightened sense of smell, or the mentally ill, who are emotionally vulnerable, or people with synaesthesia, a neurologically-based condition in which stimulation of one sensory or cognitive pathway leads to automatic, involuntary experiences in a second sensory or cognitive pathway. It could destabilise the military, who might otherwise rely on the power of scent as a new sensory language to navigate around the battlefield should they lose their other senses. The elderly could be bombarded with terrifying smells from their past, which could entice a stroke or heart attack. It could trigger an asthma attack for people allergic to fragrances, particularly in confined and open public spaces. It might increase the appetite of the obese, encouraging them to eat more.

Scents-on-a-chip could join forces with nature to create a mass orgy or mass mood disruptor. There is evidence to suggest that pheromones affect behavioural responses by modifying mood or emotion. Pheromones can also calm newborn babies, since they are able to accurately detect the smell of their mother. After a few days, babies have the ability to recognise their mother by her specific odour and, likewise, mothers are able to distinguish their own baby from others. However, this powerful bonding trust could be abused if the wrong pheromones or maternal lactation odours were sent to calm newborn babies and vice versa. The same could happen to anxious school children separated from their parents, who might otherwise find sensory clothing implanted with their parents' odour a calming and reassuring alternative to a comfort blanket.

The McClintock research on pheromones has shown that it is possible to alter the female menstrual cycle through the controlled use of pheromones. By 'conditioning' a female in this manner, *scents-on-a-chip* implanted in sensory clothing could release a 'veil' of pheromones without her knowledge. Conception could be manipulated, which would alter her hormones levels, ovulation cycle and fertility capability, manipulations which could have some impact on her subsequent behaviour.

Research in electronic nose sensing to detect levels of personal body odour has huge potential in the field of 'wellbeing fashion'. By diagnosing how a person might be feeling through stress-related body odour, clothes could potentially shield the user from negative feelings, such as fear or sadness, that they should otherwise not be protected from. This could have a positive impact for people with bipolar affective disorder because stress can trigger a relapse into depression or mania. However, if a centralised computer such as UniComp functioned in a way that allowed 'new data sensing', it could obscure our powerful (prehistoric) ability to smell and spitefully work the opposite way. It could deliberately fail to alert us if we had a life threatening disease such as cancer, or were about to eat poisonous food, or fail to relay vital medical data that can be successfully monitored through the sense of smell.

Although complex, contemporary musical scores enhanced with scents have the ability to create exciting, coherent synchronised scent symphonies. If scented soundtracks became a mainstream feature, sensory stimulation could be violated to cause extra distress with chilling effects. Negative emotions could be augmented by unexpected terrifying smells in the most mundane of films (although some might wish for this form of augmentation).

Advances in 'odourology' could lead to the shocking ordeal of losing our most intimate personal identification of all, body odour, which is more accurate than DNA or fingerprinting. The future may include a corrupt society in which pervasive computing automatically stores personal smell data in a centralised 'smellcode bank'. The authorities could manipulate this smell data to their advantage and trap people, maintaining total control over the entire population.

The stench of a stink bomb offers the military a powerful new 'offensive' weapon to add to their arsenal; not only to manipulate soldiers, but also the enemy at large. *Scents-on-a-chip* could be wirelessly embedded into sensory surveillance clothing to deliver a 'veil' of putrid odour to control a crowd. It could be embedded in uniform, to destabilise prisoners and therefore prevent them from escaping their prison cell. It could be directed in a cruel, twisted manner against colleagues, family or friends at a most inconvenient time, such as at the alter of a wedding, during exams, at an important government meeting, in an interview, and so on.

Experiments with sleep have proved that it is possible to remember a learning task through smell conditioning. It could be entirely feasible to embed *scents-on-a-chip* into specific clothes during the day and pyjamas at night. This might be seen as a form of brainwashing, because fragrances could manipulate the mind, without someone ever knowing. Repulsive, nauseating scents could also be forced on the user to encourage constant sleep deprivation and prevent relaxation.

The field of scent marketing is expected to reach a critical mass by promoting the health benefits, awareness and value that scent can play in business and society. This new field will generate novel applications for consumer product markets and public environments by offering a range of sensory services, data and recommendations to help people make smarter decisions. Major corporations are already creating individual signature scents to strengthen their brand and this will increase over the coming years. However, inhabiting a world managed by UniComp in *This Perfect Day*, the powerful and positive benefits of scent marketing could be manipulated to achieve the opposite effect. Unlike a sensory system that uses odour themes to promote marketing or display personal ambient shopping reminders, or has the capacity to improve finance skills through sensory banking methods, the 'veil' of evil scent from a deceitful computer could deliberately confuse the consumer by sending out the wrong subliminal messages to unsettle, distract, trigger inappropriate memories or forget important information. It could manipulate the consumer to catastrophic proportions, by enticing extreme overspending and consigning them to a life of misery, debt and absolute hell.

Chapter 5

Reflective Computing – Naturally Artificial

Nikola Šerbedžija

Fraunhofer FIRST, Berlin

> *The feeling of guilt with which [Chip] had left the Academy had led him to withhold himself from his next adviser, for he wanted to retain that feeling, which, though unpleasant, was the strongest feeling he had ever had and an enlargement, strangely, of his sense of being*

THIS PERFECT DAY, P. 59

5.1 Introduction

Nature has always been a major source of inspiration for technical developments. The more we understand the multiplicity of its forms and complexity of its functioning, the more we attempt to borrow from its fascinating effectiveness. The phenomenon of adaptation belongs to the most challenging, but also most difficult ones to re-create. This task requires not only new techniques but a thorough understanding of the phenomenon as well. Reflective computing is a novel paradigm that, by mimicking the process of adaptation, creates control systems naturally integrated into everyday surroundings. The major goal of the reflective approach is to gain awareness about individuals being involved in the controlled situation and to act appropriately, self-tuning its functioning to the benefit of the users. Reflective systems adapt to both social and individual circumstances, interacting with people in an instinctive and non explicit manner. The techniques and methods to achieve spontaneous man–machine interactions are discussed as well as possible impacts of the approach, taking into account both advantages and latent risks that may go beyond the initial intentions.

5.2   Motivation: What You Need Is What You Get

Indisputably, younger generations are far better prepared to accept and use new technologies than the older ones. This is so because from early childhood they have been playing (with or without permission) with remote controls, mobile phones, calculators, computer consoles, etc. That makes them fit for using more advanced devices as they grow older. The fact is they adapted themselves to new technology, becoming definitely smarter than their parents for the 'smart things'. Whether this kind of adaptation has some negative impacts, like deficiency in arithmetic, reading or reasoning, remains to be investigated.

Since computers have become an integral part of our everyday surroundings, it is necessary to re-think and re-design ways in which we cooperate with computers. To make a control system a genuine companion in everyday life, it should be enriched with some adaptation capabilities, in order to adjust its functioning to the users' needs. Otherwise, a modern *homo technicus* may experience (as any intrinsically adaptive species would, due to its permanent and enthusiastic exposure to rigid artificial systems) unpleasant retrogressive mutation.

The ideal man–machine confluence is the one that minimises explicit interaction and maximises the functionality of the system. The goal is to avoid giving commands to a control system, but rather to enable the system to understand what is needed in given circumstances. In a similar way that text editing has been revolutionised by the 'what you see is what you get' principle, the motto 'what you need is what you get' is radically changing the landscape of man–machine interfaces. The approach described here is called reflective, as it observes people in their activities and reflects their need by adjusting the control system accordingly. Observation is done through numerous sensor devices that collect information. Based on the collected information, an analysis is performed that results in emotional, cognitive and physical diagnosis. Taking into account the detected user state and the system goals, the functioning is adapted to the users' needs, making the control system naturally embedded into wider surroundings.

To illustrate the idea of reflective approach, three scenarios are considered, showing how technology blended with adaptive behaviour may be supportive any time, for any person of any age.

5.2.1 *Growing up with reflective care*

A playground in parks and kindergartens is one of the most beloved places for every kid. Equipped with swings, swing sets, seesaws, and monkey bars, a playground is the best place for children to exercise. However, energetic or unattended playing often brings a danger of injury. Imagine being suddenly left alone at the seesaw. Betrayed and seemingly abandoned, a child is in pain, both emotionally and physically. The reflective seesaw (see Fig. 5.1) should prevent that: it functions discretely, remaining neutral as long as both parties are present. If one party suddenly leaves, it senses the imbalance and reacts by compensating it with a benevolent counter-power. Technically, a reflective seesaw is easy to develop: what is needed are a couple of sensors, hydraulic counter-power and the control unit. Then a seesaw may learn each individual kid's habits and not only prevent accidents, but also assist in playing when a child is alone.

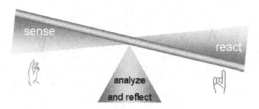

Fig. 5.1   Reflective seesaw.

The whole playground may be equipped with reflective devices that observe children as they play, increase joy and exercise and prevent possible accidents or call for help in case of need. This approach improves safety and brings more enjoyment on the playground. One negative impact may be that children become accustomed to an excess of care and become less cautious; another, at the other extreme, is that they fail to learn how to assess risk, and are subsequently disadvantaged as adults.

5.2.2   *Keep on playing with reflective assistance*

Adults, especially male adults, have their favourite four-wheel toys as well. However, real driving is not a playground and assistance is often welcome, especially in case of a long drive or heavy traffic. The reflective vehicle is a more advanced scenario, aiming to increase safety and pleasure in complex driving processes. A car is equipped with numerous sensors, e.g. cameras to detect facial expression, numerous psychophysiological measures (electrocardiogram, ECG) and a vehicular data bus system (e.g. CANbus), which offer numerous real-time data about the driving and engine condition (pedal pressure, wheel corrections, speed, etc). The sensors are used to monitor and diagnose the driver's state in a specific driving situation. The vehicle is also equipped with actuator devices like a 'reflective console' that gives warnings, a reflective media player and reflective seats (which re-shape to match the driver's or passenger's comfort) (Serbedzija *et al.*, 2008). The reflective vehicle actually plays the role of a friendly co-driver. The downside may be that sometimes a driver may develop a dislike of the 'back-seat driver' – but it seems to be a destiny of all clever clogs, anyhow.

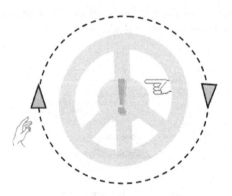

Fig. 5.2   Reflective vehicular assistance.

Figure 5.2 shows the reflective steering wheel, which stays neutral when the driver steers smoothly, and raises an alert (!) when the steering wheel corrections become more frequent, indicating possible difficulties. Further extension to the concept would be the connection to other reflective vehicles and networking with traffic control and road infrastructure.

5.2.3 Stay independent with reflective elderly care

With an ageing population there is a need to assist senior citizens in independent living. Reflective elderly home assistance is envisaged as a control system, supporting the most relevant home-living needs of elderly people. Two examples may be taken as an illustration:

- Rehabilitation at home by using guided exercise, according to the instructions displayed on television, aimed at personalised therapy. While supporting the exercise, physiological monitoring (e.g. heart rate, blood pressure, etc.) is done, with capability to adapt the training programme to real-life and personal situation and to connect to the remote medical control in case of emergency.
- Remote home appliances controlled by online state and switch off-on remote commands (e.g. for lighting, kitchen appliances, heating). This is meant to assist elderly inhabitants to assess the home situation from a distance (during social visits) or let others (friends, relatives, and social care staff) do so.

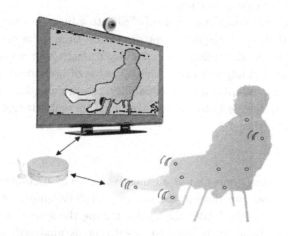

Fig. 5.3   Reflective home trainer.

Figure 5.3 illustrates the reflective home rehabilitation system, equipped with body sensor and camera to track the exercise and the TV as an actuator device that leads the person through individualised rehabilitation programmes. Extending the support to the whole reflective home, a control system for elderly people recognises their needs and weaknesses and assists and/or calls for assistance. The home system is also connected to medical assistance and friends and/or relatives. Dealing with highly personal physiological, psychological and physical details of the people involved, such systems need to be loyal, secure and well protected, which poses an extra challenge to already complex endeavour. Under no circumstances should the system be allowed to share this personal data with commercial or untrusted systems (whose aims may not be clear).

5.2.4   *Reflective control system*

A reflective control system that implements the above scenarios has to be capable of adaptation, featuring dynamic adjustment of its functioning in real-time, according to the situation. Different types of adaptation across different scales and dimensions are considered:

- Immediate adaptation – a capability of reacting in a moment when a sudden change occurs.
- Short-term adaptation – a capability to adjust to a more complex situation which requires some dimension time to be understood.
- Long-term adaptation – a capability to learn over a longer period of time and adjust to the personal needs of individual users.
- Pervasive adaptation – a capability to exchange knowledge with other systems and to act adaptively in different settings and in any situation.

Reflective control systems aim at all these varieties of adaptation.

In what follows, we discuss the design and development strategies of the reflective approach. Under the motto 'mixing the senses', a theoretical consideration of biologically-inspired adaptation is analysed, followed by the 'real-life computing' principle that offers technical blueprints of the design and implementation methodology. A strong pragmatic orientation of the approach is illustrated by a number of 'implicit and discrete' practical deployments. Interfering with nature is a tricky endeavour, so it is worthwhile to re-consider 'who is controlling whom' in a brave new technological world. The analyses of the impact of new technology help in re-examining the results achieved and in tracing new challenges.

5.3 Theoretical Consideration: Mixing the Senses

One of the most striking features of nature that ensures evolution and progress is adaptation: a capability to self-adjust according to changing conditions. In an effort to mimic the adaptation in natural systems and deploy it artificially in man–machine interfaces, this approach takes the biocybernetic loop as a starting point. Originally, the loop (Pope *et al.*, 1995) describes how psychophysiological data regarding the status of the user are captured, analysed and converted to a computer control input in real-time. The function of the loop is to monitor changes in user state in order to initiate an appropriate adaptive response.

The reflective approach extends this initial concept to a wider set of input information, thus allowing for more complex forms of monitoring, analysis and adaptation. This approach takes the rationale of affective computing and combines it with higher level understanding of social- and goal-oriented situations. This approach is multi-modal and takes into account different kinds of information, processing them in multiple loops at different time scales.

5.3.1 *Biocybernetic loop*

The biocybernetic loop is implemented with the help of a sense-analyse-react control troika (Serbedzija and Fairclough, 2009). There are three major phases of a single loop: sense, analysis and activate. These phases are repeated endlessly, where each consecutive cycle takes into account the effects of the previous one, therefore performing constant self-tuning and performance optimisation.

The first phase of the biocybernetic loop is monitoring of the user in a given situation. The collecting of information can be done by observing overt actions (e.g. location, looking, pointing), overt expression (e.g. changes in behaviour associated with psychological expression) and covert expression (e.g. changes in physiology associated with psychological expression). These options cover both visible and invisible indicators of the user state, allowing for further higher-level processing and diagnosing.

The analysis phase of the biocybernetic loop is a comprehensive process that involves psychology, physiology and behavioural sciences. It may also include learning processes and decision making. In order to make an effective use of such diversity, the reflective approach relies on affective and physiological computing and deploys simplified rule-based reasoning. The loop is designed according to a specific rationale, which serves a number of specific meta-goals. For instance, the biocybernetic loop may be designed to:

- Promote and sustain a state of positive engagement with the given task.
- Minimise health or safety risks inherent to man–machine interaction.

The capability of the biocybernetic loop to sustain engagement has been demonstrated within the context of the computer game (Rani *et al.*, 2005). The second meta-goal is concerned with health and safety. The concept of such adaptive automation is to avoid the use of automation during hazardous states of awareness, e.g. fatigue and boredom, when safety may be jeopardised (Prinzel, 2002).

The final phase of reaction is devoted to the adequate system response that is performed through a certain action of the system actuators, having further influence both on the user and the controlled situation.

Based on a better understanding of both personal involvement and social and behavioural situation of the user, a reflective system may offer adaptive control of different types and different time scales: immediate adaptation should support safety; short-term adaptation should respond to more complex states that require several steps of self-tuning; long-term adaptation should provide individualisation as a process that guarantees that the system has co-evolved with each individual user and can target its functioning to specific individual needs; and pervasive adaptation is spreading through system modification that crosses the single system boundary and is omnipresent. Pervasive adaptation may be seen as an orthogonal concept to previous types of adaptation, providing interfaces to other similar systems.

5.3.1.1 *Awareness*

Awareness implies knowledge gained through one's own perceptions or by means of information. In technical systems, perception comes through sensor devices that capture, quantify and operationalise events in the environment (including the user). In further processing, quantified and operationalised sensor measurements create an image of users and their situation, yielding system awareness. At a fundamental level, awareness describes the 'field of view' of the system, i.e. the range of events to which the adaptive system is capable of responding.

Awareness, as presented in the above application scenarios, is most often used to address the safety functions of a control system. For example:

- At the playground, reflective control should react immediately to avoid possibly dangerous situations (e.g. overly energetic play).
- In a driving situation, any driver may experience difficulties in navigating through narrow lanes in a stressful traffic situation (e.g. reduced visibility or ice). This scenario requires a higher level of concentration to sustain adequate levels of lateral control. The system becomes aware of this change in driver state via psychophysiological changes, such as increased heart rate or reduced heart rate variability, as well as frequent corrections of the steering wheel detected via vehicular computer. In this case, the warning console may provide visual feedback, disable incoming phone calls or reduce the volume of the car entertainment system.
- In the home setting, physiological monitoring should alert medical assistance in case of detected high heart rate or critical blood pressure; or location detection should set off an alarm in case of a sudden collapse or fall.

Awareness could be related to a recognition of a more complex user phenomenon (individual, social or behavioural situation), but for the purpose of this presentation it is reduced to its simplest meaning.

5.3.1.2 *Short-term adaptation*

An adjustment is a typical example of adaptation, seen as an act of change in order to become adjusted to a different or special situation. A system adjustment at a moderate time scale is implemented through the biocybernetic loop that monitors behaviour with respect to a certain goal or in achieving a planned state.

In the application domains, it may be best illustrated by achieving an envisaged application goal through adaptive control. It is anticipated that mood will be assessed via cameras for facial recognition, combined with psychophysiology. However, changes in mood take place over several minutes and the system requires a moderate time scale in order to detect a negative mood, such as anger:

- At the playground, the reflective control needs more time (and biocybernetic cycles) to diagnose positive (or negative) emotions while playing and to react appropriately.

- In driving assistance, a useful goal is comfort (positive physical state) while driving. The reflective vehicle may be capable of influencing the disposition of the driver, to prevent negative moods such as boredom or anger, and to promote positive moods of high activation (alertness) and positive affect (happiness).
- In a reflective home, the rehabilitation should go smoothly. Should the system detect a painful or stressful situation, the plan should be changed, easing the requested movements.

Short-term adaptation is the most common type of adaptation and is implanted in many control systems.

5.3.1.3 *Long-term adaptation*

Evolution can be defined as a gradual process in which something changes into a different and improved form. From the temporal point of view, evolution is a modification process that takes place over a longer time period.

An aspect of evolution is a dynamic form of personalisation, where both system and user respond to repeated exposure to one another. The system must learn how a particular user expresses anger or happiness and which type of adaptation from the system repertoire provides the best means for reducing anger or promoting positive affect for the user. As emotions are not firm phenomena that can be switched on or off, an adaptive system needs to monitor and control the success of its own reactions, re-measuring the emotional state as a function of its response, thus fine-tuning subsequent adaptations. As can be seen in the above scenarios, personalisation is a common system requirement:

- Children are different: some enjoy very active, others more gentle play. Thus, the system needs to track the child's behaviour over a longer period of time to adjust to their personal needs.
- The vehicular adjustments to the particular driver also take time to get to know the driver in the first place. Therefore, the system must continue to evolve and to experiment with different adaptive responses in order to 'refresh' the interface with the user.
- Reflective control at home cannot be successful if the system reacts in a standard way. Each person has their own limits and physiological thresholds that need to be learned through experience.

Personalisation requires system memory; a database of the previous experiences. During a longer period of time, the adaptive system should learn about each individual user; her/his habits, wishes and needs that may change over time, and should accordingly evolve, exercising adaptation at a longer term.

5.3.1.4 *Pervasive adaptation*

Pervasiveness denotes the quality of filling or spreading throughout. Pervasiveness of a reflective system is an orthogonal concept to the temporal adaptation aspects. It introduces a new complexity, namely distributed and coordinated adaptation, i.e. connecting different devices used in different systems, bringing a new (info)sphere of reflective applications that are an integral part of our technical surroundings. The concept of pervasiveness opens up the possibility of multiple biocybernetic loops running simultaneously and the capability of sharing information on the user state or preferences between distributed systems. Pervasive technology highlights issues of synchronisation (between different loops), conflicts (between different adaptive responses) and privacy (i.e. the capability of devices to share information about the user) for biocybernetic adaptation. In addition, pervasive technology brings about the potential to enrich information about the current state of the user by pooling information across systems.

In the application domain, pervasiveness brings obvious advantages in improving singular systems and yielding collectiveness into the scenarios:

- A reflective kindergarten contains both inside and outside settings, each equipped with different tools for learning and playing. If they are all connected in a common pervasive system that can also communicate with the parents' reflective infrastructure, the 'all spreading' character of the system would be achieved.
- A reflective vehicle should be connected with other vehicles and road infrastructure, utilising the pervasive character of our future environments.
- A reflective home is by definition interconnected with other systems that offer medical or friendly assistance, making it genuinely pervasive.

Finally, long lasting pervasiveness and individualisation is achieved by having the reflective technology help us throughout different stages in life, from early childhood to old age. Certainly, an alarm should be raised at this point, re-considering whether we can really trust such a personal assistant, or whether we can decide how and when to switch it off.

5.3.2 *Affective computing*

The driving force behind the analysis phase of the sense-process-react paradigm is affective computing (Picard, 1997), a rapidly evolving discipline that investigates how to capture and interpret affects (emotional states with accompanying movements), postures (the way a person holds/carries their body) and gestures (expressive, bodily movements). Some categories of affective computing rely on psycho-physiological variables (PPV), which can be measured by ambulatory devices equipped with modern microelectronic sensors. This use of physiology in diagnosing psychological states (often called constructs), by making physiological measurement a part of the processing loop, is called physiological computing (Fairclough, 2009). The analysis of the collected measurements makes it possible to precisely determine the user's emotional, mental or physical state, especially in situations of predictable behaviour. Once the user state is evaluated, the system can be tuned to provide a supportive reaction.

5.3.2.1 *Short chronology*

Traditionally, affect has always served as a fairly reliable borderline between human and machine: humans have and recognise emotions; computers do not. But the time when machines were considered cold, affectless and serious are gone. Nowadays, more and more smart devices are equipped with some means to recognise and interact with human emotions.

As is often the case, the toy industry is the pioneer of pseudo-life innovations: we all remember teddy bears and dolls that 'behave' as if they are alive. This may have been just a first step in cheering up children by imitating reality. Nowadays, cameras recognise a smile, and may be set to picture only 'happy' people, lie detectors are permitted in many countries as a routine method of police interrogation, automatic text processing can discover humour, audio analyses can tell whether the speaker is happy or not and music and lighting are 'standard' means to improve our mood.

The scientific boost for affective computing is attributed to Rosalind Picard (1997), who wrote that 'computer-based communication is affect-blind, affect-deaf, and generally speaking, affect-impaired. A quantum leap in communication will occur when computers become able to at least recognise and express affect'. Pioneering work in affective computing gained significance with the findings that emotions are tightly connected to reasoning, justifying the ultimate importance of this psychological phenomenon. In other words, understanding affect means also understanding cognitive processes – a statement that could not be ignored. The end of the last century marked the start of a new discipline.

Affective computing is devoted to creating computer systems that emulate, recognise and react to human emotions. It is a field that opens the way to previously inconceivable kinds of computer applications while at the same time threatens to disturb the relaxed time where we thought only our friends understood us. Crossing this border between human and machine, even as it creates conveniences, may potentially open a number of threats to our privacy. Sure it would be good to have a 'flirt assistant' that whistles 'she or he likes you – would you like to do something about it?' However, we do not necessarily want our own 'emotional image' to be broadcast for public display (so that anyone can see who we like or how we feel at the moment).

5.3.3 Capturing the user status

A number of monitoring techniques are available to capture the psychological status of the user. Based on the nature of affect as well as on intrusiveness of the monitoring devices, three distinct categories exist:

- Overt actions, for example location tracking, looking and pointing.
- Overt expression, like changes in behaviour associated with psychological expression.
- Covert expression, represented by changes in physiology associated with psychological expression.

These groups of monitoring cover both overt and covert indicators of the user's psychological state.

5.3.3.1 Overt actions

Overt behaviour and actions may be captured at a low- and fine-grained level of detail. The location and movement of the user may be discovered by GPS (general positioning system) or by simple acceleration body devices. User activities in terms of active engagement with software/hardware may be monitored (e.g. recording keystrokes and cursor movements) and cameras can provide details of user actions, such as eye movements and gross actions, such as standing or sitting. This behaviour can also be captured at high fidelity, such as measuring indices of productivity linked to performance. For example, how many tasks have been completed in a set time, how many levels the user has completed on a computer game per hour of play, or how many corrections a driver is making on a steering wheel while driving. Overt actions and performance represent one source of data that is open to visual or behavioural inspection.

5.3.3.2 *Overt expression*

The measurement of overt expression has been heavily researched in the domain of affective computing. A number of systems have been developed to capture the expression of emotion as manifested with respect to facial or vocal expression (Russell *et al.*, 2003) and body posture (Ahn *et al.*, 2007). These categories of expression involve subtle changes that are not always under conscious control. In this case, expressive behaviour that is overt and observable is monitored and categorised as an indicative display of key emotional states (Bartlett *et al.*, 2003). The use of a camera as a non intrusive sensor is very popular.

Fig. 5.4   Facial expressions.

Figure 5.4 shows major emotions as captured by facial expressions. A useful summary of automated detection of facial expression can be found in Pantic and Rothcrantz (2000). Some of the basic elements for facial expression detection and posture/gesture recognition are given below.

Facial Expressions
Measure: Detecting basic features from the face (eyes, mouth, muscle activity, etc.).
Psychological constructs: Basic emotions.

Body Posture
Measure: Combination of shoulder and head posture; activity level (amount of movement); position.
Psychological constructs: Derivation of hedonic tone: happy or sad posture. A high amount of movement tells something about the aroused energy level. A low amount of movements can, in combination with other measures, indicate high concentration or tension. Positioning in chair can indicate fatigue, boredom or high alertness.

5.3.3.3 Covert expression

Covert expression relies on human physiological changes as a major input parameter for a man–machine communication. The changes occur under the skin and are genuine and innate. The body emits a wide array of bio-electrical signals, from increased muscle tension to changes in heart rate to tiny fluctuations in the electrical activity of the brain. These signals represent internal channels of communication between various components of the human central nervous system. These signals may also be used to infer behavioural states, such as exertion during exercise, but their real potential to innovate human–computer interaction lies in the ability of these measures to capture psychological processes that remain covert and imperceptible to the observer.

There is literature in the physiological computing tradition (Fairclough, 2009) that is inspired by work on affective computing (Picard, 1997), specifically the use of psychophysiology to discern different emotional states and particularly those negative states such as frustration (Kapoor et al., 2007) that both designer and user wish to minimise or avoid. A parallel strand of human factors research (Pope et al., 1995; Prinzel, 2002) has focused on the detection of mental engagement using electroencephalographic (EEG) measurements of neural activity (see also Chavarriaga and Millán, Chapter 3).

Measuring physiological signals represents the most precise technique for detecting and diagnosing psychological states, though at the same time it is inconvenient, as it requires sensors to be attached to the body. Below we give some of the most commonly-used physiological measurements and their psychological interpretations.

Electroencephalography (EEG: Electrical activity of the brain)
Measure: Power in theta (3–7Hz), alpha (8–12Hz), beta (14–40Hz).

Psychological constructs: Ratio of alpha activity from frontal sites = approach/avoidance motivation; alpha activity at all sites = inverse of cortical activation = alpha suppression at frontal sites important for cognitive demand; theta activity at frontal central site (Fz) = indicator of cognitive demand.

Electrocardiogram (ECG: Electrical activity of the heart)

Measure: Heart rate in beats/min, or IBI (inter-beat interval (ms)) between successive R-peaks; mid-frequency band of sinus arrhythmia (0.07–0.14 Hz); high frequency band or respiratory sinus arrhythmia (0.15–0.40 Hz).

Psychological constructs: Increased autonomic activation and shortening of IBI = cognitive demand; mid-frequency component has been associated with mental effort; high frequency component has been associated with vagal inhibition (lowers autonomic activation). But RSA also highly depends on respiration pattern.

Blood pressure

Measure: Systolic and diastolic blood pressure once every three to four minutes.

Psychological constructs: Increased systolic blood pressure = cognitive demand and motivation.

Pupil diameter

Measure: Frequency of high frequency discontinuities per 30 seconds.

Psychological constructs: High frequency discontinuities in pupil diameter related to cognitive demand.

5.3.3.4 *Multi-modal processing*

The use of overt or covert measures to capture user state is not mutually exclusive. The detection of user states is achieved via multi-modal data collection (Pantic and Rothcrantz, 2003), where specific states are characterised by 'fusing' information from a variety of sensors, e.g. gestures, facial expression, pressure on the mouse, as well as psychophysiology. Recent work on the detection of user frustration (Kapoor *et al.*, 2007) demonstrated the utility of this approach by combining multiple measures to predict subjective feelings of frustration.

To summarise the state of the art, the psychological status of the user may be represented by overt actions/location, expressive behaviour and covert psychophysiology. This representation of user status may be captured and stored in real-time and used to direct system adaptations, i.e. to tailor the response of the system to the needs and preferences of the individual. Reflective computing deploys all of the stated techniques in a uniform approach to perform the most precise detection of the user state. In that respect it is a multi-modal approach that takes into account most of the achievements in affective and physiological computing.

5.3.4 Closing the loop

The biocybernetic loop indicates how the reflective system should function, whereas affective computing provides means for comprehensive and reliable analyses of human affects and physiology. To make the machine really responsive, a control strategy needs to take such reasoning into account when controlling the system functioning. The control systems are also equipped with numerous actuator devices that should be integrated into computer settings and should influence the whole setting, social situation and emotional, cognitive or physical state of the people involved. For example, a negative mood should be comforted with cheering music, soft-lighting and a calming aroma (see Tillotson, Chapter 4); if a person sits uncomfortably, then the seat should re-shape automatically; when a shopper stares at the product label, then the font showing the price and description should increase in size.

Adaptive system control and the use of special devices to influence the application setting and improve the personal situation in given circumstances is the ultimate goal of the reflective systems. Thus, new configurations are needed to include novel actuators that should create a positive impact on people and improve efficiency, comfort and wellbeing.

However, influencing inner user states by technology needs to be balanced and sensitive to personal, social and ethical concerns. There is a time to express emotion, and a time to suppress it; a situation to sense what others are feeling and a situations to ignore feeling. Pervasive systems, being omnipresent and active all the time, need to have a balance in exercising their own influence. This is the point at which ethical issues become crucial: it is easier to create systems that are responsive to human inner state than to make this response sensitive to psychological and social circumstances.

5.3.5   *Reflective software architecture*

Developing software to control the biocybernetic loop involves tasks like real-time sensor/actuator control, user and scenario profile analyses, affective computing, self-organisation and adaptation. To accomplish these requirements, a service- and component-oriented middleware architecture (Beyer *et al.*, 2009; Schroeder *et al.*, 2008), based on a reflective ontology, has been designed, which promises a dynamic and reactive behaviour featuring different biocybernetic loops. According to the reflective ontology, the reflective software is grouped into three layers:

- Tangible layer – a low-level layer that controls sensor and actuator devices. It offers its atomic services (sensor measurements/actuator controls) to the rest of the system.
- Reflective layer – a central layer that combines the atomic services of the lower layer with user profile and scenario description. This allows for more complex services and components that evaluate user emotional/cognitive/physical states and application situation and trigger system (re)action, according to the application goals.
- Application layer – a high-level layer that defines the application scenario and system goals. By combining low and high level services and components from other layers, application layer runs and controls the whole system.

In the next section, we discuss how this architecture has been used to develop a number of reflective case studies.

5.4   Reflective Deployment: Seamless and Implicit

The reflective approach imitates nature and makes artificial technical systems look and feel natural. This means that the man–machine interaction is seamless and implicit (as the system is capable of grasping the user's needs) and discrete (as it operates via overt and covert human expressions), making the human a part of the processing loop. The functioning of pervasive reflective applications is explained through a number of case studies. Each case study represents the stand alone system with its own reflective framework.

5.4.1 *Mood player*

The mood player is a music player that selects music to match the mood of the user, or selects music that may improve her/his emotional state.

Several steps are needed for realising the music player, which collectively form a closed-loop system. Firstly, the input of the system must be defined so that it covers the current mood, measured unobtrusively with physiological sensors. Another input to the system is the target emotional state selected by the user, e.g. to feel more positive, or to feel more energetic. The second step in the closed-loop system involves pre-processing input to obtain the significant features from the raw physiological signals. These features function as input to drive the selection of music. Thirdly, music will be selected based on the predicted influence that the song will have on the diagnosed emotional state. These steps close and complete the biocybernetic loop for the mood player.

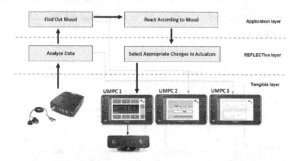

Fig. 5.5   The mood player component architecture.

The specific reflective component architecture used for the application of the reflect framework applied on the mood player use case is presented in Fig. 5.5. The tangible layer controls the devices and the corresponding processing algorithms for the physiological sensors and music player (actuator). The physiological sensors send the information to the 'acquisition and data analysis' component, which performs the pre-processing of the signals and passes it on to the 'physiological feature extraction' component. This component calculates the features, e.g. heart rate, from the signal. The 'play music' component plays the music for the user. At the reflective layer there is the 'adapt music' component that fuses the sensor data with system goals and sets the 'appropriate' music. This component receives the request to which emotional state the player should adapt to. It further instructs the 'play music' component which title to play. The application layer contains only one component – 'mood manager,' where the 'reasoning' of the mood player is implemented, taking care that the involved biocybernetic loops function smoothly (preventing possible safety versus joy conflicts).

5.4.2 *Adaptive seat*

The aim of the seat adaptation system is to monitor the postural behaviour of a driver and to use these data to detect periods of driver discomfort. In these cases, the seat should re-shape itself to counteract the perception of discomfort detected in the user.

The adaptive seat contains a number of pressure sensors that creates the pressure map indicating sitting behaviour (comfort). These raw data are processed to calculate the centre of pressure (COP), a parameter which is broadly used to study human sitting posture (Cho and Choi, 2005). Should any discomfort be detected, air pumps are activated to inflate/deflate the air cushions within the adaptive seat.

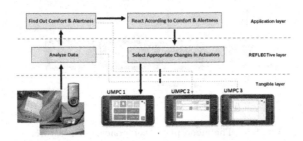

Fig. 5.6   A simplified seat adaptation system component architecture.

Figure 5.6 illustrates the component architecture of the seat adaptation or comfort system. To make the system function more precisely, comfort sensor information must be combined with the camera (for posture analysis) and the driving information (not shown on the picture). Vertical and horizontal acceleration should be taken into account (e.g. sometimes the current discomfort may be caused by sudden short-term acceleration or a bumpy road) by determining the seat adaptation strategy. The three screens are used for monitoring purposes as system functions seamlessly, re-shaping the seat automatically, according to the comfort of the driver.

5.4.3 Vehicle as a co-driver

The case studies outlined previously describe separate systems reacting upon users' emotional and physical experiences. The reflective vehicle system is a combination of both subsystems, enriched with the vehicular CAN-bus and a vehicular board computer. Such a system configuration allows for adding a third component – a cognitive monitor. This is achieved by supplementing the reflective and application layer with rules to aid cognitive diagnosis, i.e. to assess the level of mental effort exerted by the driver. The cognitive monitor uses psychophysiological sensors (e.g. heart rate and heart rate variability) as well as data regarding driving performance, e.g. lateral deviation of vehicle and steering wheel control. The driver receives feedback from the cognitive monitor via display warnings at the board console if high mental effort is diagnosed. The resulting system offers a 'co-driver' style of a support, helping the driver throughout the ride, observing her/his emotional, cognitive and physical condition.

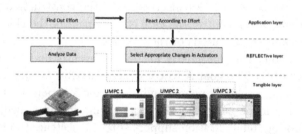

Fig. 5.7 Elements of the additional cognitive support.

Figure 5.7 sketches the elements of the cognitive vehicular support that, together with components for emotional and comfort control (the mood player and seat adaptation are used in the same way as described previously), yields a final vehicular assistance system.

Figure 5.8 shows the cockpit of the reflective vehicle with three on-board computers, adaptive seat and cameras installed in front of the driver. The system has been tested in practise and effectively justifies the pragmatic orientation of the reflective approach.

Fig. 5.8   Reflective cockpit.

5.4.4   *Reflective home nurse*

Home nursing gains in significance with increased life expectancy. As a result, more and more people reach the age at which they need some assistance in order to prolong their independence (living at home on their own). This makes home nursing a resource-intensive activity, stretching current medical care to its limits. In this situation, new technology can help. Reflective assistance is concerned with the construction of flexible 'smart' systems, which control the care environment of the elderly, adapting its functioning to the needs of the individual.

Reflective home care for elderly people is currently under development (Serbedzija, 2010). The goal is to construct a flexible 'smart' ambient to control the home for elderly people, fulfilling some functions that traditionally belong to a home nurse. The support should include: medical ambulatory monitoring; rehabilitation support (Fig. 5.3 sketches the home rehabilitation control that guides and monitors seniors through their physical exercises); seating/lying comfort; movement monitoring; home appliance monitoring; TV and media-rich entertainment control; and communication with mobile devices. A discreet and implicit functioning of the reflective home care should significantly improve the quality of life for older inhabitants, offering its assistance only if needed.

Reflective support for each of the above mentioned functionalities is achieved by embedding numerous sensor and actuator devices into home settings and by deploying reflective control to these devices:

- Medical support consists of heart rate and blood pressure measurements as a regular daily check up, with warnings displayed on TV and an emergency hotline to medical staff.

- Rehabilitation support controls exercise devices (e.g. home cycle or walking track) according to the instructions displayed on TV. Physiological monitoring (e.g. heart rate, blood pressure) is done simultaneously, guiding the exercise according to the body response.
- Movement control is done via cameras placed in each room and is used only for critical hotline warnings (in case of a sudden fall).
- Comfort control is maintained via seating and lying sensors, checking the body pressure at critical points and modifying (if necessary) the shape of the armchair/mattress via air pumps.
- Home appliances are connected to automatic switch on/off devices, allowing remote monitoring and control.
- Entertainment control consists of a mood player designed to control an entertainment centre according to emotional response.
- Communication control connects to mobile devices, allowing for urgent calls and remote monitoring.

Given this functionality, the reflective home performs many of the routine functions of a home nurse. It does daily medical check-ups, assists in active exercise and rehabilitation, cares for the inhabitant's physical, emotional and mental state, reminds and/or takes control of switching on/off the home appliances and supports mobile communication with emergency centre, friends and relatives. In summary, it assumes numerous medical, psychological, physical and social functions.

The reflective framework, with its already existing controllers for ambulatory psychophysiological measurement and diagnosis, offers an off-the-shelf solution for a number of problems that appear in the domain of remote measurements and analyses of user states. The already described vehicular emotional, cognitive and physical monitors are re-used almost without any modifications. This makes the reflective framework a straightforward means for use within the home care scenario.

Looking at the nursing home checklist (see www medicare.com) it may be concluded that a reflective assistant, as a caring home nurse, fulfils most of the requirements that an ideal nurse must satisfy: medical competence, pleasant behaviour, a good sense for temperature, atmosphere and wellbeing at home, while remaining at the same time respectful towards residents, sensitive to their emotional, physical and mental state, available 24 hours a day, and ready to communicate with friends, relatives and medical experts. Last but not least, such a reflective assistant is always ready to call for human assistance if needed.

There is further work in the extension of the use of reflective technology in a medical domain. This primarily requires refinement and enrichment of the reflective ontology in providing support at all levels of reflective programming: namely interfacing new devices, diagnosing new situations and enlarging its knowledge base. Improvements in the domain of information protection are also on the research agenda, as the system deals with highly sensitive personal information that should not be available for any other use but medical. Most often there are leaks of information that may be abused for commercial and marketing purposes. Special care should be taken in protecting the private sphere of the elderly population, knowing how sensitive they are and how easily they can become a victim of aggressive unscrupulous salesmen.

5.5   Technology Impacts – Who is in Control

The ultimate goal of the reflective approach is to make future control systems genuinely friendly, personalised and responsive to the needs of individual users. To achieve this goal, it is not enough to create interfaces that suit an average user; it is necessary to make them really personal, taking into account current necessities as well as the psychological state of the people being involved in real life. On one hand, emerging systems that are reactive to human senses can be interpreted as our technical 'sixth sense', which supports us in everyday situation. On the other, we should be aware that our personal identity is being exposed to the interconnected world, whose meta-goals may be different from what we expect. This raises ethical concerns: Are we aware how much systems know about us? Can we trust the systems? Do they respect our privacy? Do they care for our emotional sensitivity? Do they take into account our social context? What is a long term impact of such systems on us? Unfortunately, there is no single and straightforward answer to any of these questions.

A step towards a better understanding of these questions may be found in looking at some of the contradictions in a more mature technology domain, like the Web 2.0.

5.5.1   *Web used to be anonymous and distributed*

Knowing how interconnected the digital world is (Norman, 2007), recording what we buy and eat, where we travel, sleep, rent cars (e.g. credit card institution), what our interests are (e.g. Google), what we read (e.g. Amazon), how we communicate (Internet provider), how we spend our spare time (e.g. Flickr), how we socialise (e.g. Facebook), what our biometric signature is (e.g. custom control), and what our medical records (e.g. health insurance smart cards) look like, we can fully relax and let e-systems assist us in most of our everyday activities. The digital divide is sharpening, 'digitalise or perish' seems to be the motto – those who are left behind are the digitally excluded.

However, one should not forget that the world wide web used to be an anonymous forum which was, in the beginning, one of the main reasons for its wide acceptance. Somehow, it seems that, in the process of use, we all almost willingly traded our virtues and values for speed and services. The emerging problem may be that young people growing up with the Internet do not care for these virtues and values anymore.

A web browser may be used as an entry point to a massively distributed system, a bazaar of interconnected and interlinked information and services. Nowadays a web browser is almost a 'dumb' terminal to a couple of 'main frames', also known as social networking sites. It seems that the major characteristics of the web, taken for granted from the very beginning, are quietly diminishing.

5.5.2 *Computers used to be trustworthy*

When visiting a bank, post office, government or insurance institution, most of us have experienced the unpleasant administrator answer: 'sorry the computer does not allow that ... '. Somehow that implies: 'maybe we could do it, but it is wrong and the computer would not permit it'. And often people believe it, since in general we all do trust technology. This is not without a reason: initially, computers were used as devices for computing, being so fast and precise in arithmetic they proved to be much more reliable than humans. But nowadays, computers make decisions, translate texts, speak and do many complex things at which they are not necessarily better than we are. In the digital jungle with greedy businesses and dangerous hackers, we experience that computer systems are vulnerable and are only as trustworthy as those who program them.

5.5.3 *Computers used to preserve privacy*

Taking part in so many e-businesses, a modern 'e-individual' is overwhelmed with different passwords and may believe that they are acting in a protected world. Despite significant and mostly successful efforts to guard online pro-

cesses and ensure authentication of parties involved, many e-society forums
leave too many leaks, basically neglecting privacy protection for the sake
of data mining, profiling and advertisement. Obsessed with attractive and
popular services, most people willingly or naïvely give up their privacy.
And the new generations are adapting their attitudes towards privacy using the wrong examples. It is often argued that sensibility towards privacy
is a cultural issue: some societies are more sensitive and others less so.
Nevertheless, the countries with the oldest privacy protection laws nowadays have the most surveillance cameras per capita. In the process of digital
revolution, even the Peeping Tom ceased to be a negative legend and eaves-
dropping is considered not as bad as it was seven centuries ago. Not only
that, computer systems are weakening their protection mechanisms, and it
seems that users are following the same pattern.

5.5.4 *Networks are supposed to be collective*

Social networks are by definition meant to promote social virtues. It is
logical to expect that individuals who have a lot of friends, who are beloved
and popular among others, are ideal social figures. However, if measured
by Facebook parameters, there may be a contradiction: if you want to be
successful online, there is not much time left for real experiences off-line.
Furthermore, constant exposure to the 'yuck' and 'wow' of the web may
substitute cognitive with colourful values, may endorse exhibitionism and
favour virtual over real experience. When all of these happen at an early age
and over a long period of time, the social consequences of social networks
become questionable (see also Colombo *et al.*, Chapter 7).

The lesson learned from mature technology is that many of the initial
principles that drive and motivate development and deployment may be
given up in the process of use and commercialisation of the technological
trends. In our fascination with trendy technological possibilities, we only
look at what we can do with modern technology, forgetting to consider
what it can do to us. The privacy loss may be seen as collateral damage, but the real danger lies in the long-term impact technology has on
us. In one of his articles, Floridi (2007) invented a neologism Infosphere
as a collection of informational entities, which inevitably constitute the environment that supports our life. To further understand the influence of
the Infosphere upon us (as Inforgs – informational organisms), the author
introduces 're-ontologisation', referring to a fundamental transformation of
our environment as a consequence of digitalisation and the Infosphere.

Within the information society, it seems that we are modifying our ontological perspective from a materialistic one, in which physical objects and processes still play a key role, to an informational one, in which objects and processes are dephysicalised, typified and perfectly clonable. The right of usage is then perceived to be at least as important as the right of ownership; and the criterion for existence is no longer being immutable (Greek metaphysics) or being potentially subject to perception (modern metaphysics), but being *interactable*.

Floridi's reasoning behind the meaning and the ethics of the Infosphere as a non-avoidable part of our ecological system may help us to understand that the impact of new technology is enormous and should not be neglected.

With the technology described here, as well as with neuroscience that is making huge progress in the domain of brain–computer interfaces, we are about to yield the last defence of our privacy to the 'digital deliberation', namely our feelings, mental integrity, even our thoughts. This raises serious concerns and calls for a wide-spectrum approach to re-think the rules and the roles computers should play in society. The problem is not only whether the private information can be abused, but, even more seriously, whether our personal and social integrity will suffer changes that cannot be reversed.

Certainly, the use of modern technology facilitates everyday life and provides efficiency, comfort and smooth communication in a way it could not even be perceived a few decades ago. Especially the applications in medicine and ambient assisted living represent encouraging justifications for the recent achievements. Nevertheless, the potential for misuse is huge and what is even more disturbing, neither possibilities nor risks are properly understood. In this context, the final observations given here focus only at a small segment of the problem – that is where technology may help. For example, making reflective systems closed by strict separation of psychophysiological and administrative data, and making it technically impossible to exchange information with other (e-business or administrative) systems, would be a step in a right direction in protecting privacy. Furthermore, the reflective ontology should be extended with the loyalty concept. Assigning different levels of protection (for example, anonymous, familiar, friendly) to physiological features and psychological constructs may ensure that the data exchange happens only at the same fidelity level and with explicit permission of the user.

However, a controversial impact of the new technology on our life is a far more complex issue and needs to be addressed from different viewpoints, involving wide and cross-disciplinary discussion. The roles in this discussion are traditionally divided among:

- Artists who picture the universe in a free and imaginative way with a free mind, calling for re-thinking, re-consideration, re-involvement, aesthetics, and even de-construction.
- Scientists and technology providers who are responsible not only for the development of novel ideas but also for hints on how to technically deal with possible ethical concerns.
- Philosophers and sociologists as leaders in considering the impacts of new technology on the society (Floridi, 2007; Rulon, 2006).
- Law makers and politicians to ensure efficient legal background and deployment (Hettinger, 1989).
- Practitioners and industry to respect regulations and ethical norms, while making commercial and other uses of modern technology.

Even though the fully justified privacy concerns have already been recognised and partially taken into account, the major threat has been completely neglected. Namely, what is the long-term impact of new technology on us as individual and social beings? Are we experiencing changes due to constant exposure to technological advances and are those changes good for us or not? Do we control the technology we made or is the technology taking control over us? These are the critical issues that require thorough consideration and clear answers.

5.6 Conclusion

The reflective approach, being highly user-centric, makes a person's physiology and behaviour a part of the processing loop and body area network an integral part of a wider system. However, an uncontrolled deployment of smart technology may bring about dangers and have undesirable consequences. The use of massively interconnected digital devices endangers our privacy, exposing all aspects of our behaviour, from the everyday activities, working competences, habits, feelings, intentions and even our emotions and thoughts. Concerns are raised to ensure that the 'digital victory' does not turn into a Pyrrhic one. Negative consequences may be prevented, if the new technology takes privacy protection seriously and integrates protection mechanisms into systems in all phases, namely design, development and deployment. Furthermore, emotional phenomena should be treated naturally and not just as measurements that are genuine and thus practical for interaction improvements. This means that social norms and 'emotional behaviour codex' as known in society, should be deployed in smart systems as well.

It seems that one of the main controversies a modern society is confronted with is not the rapid technology development that sometimes goes even beyond science-fiction, but rather the slow pace at which humanities answer to the new moral challenges. Their main task remains to be to warn about possible nightmare scenarios. Orwell's greatness (Orwell, 1949) cannot be measured by the fact that he envisaged many abuses already present nowadays, but rather by his warnings, which helped ensure that his worst predictions have not come true, although arguably actuality is far more insidious than that (Morozov, 2011). This book illustrates that the fiction from *This Perfect Day*, as far as technology is concerned, is *under*-estimated. Nowadays technology can do much worse things than those envisaged in fiction. The nightmare of having a central power that governs the world seems also to be exhausted. The major danger is inside us. Our wish to imitate and prevail over nature may rebound on us, if we forget that we are part of that nature and whatever we do to influence and change our environment is having an impact on us as well.

The spectrum of further challenges that still need to be researched in the reflective domain is wide and crosses various disciplines. Psychology needs to offer more expertise on diagnosing different emotional and cognitive states. Better methods and tools are needed to analyse and filter out raw sensor data in order to get clear features (that may lead to more precise determination of different psychological states). Social sciences and philosophy should investigate the impact that such user-centric and personalised approaches may have on us, as it is clear that we also do change and evolve through constant exposure to technical systems that surround us. Finally, technology providers need to take into account not only technical benefits that envisaged systems should bring, but to try to find technical solutions that support privacy, trust and ensure positive impact on us as biological and social beings. In other words, our future artificial systems should be much more natural.

Chapter 6

Healthcare in a Pervasive World

Simon Dobson and Aaron Quigley

University of St Andrews

> *"Not without giving Uni a good reason, I can't,"*
> King said. *"One fuzzy move, brother, and the doc-*
> *tors will be examining* me. *Which would also mean,*
> *incidentally, they'd be reexamining you."*

THIS PERFECT DAY, P. 116

6.1 Introduction

Consider the following scenario:

Jack is 85, but still in good health – what 65 was for his grandfather's generation. He has a wide circle of friends, many of whom, like him, live in picturesque country villages. The average age in Jack's own village is well over 50. He didn't grow up here: he moved here when he semi-retired 15 years ago, and started working as a consultant to a firm overseas.

Although his friends don't live locally, Jack is far from isolated. He's in contact with people all the time, either by video calls or letters, and gets a peripheral awareness of the health and activities of those closest to him through his TV and through a digital photo frame that can add annotations to people's pictures as they are displayed. Jack doesn't worry that he won't get help if he needs it, because he knows that his friends are getting the same information about him, and will notice if he starts to decline – just as they would if they saw him every day. And the system watches him too: not intrusively, but it would notice if he became less talkative or less engaged, and would send one of the community nurses to check up on him.

There's always someone organising a trip out or a meet-up in town, which makes going out all the more pleasurable: it's easy to arrange meetings, so he can make the most of them. In many ways it's easier to meet up now than it ever was: Jack has the time to devote to his friends and his hobbies, helped by his Internet connection. He once heard this technology, that he treats as normal, being called 'assisted living', but he doesn't think of it that way: it's just living.

The aim of this chapter is to describe the trajectory of pervasive computing, as applied to healthcare, that will bring about this transformation from 'assisted living' to just 'living'. In doing so, it will identify a number of technological and societal challenges that will need to be addressed.

6.2 The Changing Face of the Elderly in Society

Imagine a map of Europe, like a weather map but where the colours indicate the average age of the population of an area rather than its air pressure. What would such a map look like? The answer tells us a lot about the shape of the future world.

Firstly, there would be substantial variation across the EU. For example, some countries, including Ireland and France, still have growing populations and a relatively large percentage of younger, working-age people. Others – Italy, Greece, and others – have a rapidly ageing population and a lower percentage of working age.

Secondly, if we continue the weather analogy and look at the change over time of population age – the 'wind in the demographics', as it were – most countries' populations are ageing (see Fig. 6.1), with those with older populations ageing more rapidly. Grey countries become greyer and their population growth rates decline – a positive feedback within population dynamics that is hard to reverse. Immigration can dent this trend in the short term but cannot be relied upon to do so over the medium term.

Thirdly, within countries there would be substantial variation between regions. Highly urbanised countries such as the Netherlands and the UK have large proportions of their older citizens living in towns. More rural countries, including Ireland and Spain, have lower population densities and older people living a more scattered and potentially isolated existence in the countryside.

Not all healthcare is driven by the elderly, of course – children are also significant service users – but the demographic trends are such that these two age groups may swamp other users, with the elderly making up the largest and most influential segment.

From these largely anecdotal views we can distill several trends. The first is the *dependency ratio*, the proportion of children and the retired to those of working age. World Bank data from 2008 suggests that no country in the EU-16 has a dependency ratio below 40%, with most being in the 55% range – roughly one dependent for every two workers.

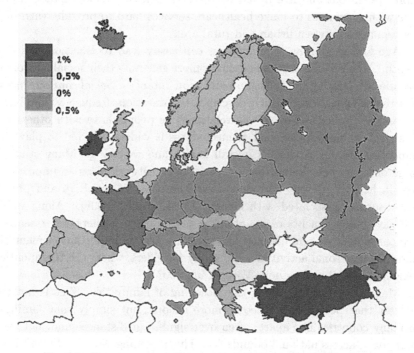

Fig. 6.1   European population growth in 2010 (source: Wikipedia).

The dependency ratio has a number of effects on healthcare provision. Since children and the retired are disproportionately heavy use of healthcare services, a higher dependency ratio correlates with an increasing burden of healthcare. However, the implications go deeper than this. A single healthcare professional – nurse, doctor, community therapist – can deal with only a small number of individuals. An increasing dependency ratio means that, all other things being equal, more healthcare professionals are needed as the population ages. These individuals are then not engaged in other activities that might be more economically productive, producing an economic drag.

This trend is exacerbated by the population distribution mentioned above. The efficiency (in terms of individuals cared for) of a healthcare worker is strongly affected by the population density of the individuals being cared for. A community therapist in London, for example, has less far to travel, and more transport options, when visiting people than the same therapist would have in the West of Ireland, where the people are more spread out and live in harder-to-access places. Demographics interacts with economics to make healthcare services hard to provide, with big discrepancies between urban and rural areas.

Age and geographical remoteness can easily lead to isolation and ill-health. An individual's social circle (or more generally their social network) includes friends, family, colleagues and acquaintances. *Social connectedness* is a psychological term which describes the duration, frequency, familiarity and reciprocal nature of the relationships people have with others in this circle or network. Social connectedness is widely believed to play an important role in a person's overall health and wellbeing. Many studies in gerontology have found that a strong social network plays an important role in helping prevent and slow down the onset of cognitive and physical disorders associated with ageing (Dara-Abrams, 2008). Along with the day-to-day benefits of maintaining a vibrant social network, research demonstrates that reminiscence activities are also an important element of many interpersonal activities – especially for elders, where the therapeutic benefits are well understood (West *et al.*, 2007).

Many countries are seeing the loosening of family ties. This is not to suggest that people have become more callous, but simply that families in many countries live apart, often over significant distances and, not uncommonly, across national boundaries. This loosening seems to be cultural rather than being strictly affected by the population density: cities are often anonymous, whilst people must often leave villages to seek work. In either case, in many countries the responsibility for individuals' healthcare often begins to fall more on state services than on extended families than was once perhaps the case.

Against these largely negative trends we can set the increased participation of elderly people in the information society. Whilst it is hard to get reliable age breakdowns, a recent study[1] suggests that 13% of US Internet users of social media are over 55. One needs to be careful about extrapolating from this any specific figure for general Internet usage, but it seems safe to say that older people are increasingly comfortable using online services. Furthermore, broadband provision and penetration levels are increasing, although figures for uptake and bandwidth in rural areas lag behind – often very significantly – figures for urban locations, and this may act as a brake on participation by elderly rural users. Nonetheless, it seems likely that the elderly are, and of necessity will increasingly become, mainstream users of Internet technologies.

Taken together, we see that geographical dispersion and increasing (not necessarily voluntary) independence creates challenges for healthcare, but is being coupled with an increase in technological familiarity. Many of the challenges are social or political, but many can usefully be supported by technology. How, then, can pervasive technology best be deployed in the service of healthcare?

6.3   The Domain of Pervasive Healthcare

6.3.1   *Bioinformatics*

The application of computers to healthcare is often considered under the general term *bioinformatics*, which includes the provision of patient records, data analytics, medical devices and other services. The deployment of such services – despite them being what might be termed 'traditional' computer applications – has been extremely slow, due to the complexity, diversity and criticality of the information being managed (Cantrill, 2010).

One might observe that such services often focus on *acute* healthcare, intervening when things go wrong. Preventive care for *chronic* conditions (including simple ageing) is a 'softer' area that is more tolerant (within limits) of errors and omissions on the part of the software services. We might therefore focus our attention on the application of pervasive technology to the monitoring and management of chronic conditions, especially ageing and the social exclusion it can engender.

One could criticise this focus by saying that it simply side-steps the issues that challenge other areas of medical informatics. However, by focusing on ageing and chronic conditions we focus on an area that is under-served

---

[1]'Ages of social network users'.
http://royal.pingdom.com/2010/02/16/study-ages-of-social-network-users/

by technology but that is enormously economically and socially significant. The need for improved acute services, for better interventions and monitoring of outcome measures, and for improved medical devices are well understood and well served by vocal and influential lobby groups. By contrast, otherwise healthy home-dwellers are easily overlooked.

Healthy home-dwellers do not remain so for ever, of course. Many conditions of mid to late life are characterised by slow degradations of function, sometimes punctuated by acute events. The first is that the degradation of an individual's function can be almost imperceptible day by day. We have all had the experience of meeting someone we have not seen for some time and being shocked by their condition, while those who see them regularly have not noticed the changes. In a healthcare setting, this corresponds to the inability of carers to monitor individuals over long periods and with high temporal resolution in their own home environments. Such monitoring (repetitive, frequent sampling over a long duration) can be made possible using pervasive and sensor technology, integrated unobtrusively.

The second consequence is that relatively minor interventions can prolong an individual's ability to live at home and so prolong their independence. Independent living is both a goal in itself and an important economic target, given the costs of nursing homes and care. Pervasive technology can therefore act both as a monitoring and diagnostic tool, and as a supportive enabler of independence for ageing people.

6.3.2 Niche areas

What, then, are the needs of such individuals? Which needs can most effectively be addressed using pervasive technology?

We should first set out the overall structure of pervasive healthcare in this domain. Technological support for independent living, whether at home or in a more managed setting, needs to fit seamlessly into the lives of those involved. No other system approach will be widely acceptable. In order to be economically feasible, we should make use of technologies that are mainstream and so affected by economies of scale. This suggests that using very simple sensors and commodity wireless networks are preferable to more expensive devices. As technology improves, the cost/benefit analysis will change, so the technology needs to be a platform that can grow and evolve as new devices and services become affordable. Mainstream software services are also preferable, both to avoid duplication and to leverage network effects.

6.4 Technological Avenues

6.4.1 *Context and situation*

Most pervasive systems are intended to collect data from their environment and use this in providing services, whether physical or digital. These two aspects are tightly interconnected, but operate in tandem. As a general rule we can view a pervasive system as a feedback loop (Fig. 6.2) in which data is *collected* and used to populate and maintain a model which is then *analysed* to drive *decisions* on the appropriate *actions* to be performed.

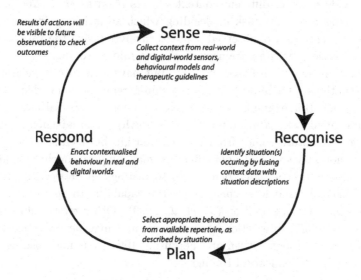

Fig. 6.2 The pervasive systems loop.

The data collected by a pervasive system is generally referred to as *context*, which can be regarded as 'the state in which the system operates, understood symbolically'. Context is generally dynamic, reflecting changes in the outside world, and brings together data collected from physical sources through sensors and online sources through web queries. Each individual piece of context is affected by the fidelity of the way it is collected, and will typically be imprecise, inaccurate, noisy and untimely. Each observation provides *evidence of fact*, rather than being facts themselves.

Coutaz and Rey (2002) further distinguish between *primary* context collected directly from sensors and *secondary* context inferred from this raw data. The process of inference is dominated by the need to manage uncertainty, since much of the contextual information collected is approximate and noisy.

Context is essentially observational data about the real world, coupled with basic inference. It is *not* the information needed by designers when discussing systems, who might talk about a user being asleep, eating, meeting with friends, and so forth. These constitute interpretations of the context data, and are generally referred to as *situations*. A situation is a semantically meaningful interpretation of collected context, and will typically draw upon a wide range of different context sources (Coutaz *et al.*, 2005). *Situation recognition*, the task of deciding which situation(s) are currently happening based on the observed context, involves fusing the various context observations within a framework of uncertain reasoning.

Situations are not isolated concepts but have structure in relation to other situations. One important relationship is refinement, in which a general situation (for example, eating) has a number of special cases (such as eating breakfast, eating dinner and so forth). The advantage of this lattice-like structure comes from the relationship between situations and context: noisy sensors and poor inference may support conclusions about a general situation without being able to distinguish between its refinements. This allows at least *some* inferential capability to be retained, and supports graceful degradation (Ye *et al.*, 2009). Other relationships stem from the temporal interaction of situations, and may be described using interval temporal logic (Allen and Ferguson, 1994), but may also need to make reference to real-world timings.

6.4.2   *Healthcare situations and behaviours*

We observed above (section 6.3.2) that we may wish to view both degenerations of function and 'episodes' that can be of significance. We can refine this view a little using situations, and explore how such situations might be constructed.

A first example is preventive medicine, where the goal is to maintain some aspect of lifestyle in order to promote better health. From a pervasive systems perspective, this might involve observing ongoing activities and logging or commenting upon them. Many drugs need to be taken on a well-defined schedule. A situation of 'taking drugs' might be triggered by a person opening their medicine cabinet or drug container, which might be sensed using a variety of technologies. (To repeat: the sensing of the cabinet door or the drug bottle is context; the interpretation of this as a 'drug-taking event' is situation.) The individual's prescriptions might require that they take several drugs during the day, which may be represented as the appropriate drug-taking situations occurring within a larger medicating scenario. If some situations do not occur, occur too often, or occur at the wrong times, an appropriate behaviour can be triggered, for example warning the individual or their carer that some 'variation from the script' has occurred.

A second scenario is long-term monitoring of individuals' functioning over time, a task usually conducted by occupational therapists. In this case, the situations of interest might include cooking, cleaning and other tasks. We might offer support to these activities, for example using visual cues or instructions, and instrument various home items in order to detect their use. (An excellent example can be seen in the development of the Ambient Kitchen (Robinson *et al.*, 2008).) However, as well as supporting the individual, we are equally (or more) interested in examining how they perform their tasks: what delays occur, how well do they use knives, do they get lost in the process? Such data is invaluable in assessing people's ability to live independently, and is currently assessed only periodically, rather than on a near-continuous basis. More frequent observations can be used to support better tracking of a person's condition, and can inform future therapies.

To illustrate episodic or one-off situations, a third example is detecting when someone has had a fall. This is surprisingly difficult to detect directly, unless the individual is wearing a panic button or a dedicated sensor, but can be inferred from circumstantial evidence, and provides a great example of how sensor fusion works. The key observation is that people at home perform a range of common activities, and the *absence* of those activities can be used to detect problems. If, over the course of a few hours during the day, the lights and kettle are never switched on, the fridge door remains closed and the toilet un-flushed, *and* we know that the person is at home, then we can be confident that there is a problem – a 'negative situation' in which the *absence* of context is detected.

The behaviours that should occur in response to these situations will vary enormously. In some cases they can be used purely for monitoring, or for providing 'peripheral vision' to relatives and carers that their charges are still OK. Other cases might be more interventionist, such as providing support for those with early-stage dementia, whilst simultaneously assessing competence (Robinson *et al.*, 2009). From the perspective of pervasive systems, the recognition of a situation can be separated from the behaviour that this recognition gives rise to, allowing for substantial tailoring to individual conditions.

6.4.3 *Avoiding social isolation*

Social network services offer interactive web-based environments for enabling people to connect and maintain social connections, thus supporting the mirroring of real communities into virtual ones. They can form a significant part of a pervasive approach to healthcare.

Initially, online social networks were the playgrounds of young people from early teens to mid-twenties (Boyd and Buckingham, 2008), but this has changed rapidly. With the ongoing niche stratification of the social network space there are many social network services targeting specific audiences, e.g. Eons for those aged 50 and over and LinkedIn for maintaining and creating professional ties. It is therefore possible to envision a spread of social network services targeted at ageing people, who are more likely to suffer from emotional isolation. In recent years, social networks have exploded in popularity and diversity, with rough estimates indicating online social networks are a regular lifestyle choice in hundreds of millions of people's personal lives, and increasingly common in professional fields.

Specific features of online social networks enable people to:

- Create online personal profiles.
- Form connections with friends who have also created personal profiles, i.e. have a large circle of friends on a social network.
- Easily update their profiles to share what is happening in their lives with their friends, i.e. profile updates and blog updates.
- Share content, such as photographs and videos.
- Engage in shared conversations between multiple groups of friends, e.g. share comments about shared photographs.
- Communicate privately.
- Create and engage in online interest groups.
- Play games together e.g. FarmVille and playfully interact, e.g. giving each other virtual flowers.

Boyd and Ellison (2008) defined social network sites as web-based services that allow individuals to construct a public or semi-public profile within a bounded system; articulate a list of other users with whom they share a connection; and view and traverse their list of connections and those made by others within the system. The nature and nomenclature of these connections may vary from site to site. What differentiates social networks from previous social technologies, such as newsgroups and bulletin boards, is that social networks help members make their social ties visible.

Gerontological studies have found that strong social networks play an important role in helping prevent and slow down the onset of cognitive and physical disorders associated with ageing (Glass *et al.*, 1999; Hyyppa and Maki, 2003). When designing technologies for the elderly, there is a danger of assuming overly simplistic models of what it means to be old, and what the needs of older people are (Lindley *et al.*, 2008). A deep understanding of why offline social networks are beneficial, and what the important properties of them are, is required when designing online social networks for elderly people.

Social network sites are commonly used to reinforce existing relationships, rather than building new friendships, though sometimes interest groups can organise meet-ups, where members meet in a cafe or bar for offline socialisation. When considering social networks in terms of elders there are opportunities to investigate and build networks that strongly intersect with the physical world, such as enabling an elder to continue independent living, while enabling their extended network to act as a loosely bound social group, remotely interacting with and monitoring the elder. The elder's status could be automatically updated via passive health monitoring technologies, etc. Noteworthy elder social networks include Eons and Boomj, which are US-based elder networks, while Platinnetz is based in Germany and remains a vibrant network. Another, Saga Zone, came out of the UK's Saga Publishing Group, which has been publishing magazines aimed at the elder market for many years.

What do older people gain, then, from social networking, and how can it be improved using pervasive technology? Firstly, social networks reduce isolation and (indirectly) dependence, since they support independent or peer-aided searches for information. In this way, they can also provide reassurance by connecting those with particular conditions to other sufferers. Secondly, a social network improves the visibility of an individual to their family and carers. With suitable privacy controls in place, it is not unreasonable to allow sharing of certain information with a sub-group of the social network to provide a view onto a person's overall state of health. Thirdly, the rise of online government offers the possibility of making a

social network a 'one-stop shop' for services – in much the same way as
the rural post office in times past served both as a social locus and as a
gateway to the state.

6.5   Challenges Remaining

Pervasive technology in healthcare does not suffer to the same extent from
the problems of safety and reliability that have plagued the deployment of
computing in medicine. By focusing on the diseases of ageing, and further
focusing on the management of chronic conditions over time, we believe
that even today's pervasive technology can be deployed in the real world
and make a significant impact on healthcare and outcomes.

Some enormous challenges remain: some generic to the area as a whole,
and some specific to healthcare. Perhaps the most pressing problem is the
notion of a user. Many systems in the literature rely on there being *one
user*, clearly identified. The reason for this is simply that many sensors
cannot distinguish between the actions of individuals, even if they can distinguish that several people are present and perhaps even their identities.
This is something that can be solved with better sensor technology, for
example the use of fiducial tagging (Harle and Hopper, 2006) – at a cost
of intrusion, expense and consequent reduction in acceptability. Alternatively, it can sometimes be solved with better reasoning, especially when
dealing with structured situations – although the proper treatment of more
complex situation construction still remains open (Ye and Dobson, 2009).

Pervasive technologies share with other information systems the need
for clear, *ab initio* privacy and security systems. Despite years of work, privacy and trust remain misunderstood and complex: indeed, adding privacy
features can complicate software to the point of uselessness. But it is essential for the acceptance of pervasive systems that they are not regarded as a
surveillance tool, but rather as an assistive part of everyday living. Better
access to, and familiarity with, pervasive technology often allays such fears,
but they remain real and pressing. The tendency to treat privacy as a late
add-on needs to be resisted if we are to avoid unnecessary system failures,
especially with potentially highly personal information that may also have
a major economic component in the form of health insurance premiums.

Finally, in moving towards ever more complex pervasive healthcare, we
should not neglect simpler technologies. Even simple computer-aided systems can provide great benefit, if used intelligently (Creeger, 2006). Con-

versely, many simple operations resist technological solution: mechanical hoists that can get a person from bed to chair are difficult for a young carer to use, and impossible for an aged partner. In no sense does pervasive technology represent a magic bullet for caring for an ageing population. But its extensible, insidious nature makes it a great candidate for progressive deployment in tackling what is likely to be one of the most pressing social challenges of our coming times.

Chapter 7

Social Networking in Mobile Pervasive Environments

Gualtiero Colombo, Stuart Allen, Martin Chorley, and Roger Whitaker

University of Cardiff

> *That Friday night, a few minutes after the last chime, Snowflake came into his room. "Don't mind me," she said, taking off her coveralls. "I'm just putting a note in your mouthpiece."*
>
> THIS PERFECT DAY, P. 93

7.1 Introduction

Online social networking plays an increasingly important role in people's personal and professional lives. With small portable devices such as mobile phones, MP3 players, sensors and PDAs (personal digital assistants) being nearly ubiquitous in our society, the paradigm of social networks has evolved from a pure set of social relationships, often restricted to a limited circle of friends and acquaintances, towards a more extensive and dynamic structure.

This chapter will focus on recent applications of social networking in mobile and pervasive environments. The pervasive and light weight nature of social networks makes them particularly successful in societies where their use can help and sustain personal feelings and relationships, as well as reinforce existing professionals links, create new ones, and promote and enhance information diffusion. The discussion is motivated by a significant example, which considers an application of mobile micro-blogging services.

113

Although already very successful in their original online Internet version, these services have the potential of maximising their efficiency in pervasive dynamic environments.

7.2　A Future Application: Social Micro-blogging Services

7.2.1　*Online micro-blogging services*

Online micro-blogging services have been very successful since the launch of Twitter in 2006 (see also its competitors, Tumblr, Plurk and Blauk). They are becoming increasingly popular in comparison to other online social networks (OSN) offering more traditional blogging facilities. Their success is largely due to the very small overhead (e.g. Twitter allows text messages up to a maximum of 140 characters), requiring relatively small cognitive effort to read and post new updates. This implies lower effort from users, thus reducing the risks of constituting a threat to our 'real' life in terms of diverting a vast amount of time from our social and professional activities.

The broadcast nature of these services allows users to share messages with their friends (followers) from a range of devices (PCs, laptops, smart phones, PDAs) in a flexible and pervasive fashion: new updates can be written in real time during a particular experience (e.g. conferences, work meetings, social events such as concerts and festivals) and valuable information can be received directly, without the need for any search (simply by following other users that are in the same area of interests, even including prominent public figures and celebrities). Micro-blogging users can assume different roles, varying from sources that report and broadcast news about specific topics, to seekers of information about very specialised topics, to friends having daily conversations and chats (Java *et al.*, 2009).

Sharing information about personal activities and interests also sustains feelings of emotional closeness in our local sphere between friends and work colleagues, by improving connectivity and building common grounds of interests that would not be exploited using other information channels (like phone, email, etc. (Zhao and Rosson, 2009)). However, some aspects of the service can still be the object of improvements, such as enhancements in security and privacy issues, filtering and grouping of messages, building views and aggregation communities (Passant *et al.*, 2008).

Note that this idea of grouping user's updates and differentiating between the groups who can read them and those who cannot, depending on their content, is a common trend recently introduced in many other social networks, such as the new privacy settings introduced in Facebook. This aligns with other features oriented towards preserving the privacy of data, mainly by increasing awareness in the users, together with the more transparent mechanism to find out what applications are handling their personal details, and when and how much of them is actually used. There are also studies which show that experience and skill are significant determinants in how users approach their privacy settings (Boyd and Hargittai, 2010).

The application of this scenario to a mobile domain opens up new opportunities for sharing micro-blog posts directly between local devices, rather than using the Internet as a central store. The use of social markers such as 'tags' allows users to send and receive updates even without predefined follower relationships, while considering common local content (locality tags) that users are participating in (e.g. during a festival or a journey on public transport), as well as self-organising the flow of information around ad hoc subjects (topic tags).

In this scenario, information is not intended to be addressed to specific recipients, but the content itself determines whether its receipt is of value to an individual. Sharing information about interest preferences among friends can subsequently be used to forward valuable content on the basis of this acquired 'social' knowledge. Micro-blogs can be automatically generated data of any type, and are not confined to user-penned text messages, see for example 'the house that twitters' (Alleyne, 2009), where a set of sensors is constantly monitoring the house environment, whose data is published in real time as Twitter updates. It is this real time feature that opens up new high potential scenarios, where individuals can infer knowledge about situations and events based on both real time data monitored on site and transmitted by sensors and the (not necessarily online) tweeting, gossiping, and talking about the events themselves. Events can be either positive, such as a festival or a spot event, or negative, like road accidents, weather disruptions, or even emergency situations (see for example the recent riots in Egypt and Libya, as well as the devastating earthquake and tsunami in Japan). Outcomes can be beneficial (finding popular events, avoiding traffic congestion) or possibly invasive – if a smartmeter started tweeting usage data, or a smartphone started tweeting GPS location data.

Emphasis is given to both the spatial and temporal aspect of these services. A recent study (Kwak *et al.*, 2010) shows how a large number of users tend to participate in trending topics (whereas long-lasting topics do not always attract new users to the discussion), as well as finding a positive correlation between the 'following' relationship and the geographical location of users. The same study also highlights how micro-blogging is turning into one of the most effective tools for information diffusion similar to news media services.

A positive example of Twitter use comes from the so-called 'Trafigura super-injunction'. This was a case of toxic waste in Ivory Coast by the multinational company Trafigura during the late summer of 2009, causing many deaths and serious health consequences. The British newspaper *The Guardian* (Leigh, 2009) reported that it had been prevented from covering remarks made in Parliament by a legal injunction taken out by the law firm Carter Ruck. However, a group of Twitter users found that Trafigura was behind it and exposed this in their tweets and re-tweets (here a fundamental contribution was given by very popular users like Stephen Fry). These actions gave the case a high profile, eventually leading the company to give up and withdraw the injunction and illustrating the ability of a crowd-based distributed service to have a real societal effect.

Another valuable application is within a healthcare context, where the constant processing of information, such as monitoring simple actions and behaviours carried out daily in their own houses by observed patients, can be used to raise warnings and alarms about possible sudden health problems (see Dobson and Quigley, Chapter 6). Micro-blogs may also have a learning function so that our interest preferences change over time, related to current and local events, and we can become increasingly interested in new topics or content. Here, tweets can have a goal themselves and influence positive behaviours. This is a concept known in sociology as 'persuasion', which is the process by which people guide themselves or others, by rational or symbolic means, toward the adoption of an idea, attitude, or the performance of a specific action.

7.2.2   A near-future utopian scenario: This Perfect Day

To effectively take advantage of this increasing and continuous flow of information, further aspects still need to be considered and implemented. Sensor data can be subject to noise and some micro-blogs can either be of scarce interest for a specific user or even turn out to be unreliable and misleading. This opens up issues such as misinformation spreading, a phenomenon present since the advent of so called 'mass media'.

An example of this is the DDT (dichlorodiphenyltrichloroethane) ban case. DDT is a synthetic pesticide that was very popular until the early 1960s when Rachel Carson's environmentalist book allegedly claimed potential damage to both environment and human health (Carson, 2002). As a result, its use was gradually restricted and then banned, firstly in most developing countries and then worldwide. In recent times some prominent scientists (e.g. J. Gordon Edwards) began criticising the original ban as the consequence of 'junk-science', claiming that its justification was based on false beliefs (especially on DDT's carcinogenicity). This claim received greater attention later thanks to a number of 'blogging' web sites, reinforcing the idea that the ban was responsible for causing thousand of unnecessary deaths due to malaria. This eventually lead institutions such the United States Agency for International Development (USAID) to renew support, and currently fund the use of DDT in some African countries. Far from being concluded and followed by the response of another group of 'blogging' sites heavily contradicting these latest theories, this debate confirms how delicate and fragile scientific consensus can be as a result of an increasingly faster and more accessible flow (now allowed by the new technologies) of types of information (such as scientific reports), whose access was in the past restricted to a limited number of specialists. Other examples of using 'junk' science, while claiming counter-arguments are 'junk', and mis-use of the scientific method are reported (Oreskes and Conway, 2010), compounded by manipulation of public opinion through poor journalism after conducting perfunctory research (sometimes referred to as 'churnalism' (Davies, 2009)).

Therefore new measures still need to be taken (which could be in a form of automatic application) in order to maximise the most valuable updates for particular users (this may be related to current location, time and specific interests), thus reducing the amount of noise and unwanted information received. For this purpose Twitter itself has very recently introduced new features, such as the addition of locality information, and personalised suggestions and recommendations of people to follow, but much more could be done in this direction.

This chapter will also attempt to make a comparison between the state of the art described above and the future scenario described in *This Perfect Day*. As described by Pitt (see Chapter 1 of the present book), the book depicted a utopian scenario in which individual activities were constantly observed, monitored and kept under control using, amongst other methods, sensors and other types of 'pervasive' devices. The book's idea of retrospective data analysis, centralised planning, passive monitoring and reactive decision-making are rather different from the actual development of mobile social networking, which is based on real time information continuously acquired and distributed by and among disparate social groups (a well-known TV comedy actor bemoans that a trip to the supermarket now leaves a trail of 'tweets' in his wake, each saying 'I saw X in supermarket Y buying product Z').

In the science fiction book however, the author portrayed a scenario with effectively one social group, the 'Family'; itself composed of many instances of atomic two-adult two-children family units, couples and individuals (not everyone was allowed to marry, and not everyone that married was allowed to have children; this was how population control was enforced). A social group of some kind was however formed, consisting of 'unusual' family members interested in resisting the authority and determinism of UniComp, although their form of communication was primitive (i.e. handwritten notes). Pervasive technologies were only used in order to reinforce the power of the existing authority and other members were prevented from making any other possible use of them.

The findings of the research presented in this chapter are, however, considerably different. Networks appear able to self-organise themselves in social groups of cooperative individuals and reach equilibrium status in which malicious behaviours and selfish nodes are ostracised without the need for any external authority. In contrast to the book, spontaneous formation of multiple social groups can be observed which may relate to trust links (friendship), similarity of interests, or frequency of encounters.

Of course, the book did not foresee the rise of ubiquitous mobile computing. We have now begun to witness how this can encourage cooperative sharing of information and resources and potentially lead to the formation of a more democratic and fairer society. We can also see how, on the other hand, the same technology can be used to entrench an autocratic or oligarchic society.

7.3   Social Networking: A Brief Background

Online social networking has become an increasingly important component in our everyday life. This originates from the inherent needs of human beings and the pervasive nature of this form of networking. This section will investigate these issues from the point of view of behavioural science, with a brief analysis of the social network structure.

7.3.1 *Recent observations from behavioural science*

Research in behavioural science has shown that, in human societies, individuals tend to form social groups of a limited size and cooperate with each other. In particular, in the early 1990s Robin Dunbar collected diverse evidence that there is a limit (of approximatively 150 in total) in the number of social links that individuals can maintain, correlated with the cognitive ability of the human brain to deal with a different number of 'social friends' (Aiello and Dunbar, 1993; Dunbar, 2010). Moreover, these relationships exhibit distinct 'layers' within their structure that are related to levels of 'emotional closeness' of the social relationships (e.g. kinship, friendship). Each 'ego' has a relatively small and constant number of contacts and stable relationships that an individual can maintain for each layer.

Inner layers contain the support circle (approximately five individuals) and sympathy circle (approximately 15 individuals), and are usually largely composed of kinship links, which typically represent stronger and more durable relationships. However, when the number of kin is not large enough to cover the inner circles, some friends may replace them and assume the same intensity of relationships (Roberts *et al.*, 2009). In any case, the 'emotional closeness' of a relationship is strongly linked to the 'frequency of contacts' (Dunbar, 2003).

Outer layers are composed of the so called 'weak links' (individuals with a low frequency of contact, or with whom we share only a limited number of interests). Although their emotional closeness is low and their strength decays over time, these are also important since they introduce more variety in the structure of our social relationships.

In a well-known study from the 1970s, Granovetter (1973) described how, in particular situations, 'weak links' can be twice as effective as stronger contacts. An example of this is the process of finding or changing jobs, in which often the best opportunities arise by getting in contact (through a weak link) with a whole network of people whose existence may be previously unknown to us, whereas the circle of closest acquaintances could no longer be exploited.

The introduction of electronic communication and online social networks, such as Facebook, Myspace and Twitter, has allowed the size of our communities to grow almost indefinitely. This is a direct consequence of the reduced effort to maintain relationships within these networks, as well as their broadcast nature. The findings of Dunbar have shown that entities like the single 'Family' are too large to contemplate and reduction to the 'nuclear family' is too small to be significant, thus humans seem to have evolved to have 150 acquaintances; any less and they feel lonely, any more and they are overloaded. Given the fragmentation of geographical and communal relationships, the use of online social networking allows the restoration of these links, and the addition of mobile features may allow individuals to reconnect with their geography.

However, recent studies have shown that these 'virtual friendships' behave differently and the upper limit remains essentially unchanged. We cannot consider a close friendship with somebody with whom our only contact consists of receiving updates about his daily activities via Twitter. What has increased is the flow and amount of information (i.e. the number of messages we send over time), but the total number and emotional closeness of our friends remain almost unvaried (Lu *et al.*, 2009).

7.3.2 *Structure of social networks*

Social network analysis is a burgeoning research area that maps, measures and studies relationships and flows between individuals, groups, organisations and other connected sources of information and knowledge (e.g. computers, electronic devices, web links, etc.) (Freeman, 2004). Networks are given a graph representation, with nodes representing individuals and links representing the relationships between them.

Despite the recent growth of research in this field, its origins date back to the beginning of the 20th century, within the field of sociometry. At that time, Moreno published his book *Who Shall Survive? A New Approach To the Problem of Human Interrelations*, in which, for the first time, he tried to explain how individuals group together and how they relate to and influence each other inside and outside their 'social group', through an extensive series of sociometric studies (Moreno, 1934). However, other analysts suggest that significant contributions were previously given in the early 1920s by a group of researchers involved in educational fields, through a series of experiments with school and preschool children by observation of their play activities. They also conducted a series of tests in which they were asked questions such as 'which schoolmate would you invite to your birthday party?', which suggested a tendency to homophily (the attitude to associate and bond with similar others) in their companion choices (Freeman, 1996).

In the 1960s, the famous 'small world' experiment conducted by Travers and Milgram (1969) asked a number of people in the USA to deliver and forward mail to a location on the other side of the country, using only direct human contacts. This aimed to investigate how we can potentially connect with any other individual in the world through only a limited number of interactions with any other distinct subject. The results were ground breaking, as most of the letters were delivered requiring only a small number of connections (hops). This concept, commonly known as the 'six degrees of separation', has been at the base of many algorithms and computational procedures regulating the flow and search of information in social networking, and is apparent in diverse areas of sociology.

It is important to mention that six hops was not the absolute result of the experiment and some letters remained either undelivered or took many more hops to reach their destination (for nodes with few or no contacts). However, the majority required an average of six hops, with many letters delivered in only three hops for the most highly connected nodes. Nodes with many connections served as a support to quickly sort out the letters and convey them to destinations nodes. This confirmed the particular structure of social networks characterised by the presence of 'hubs', one of the most significant research findings in this field within recent decades.

Barabasi (1999) has shown that small world properties are a fundamental characteristic of 'scale-free networks', such as online networks (including the world wide web), whose structure follows a 'long tailed' distribution of links (i.e. almost all of the network elements have links with a small number of other nodes, whereas only few nodes have links with a large number of individuals). Formation of such groups can be modelled by preferential linking with the underlying idea that a new node joining the network is more likely to form links with nodes already having a large number of connections, thus further increasing their number.

This phenomenon is also known as 'preferential attachment' or 'the rich get richer' and, when applied to the web, it has been used to justify the success of web services like Google (the process can be reversed only if new events occur, such as the introduction of a new technology, giving somebody else a chance to compete). This leads to the formation of few websites having many links (hubs), while the majority of nodes have in general far fewer connections. This explains the particular 'scale-free' structure of the web described above. The same structure can then be recognised in some of the most popular online social networks, in which hubs may, for example, be identified as Facebook users having a large number of 'friends' or Twitter users with many 'followers'. This generally confers to online social networks the property of being 'searchable', thus suitable for quickly finding destination nodes in data delivery applications (Watts et al., 2002).

Even if not all online social networks show the 'small world' behaviour described above, there are underlying structural features 'hidden' in any massive social network (such as assortativity, dis-assortativity, centrality, etc.), thus combining sociological perspectives with the scientific analysis of physicists (Newman *et al.*, 2006; Strogatz, 2001).

7.4 Social Networking in Mobile Pervasive Environments: Push vs. Pull

Wireless and mobile devices such as phones, MP3 players, sensors and PDAs are becoming increasingly capable of creating and sharing content. This has been also further supported by the introduction of unlicensed wireless connectivity protocols such as Wi-Fi and Bluetooth.

Resource sharing in peer-to-peer (P2P) online networks (sometimes with some centralised infrastructure) was originally based on polling, i.e. on requests issued by users, discovery of paths towards a specific resource's location, and the final retrieval of these desired resources.

In emerging pervasive environments which are composed of mobile entities, such as delay tolerant networks and opportunistic networks, end-to-end connectivity is no longer guaranteed and resources are carried, shared and forwarded directly by devices with no centralised infrastructure required. Content is transferred via isolated pairwise interactions using short range wireless links (e.g. Bluetooth), thus the dissemination of content is regulated by the mobility of individuals through the network. For this system the traditional polling approach needs to be integrated with more proactive protocols in which nodes opportunistically 'push' valuable content to others in proximity of hypothetical destinations, in order to facilitate the retrieval of the desired resources when an online connection becomes available (Boldrini *et al.*, 2008). Note that a combination of push and pull has also been used in other applications, for example to increase efficiency and reduce delay in live streaming based on peer-to-peer technology (Locher *et al.*, 2007).

Social networking between mobile devices offers a new, yet challenging, opportunity for content provision and data forwarding in these pervasive computing environments. Individuals can organise themselves into social communities that could be based on 'homophily' (including nodes sharing similar interests) and/or 'familiarity' (including those they are most frequently in contact with), in order to share information within their social group and then use this information to effectively push each other valuable content ('social pushing') (Allen *et al.*, 2010b). Other examples are original 'mobile peer-to-peer' platforms such as PeopleNet (Motani *et al.*, 2005) and 7DS (based on the seven degrees of separation approach) (Srinivasan *et al.*, 2007), as well as more recent applications in opportunistic networking (Conti and Kumar, 2010).

Further studies indicate an analogy between the way data is spread and disseminated throughout social networks and biological phenomenon such as epidemics, see for example the 'susceptible—infected—recovered model' (Newman, 2002). Within social networks in pervasive environments the spreading of information is achieved via social contact, thus making social networking in this context more suitable for content based and information dissemination applications, rather than data or message delivery based on the searchability property of traditional online social networks.

7.5 Trust and Cooperation

Decentralised systems, such as P2P, auctions, mobile ad hoc networks (MANETs) and opportunistic networks, depend on parties acting on behalf of others without directly benefiting themselves. Notions of cooperation and trust are widespread in human society, for example kin selection, group selection (Lehmann *et al.*, 2007; Traulsen and Nowak, 2006) and reciprocity (people are inclined to return a favour (Trivers, 1971)). For effective decentralised networks, these concepts need to be translated to interactions between devices.

To be useful in this context, social links must be based on strong trust relationships in order to maximise cooperation within social communities and ostracise uncooperative and malicious behaviours. The 'socialnets' approach is based on the idea of forming, utilising and maintaining social structures to incentivise cooperation.

In P2P systems, incentives are often introduced in terms of economic models and rewards (Wolfson *et al.*, 2004), as well as punishment mechanisms imposed by third parties (for example penalties imposed on newcomers (Feldman and Chuang, 2005)). Direct reciprocity based on previous interactions and indirect reciprocity based on reputation schemes among trusted peers are also used to incentivise cooperation and detect free-riders. Concepts such as reputation work as indicators for trust in the system and may themselves be susceptible to mis-behaviour. In this sense direct reciprocity, based on an individual's past history of interactions with other specific parties, is a much more reliable notion. Axelrod's seminal work 1984 showed that a sufficient number of repeated interactions is necessary, so that long term benefits of cooperative behaviours overcome the short term benefits of selfish strategies.

7.5.1   *Social networks of trust*

In Allen *et al.* (2010a), cooperation between mobile devices is modelled by a network of repeatedly interacting agents which build up and maintain a dynamic social network of other trusted peers, based on similarity of behaviour. This demonstrates how naturally forming social groups can maintain high cooperation without requiring any external enforcement mechanism or punishment protocol, in stark contrast to the dark futuristic scenario of ostensible total social conformity in *This Perfect Day*.

This model represents a resource sharing scenario in which nodes repeatedly meet each other and (if they cooperate) share one of their resources with the opponent. The simulation is conducted by a sequence of sessions of the Iterated Prisoner's Dilemma game (IPD) (Axelrod, 1984). When a node receives a resource it scores a positive utility, defined by the original payoff matrix of the PD. In order to push resources, nodes have to pay a cost, which is equal to the half of the score obtained from receiving one resource. When a node defects, this will then provide double utility in case its opponent cooperates and shares one of its resource (since the defector will not pay any cost). The model also assumes that each node has its own cooperation level (i.e. a probability to cooperate in an interaction).

In the proposed model, each node keeps track of the scores, resulting from the latest interactions with each opponent it has played with. This information guides it to form social groups with those nodes that it would prefer to interact with in the future. Social links are used to prioritise selection and to take a decision on playing (or refusing to play) PD sessions, with the goal of encouraging interactions among the most cooperative peers.

Results show that the model works effectively when social groups are formed on the basis that 'nodes seek to interact with others which are at least as cooperative as themselves'. Motivation for this choice comes again from sociology and the *projection hypothesis*, which is evidence of the disposition to 'expect others to do what you intend to do yourself' (Orbell and Dawes, 1993). Another relevant observation from behavioural science is reciprocal altruism, or social exchange, where individuals assume altruistic behaviour in the hope of the behaviour being reciprocated (Trivers, 1971).

When the selection of nodes happens randomly and they are always forced to play a PD session, after few iterations the most defective nodes will be those scoring the highest utility, thus exploiting the cooperative behaviour of others, which end up being heavily penalised. However, when the PD sessions are played following the proposed protocol, this tendency is reversed, with the most cooperative nodes receiving the highest payoffs and defectors being ostracised by the rest of the population and scoring little or no utility.

7.5.2 *Privacy and security*

Another aspect related to trust issues is that of privacy and security in social mobile pervasive networks. We have seen how autonomic and opportunistic scenarios require frequent content sharing. Privacy becomes of major concern for norms and protocols for acceptable behaviour in pervasive networks, because of their inherent characteristics. For example, a node would agree on sharing all or part of his context information with his social friends, but he would not like seeing his context accessible to less trusted nodes.

Furthermore, forwarding decisions are directly taken over the content of the packet, but content publishers or receivers may not wish to reveal this content to intermediate nodes whose only task is forwarding. Besides, trust establishment can be very delicate when it involves the exchange of particularly sensitive information. Therefore, traditional protocols like Secret Handshakes and Matchmaking that have been proposed for this problem, implementing solutions for secure initial exchange in online scenarios (assuming continuous end-to-end connectivity), need to be re-designed for mobile dynamic environments (Shikfa *et al.*, 2010).

In general, social network users have scarce knowledge about who and for what scope their personal data can be used and are generally unaware of the business models lying behind some social networking sites. Users' behaviour and access can be tracked by companies known as 'aggregators' for marketing purposes. The leakage of privacy in OSNs has been investigated in a group of publications showing how personal identifying information can be forwarded directly to third-party tracking sites (for example through request headers), whereas users only agreed to share their private data exclusively among 'friends' of the specific social network they have joined (Krishnamurthy and Wills, 2008, 2010a).

Bonneau *et al.* (2009) introduces the concept of a 'social graph privacy', which prevents data aggregators from reconstructing large portions of the social graph composed of users and their friendship links (this can be more difficult to achieve than simply protecting the private data of individual users). It seems that it is possible to recreate substantial information based on the small subsets of data that social networks make public, for example Facebook exposes to search engines public view of user profiles that includes up to eight of the user's friendship links.

More recently, the extension of social networking to the mobile domain has introduced further privacy concerns (Krishnamurthy and Wills, 2010b). For example, the automatic disclosure of user presence and geographic location (e.g. Foursquare, Gowalla, Loopt) can lead to undesired consequences (a website called Please Rob Me (Hough, 2010) aims to track the location of empty homes based on updates posted on social networking sites). Moreover, users are not necessarily aware that sharing information with mobile online social networks (mOSNs) that allow connections to other traditional OSNs (e.g Foursquare can link posts to Facebook and Twitter automatically) can have their information directly visible for users of the specifically connected OSNs.

In general, it appears that the market for privacy in social networks is highly dysfunctional because of the large variation in sites' privacy controls, data collection requirements and legal privacy policies, all of them not sufficiently conveyed to users (Bonneau, 2009).

Finally, there is the important issue of the validity and reliability of the information itself which may allow constructing and re-constructing multiple Internet personas and accounts without a proper verification. This frequently happens within the teenagers' sphere and the way they can 'poison' their personal data. However, phenomena like *cyberbullying, grooming* and general abuse of social networking sites are not exclusively restricted to teens: any children or minors accessing them without adequate parental guidance is potentially subject to being bullied, turning into bullies themselves or becoming victims of online predators. It has been reported that complaints about grooming and bullying on one of the most popular websites has increased four times during the year 2010 (Edwards, 2010).

7.6 Further Applications: Key Opportunities for Social Networking

Social links are not only exclusively formed to preserve cooperation between individuals, but also to share information about useful and desired content. Beside the applications for content dissemination and resource sharing described earlier, we have identified three key opportunity fields for the exploitation of social networking in pervasive environments. These are: social micro-blogging, social network services in developing regions and opportunistic computing.

Since an example of application based on social micro-blogging has been extensively described within the introductory section, the rest of this section will focus on briefly describing possible applications for the further two exploitation perspective areas.

Social Network Services (SNS) in developing regions. Cellular and satellite networks in developing regions are usually very poor and expensive, due to the lack of coverage in many rural areas. It is not realistic that applications that feature friend browsing functionality (such as Facebook, Myspace, Orkut) would become popular there. It is the frequency of interaction against closeness that is relevant here, since the cost of communication is a barrier to forming links of sufficient strength. Therefore SNSs suitable to these regions only fall under four main categories: friend searching, resource sharing, information seeking and product marketing. Nevertheless, SNSs can improve standards of living and communication by introducing new services that use existing social links and interactions within the members of the communities. An example of this application can be found in Vallina-Rodriguez *et al.* (2009).

Opportunistic Computing. Opportunistic computing is described as distributed computing with intermittent connectivity and delay tolerance. Here, the main challenge is to effectively utilise opportunistic contacts to make information available and accessible, together with providing collaborative computing services and applications. Middleware services may then be needed to compensate disconnections and delays, manage heterogeneous computing resources, and control data and services access and placement (Conti and Kumar, 2010).

7.7   Conclusion: The 'Socialnets' Paradigm

This chapter has described how mobile pervasive environments present pe-
culiar characteristics and require a different approach to build social networking applications. In particular, the concept of resource for potential
sharing is now broadened: content is diverse and can embrace pictures,
data from sensors, news feeds, caching of web pages from the Internet,
message, audio and video files. This diversified content is now carried by
mobile devices that use short range wireless technology for forwarding and
sharing, thus aiming to achieve full integration between human activity and
mobility. To accomplish this we require the definition of new decentralised
self-organising systems, self-adaptive cooperation and security protocols.

Individuals will then need to use the concept of social networks to structure the provision of content. Firstly opportunistic networks will be formed
to exploit human mobility and allow devices to interact. Then, the system
should allow devices to build up and use social networks of other devices to
provide knowledge of content. Knowledge can be of different natures, from
type and quality of content to information about cooperative and trusted
individuals, either directly acquired or recommended by third parties. Finally, nodes will use the acquired information in order to maximise utility
when interacting with network peers, as well as detecting and ostracising
malicious and uncooperative behaviours.

Possible application fields range from resource sharing and mobile peer-
to-peer scenarios (example resources are photos, MP3, videos, dealing in
general with high payloads) to microblogging (using resources with much
lower payload) to applications in rural and developing regions, where opportunistic computing techniques can allow content dissemination, even
where Internet connection is either not or only intermittently available. In
general, social network applications will not be ideally suited to guaranteed
traffic from source to destination (as in online social networks), but will
focus on content dissemination scenarios in dynamic environments.

Finally, a number of aspects still need to be investigated and eventually
implemented. For example, issues related to the persistence of content –
how long for and what specific content should be stored, should some of the
content be permanently conserved, etc. – and, in general, to the relevance
of content to devices (based on interest, time, and spatial information) and
the reliability of both the sender and the received information. This could
be achieved through models of cognitive mechanisms of inference, belief,
cooperation and trust.

Chapter 8

Smart Sustainable Futures

Joan Farrer

University of Brighton

> *"The Family can afford a little waste where a member's health is involved."*
>
> THIS PERFECT DAY, P. 91–92

8.1 Introduction

The purpose of this chapter is to use Ira Levin's concept of 'coveralls' as a catalyst to examine and discuss what are the critical and philosophical issues surrounding contemporary thinking about sustainability, in particular design solutions, in relation to the sustainable fashion and textiles industry. The focus of this line of thought is to re-consider what is meant by 'impact' in terms of research, to consider how clothing (or indeed any everyday object) might be employed to enable interdisciplinary and non expert players, such as commercial designers, to participate in and contribute to potential solutions of achieving a more sustainable society, which is an ongoing and significant issue. With the benefit of 40 years hindsight, since the time of the book's publication in 1969, we discuss Levin's acknowledgements and omissions, with regard to the principles of sustainability, design innovation, and waste. In particular, we reflect upon the importance (or lack of) given to fashion, textiles, design and consumption at that time, in relation to the

importance and scale of the global industry today. We analyse the emergence of 'smart' and 'intelligent' materials, which have appeared since the
1960s, in conjunction with mobile and pervasive technologies and discuss
how these, unlike their predecessors, have the potential to be used to promote sustainable principles and consumer engagement with the sustainable
agenda. We discuss the subsequent development of thinking and products
in the sustainable and 'smart' textiles arenas and assess how they could
offer part of the solution for a more sustainable society. Finally, there will
be a summing up of the 'what if' question with regard to blue sky thinking,
predictions and the potential of the imminent 'smart sustainable' future
concept.

8.2 Levin's Vision of Fashion in the Future

The concept of *coveralls* in the novel is the obvious choice to focus our
discussions relating to sustainability in fashion and textiles. These coveralls, which were the utilitarian garments worn by the inhabitants of the
futurist society, reflect the philosophy and general opinion of the characters
in the book, who value uniformity and simplicity over individuality and
artistic expression of ideas. The central concept of a single garment, designed for ultimate efficiency in production, consumption and disposal, was
presented as a utopian ideal, even though 'coveralls' were certainly limiting
in terms of design aesthetics and individual expression. However, in terms
of sustainable manufacturing, production, consumption and disposal, the
premise has potential when considered with the actuality of technology now
available. As this chapter will discuss, the concept of fewer garments with
a longer life-span has significant potential for thinking about sustainability
and use in a different way.

A second way of thinking about sustainability in the future is embodied
in the concept of UniComp, the idea of technology as the all-powerful,
all-knowing computer used as a means of controlling the use of resources
(both human and non-human) for ultimate efficiency. With the realisation
that the amount of data that are being generated, collected and made
available to us today, the reality becomes one of finding means by which
the consumer can reach an informed decision about the sustainable nature
of products, without the need for becoming educated in sustainability issues
and an expert on the complexities of the sustainable agenda. This premise,
although not without problems, which will be discussed here, is another

way of thinking about how to enable consumers to make better choices in terms of sustainable product purchases.

Finally, the polarisation of the society in the novel, the 'haves' and the 'have-nots' should be discussed in particular to its relationship to sustainability, then and now. In fact, the model presented in the novel is quite opposite to the polarisation that has developed in present-day society. This discussion will consider how the balance is reversed and what the consequences are for thinking about how we can be more sustainable in our practices. It is apparent that much of the thinking around sustainability in terms of fashion and textiles is being put forward by post industrialised thinkers, providing possible solutions for a post industrial society. However, this polarisation is key to any discussion about sustainability that replaces the model of international trade and global economies with the model of source, make, shop, sell and dispose of within a local geographical unit.

8.3 Sustainability

Discussion and debate surrounding the topic of sustainability (as it has now become known), has been largely concentrated into the period spanning the last 50 years, despite having roots as early as the 16th century. The first authoritative engagement with the general public was through Rachel Carson's ground-breaking *Silent Spring* (Carson, 2002), which brought together research on toxicology, ecology and epidemiology. It linked the fact that agricultural pesticides were building to catastrophic levels, with damage to animal and human health. Since then, well-publicised, large-scale environmental crises such as the 1985 discovery of the hole in the Antarctic ozone layer by British and American scientists, the 1986 nuclear disaster at Chernobyl in Ukraine, and the 1989 Exxon Valdez oil spill over the pristine coast of Alaska's Prince William Sound, have meant that environmental protection and conservation have become synonymous with sustainability.

One of the most cohesive descriptions given more than 20 years ago in the Brundtland Report (World Commission on Environment and Development, 1987) was that 'sustainable development is development that meets the needs of the present without compromising the ability of future generations to meet their own needs'. This emerged as a pivotal text around the enormously complex issue of sustainability. This report, commissioned by the council for sustainable development, was primarily concerned with alleviating social poverty and creating global equity. However, the resulting report highlighted three fundamental components to be addressed towards sustainable development, which included social equity, itself inextricably linked to environmental protection and economic growth. Although there are many different definitions of sustainability, the definition included in the Brundtland Report remains the most eloquent for our purposes here. In simple terms, the concept of sustainability can be explained by the milking stool model of the three 'legs' or pillars: people, profit and planet, supporting the seat or platform of sustainability, where all elements are as important as each other.

8.4   Technology and Sustainability

As was the case. in Levin's vision, a common theme that has emerged in versions of the future from science fiction writing, is that resources are not inexhaustible and have to be managed. In addition, the world's population would expand exponentially unless measures were taken to control it. The use of technology appears to have been central to these ideas, in so far as, for the first time, it became conceivable that computers would have the ability to store, access and evaluate huge quantities of data over long periods of time. In the book, the technology itself may appear quite 'clunky' and in fact by today's standards, 'dumb'. Levin's 'nameber' bracelet was a version of 'clunky' wearable (or portable) electronics, which is a term first coined by Philips Electronics in 1995. Phillips Laboratory UK then established a unique multi disciplinary team of computing and electronic engineers, textile and garment designers to work on early wearable technology prototype ideas for Nike and Levi, international brands with money to invest in research. These experiments were an early example of the 'bolt-on technology', which is available in the market now, primarily to gather and communicate data to and from an external source for a variety of applications from entertainment to wellbeing. Two key examples are: the Nike Air Trainer with energy-harvesting equipment to support iPod technology that records activity and movement and downloads to iPhone applications; and the Zephyr Technologies Ltd NZ body Bio Harness developed for monitoring vital signs such as heart rate and body temperature for first responders such as fire fighters and military personnel. This product has specially developed software as part of the package.

Fig. 8.1 The LilyPad Arduino, which is bolt-on wearable technology for 'build your own' interactive fashion. AUT University, New Zealand.

There is confusion about the distinction between 'wearable' technology and 'portable' technology, such as the examples above. Wearable technology is sometimes used as a misnomer for miniaturised portable technology or for portable technology that has become miniaturised. Just because the functionality of a full TV set, stereo, video cassette recorder and telephone strapped to one's back has been replaced by an iPhone for a desk dock station or pocket does not mean it is 'wearable technology' – it remains 'bolt-on' (see for example the LilyPad Arduino, Fig. 8.1). Wearable technology should refer to integrated technology within 'smart' fabrics and is the development of interactive materials triggered by conductive fibres, surface phase change film and pigmentation or nano-technology embedded in man-made fibres that are then made into fabric (cf. Jefferies, Chapter 9 and Tillotson, Chapter 4). The term 'smart' is being used to describe technology that goes beyond the limits of 'counting things' and becomes ubiquitous, or, in other words, becomes as one with the user, seamless but interactive.

The convergence of textiles and electronics is exemplified by the development of a smart material, which is capable of accomplishing a wide spectrum of functions found in rigid and inflexible electronic products today. Smart textiles could serve as a means to increase the wellbeing of society and they may lead to savings on the health budget. They are a high value product and also an immaterial concept which satisfies such consumer needs and demands as creativity and emotional fulfilment (Schwarz *et al.*, 2010).

The potential of the reality of this kind of technology means that, rather than automatically rejecting the fashion proposition of a single garment design that is uniform, 'smart' textiles are demonstrating an ability to experiment with the integration of technology into garments for aesthetic and expressive purposes, as opposed to purely functional. Textiles and clothing can use a variety of intelligences to build up a smart textile system, sensing, actuating (powering, generating and storing), communicating, data processing and interconnecting. The integration of intelligent agents like conductive fibres, which are a key element in wearable technology, enable textiles to become electronically conductive, allowing audio, data and power which can be integrated in various ways: for example by using metal content wires in the weave or knit; printing surfaces with conductive inks to create soft electrical circuitry; or using fibre optics to enable power to be moved about the fabric for different functions, as specified by the designer and programmer.

Incorporating electrical elements into conductive textiles, such as sensors, enable the fabric to 'feel' changes in the environment, such as pressure, velocity and temperature, whereupon this information can be transmitted to and from an external source in an electrical signal. Such signals can then be actuated by emitting sound, changing a textile shape, creating heat or cooling and can be realised by the chemical actuator being bound to electroactive polymers such as carbon. Invisible elements with built-in functionality will create interactivity or an interactive platform for the wearer to download, design and individualise body coverings on a daily basis. This research is in development through active camouflage for military applications at Massachusetts Institute of Technology (MIT), who propose to use liquid crystal and electrochromic technologies to alter molecules. The idea is that built-in sensors would detect the soldier's immediate environment and modify the colour and texture of the clothing in order to blend in (Hibbert, 2006).

The need of individuality in fashion is a key aspect that is unlikely to change, despite the knowledge that the over-production and consumption of fashion causes immense problems for sustainability. The adoption of different methods of achieving this individuality is crucial to developing new solutions that address the treadmill of over-production, consumption and sustainable disposal, which remains a problem for the discipline of design.

8.5 The Potential of a Standard Garment Solution

In recent decades, it has been the fashion retail trade and market-based economics pushing an aspirational lifestyle which were at the core of fashion
and textiles consumption. Retailers produced ever growing collections and
fresh ranges, often of dubious quality, believing the consumer would continue to blindly buy goods if constant newness prevailed. Now, although the
consumer is more 'choosy', they still demand vast amounts of new collections which are now well made, well designed and are still buying (literally)
into the notion of a lifestyle for maximal consumption. The desire to consume is still promoted by the fashion retail trade, coupled with the desire
to consume by the ordinary customer in the developed world, which has
resulted in an insatiable appetite for fashion. Inevitably, this frenzied spiral
of production and consumption is creating increasingly disposable fashion,
where a lack of emotional attachment to clothes has led to the consequent
dumping of perfectly good clothing, with 30 kilos of textile waste per person
reaching UK land fill sites each year (Allwood *et al.*, 2006). At the same
time, neither wish to feel responsible; no-one wants to take responsibility for
over-production or over-consumption, certainly not the short-term interests
of the retail trade, who are trying to maximise profits, nor the consumers,
who want good, exciting merchandise on the cheap. Unfortunately, it is
consumers who can be considered one of the major obstacles to achieving
a sustainable future and it is changing their purchasing habits which will
be at the heart of any movement for change.

Our current perception of disposable fashion items is that they are by
nature cheap products, in terms of both the raw materials and construction methods used, and as a result we have no respect for them. They
are produced to be inexpensive and demonstrate a built-in obsolescence.
However, the end retailer is concerned primarily with profit and, despite
the inexpensive retail price, endeavours to achieve maximum profit mar-
gin. Unfortunately, this means that the cost efficiencies are usually made
at the expense of the labour force, as prices for raw materials and freight,
for example, are not as flexible. This requires a production system of ex-
traordinarily detailed efficiency in production costs and logistical terms.
To develop this efficient and more sustainable system, leading fashion and
food retailers such as Marks & Spencer (UK) and WalMart (USA) have
developed smart tagging of goods through the supply chain and stock control via radio-frequency identification (RFID) technology. This system is
becoming as widespread as barcode technology, as it enables the store and

the consumer to communicate with each other through scanning and mobile phone technology. Interactive labelling using RFID in clothes will ubiquitously communicate with technology in our daily lives, such as our washing machines to wash clothing appropriately.

The idea that we could develop one standard garment that would satisfy the needs of consumers and replace the practice of buying disposable fashion is being made more desirable with the latest developments in fibre, textile and computing technology. The key will be to make a particular fashion look that is temporary, interactive and replicable, without the necessity of physically making a new garment. This garment could be produced to take advantage of efficient production methods using computer-aided design (CAD) and computer-aided manufacture (CAM), and to have a long and useful life, which may change and adapt towards a pre-considered end use, such as being programmed for composting and/or materials and energy recovery. The potential of technology now is to enable garments to change shape, to project different surface patterns and textures, to react to different environmental stimuli and to interact with the wearer aesthetically or emotionally. The following are examples of how this is being achieved in some close-to-market applications.

8.5.1 *Shape memory textiles*

If we did attempt to adopt a 'one style suits all' approach to clothing, the minimal supply chain would be given a 'one size fits all' production model as well. The problem with producing such clothes, as represented by Levin's coveralls, is that, unlike in *This Perfect Day*, where people were genetically engineered to be identical, in our society people are obviously not the same size and shape. This has been somewhat overcome by the development and adoption of standardised sizing systems that have allowed garments to be produced in numbers suitable for mass production. However, different geographical areas and anatomical body types mean that even standardised systems are struggling to get it right. There have been some interesting developments in research around body scanning technology, in particular combining body scanning technology with knitted whole garment technology, which also eliminates fabric waste (see Fig. 8.2).

The possibility of an oversized shape being moulded to various other incarnations offers a potential solution to this ongoing problem of sizing, as well as providing the potential for garments to be redesigned in terms of silhouette (aesthetic shape), for fashion purposes. A 'clunky' example of

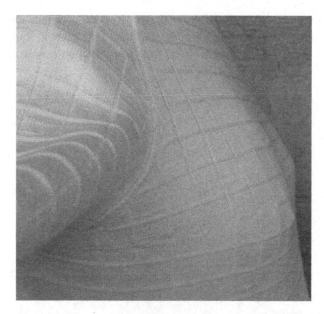

Fig. 8.2 'Knit to Fit' Whole Garment Manufacturing Technology.   University of Brighton, UK.

this silhouette reshaping can be seen in the work of Hussein Chalayan in the 'transformer dresses' from his Spring/Summer 2007 collection, which includes a shift shape dress that is capable of converting to a full skirted shape through a series of computer-operated automated pulleys, known as animatronics. However, the latest developments in textiles technology are forging ahead to include shape memory fibre and metal composite developments that have the ability, depending on their programming, to maintain a shape or change shape in response to environmental conditions, such as a variation in temperature. The potential for developing garments that are transformable is now imaginable, if not possible, in the near future. The nature of the fibres could also mean that various textures could be achieved through one cloth, for example a crepe-like finish could be applied for a particular garment shape and yet a soft, fluffy angora finish might be more suited to another style incarnation (see Fig. 8.3).

Although these developments sound as though they are also the stuff of science fiction, these new intelligent technical developments are in the research and development stage, and these 'blue sky' concepts are becoming more and more likely. Given the shift in consumption, the business model for the fashion retail trade would be more in line with high price 'haute couture' methods, where quality of make, functional design and flawless aesthetics drive price up and quantities down. These iconic items are non disposable, repairable, and a heritage purchase, with an ingrained value.

Fig. 8.3   Nitol shape memory alloy woven textile. University of Brighton, UK.

8.5.2   *Light emitting, Fibreoptic and conductive textiles*

Another development is in the genre of techno textiles (Braddock and O'Mahony, 1999). In these products there are fibres capable of reflecting light or, when connected to a power source, such as a lithium battery or solar power cells, conducting light, changing colour and creating light rhythms (see Fig. 8.4).

The potential of this technology is in the ability to weave fabric that is capable of projecting a pattern or image. This would enable our standard garment to change colour, or to display a particular pattern or perhaps play video images. The possibilities are endless for this kind of technology, but from a purely aesthetic point of view it would add many more possible combinations and permutations of design possibilities for the individual to customise. In addition to light emitting textiles, there are fabrics which can conduct and make sound to act as a speaker, for instance, or to play musical notes as you stroke the surface via sensors and actuators.

Fig. 8.4   Light-emitting textile using fibre optics. Herriot Watt University, UK.

8.5.3   *Aesthetic applications*

An application could be developed to transform our standard garment shape by turning part of the fabric into a lace pattern and texture and other parts into a watermark taffeta. The watermark pattern would be projected and the sound effects of rustling taffeta would be broadcast in time with the movement of the body. We have to consider how this design would be created, and recognise that it would involve interdisciplinary teams to develop the fibres, fabrics and garments to be programmed to perform. This presents two issues. Firstly, how users would be able to access their virtual wardrobes. Of course this is no longer that hard to imagine if we think about how many of us currently access our CD collections via iPod, iPhone and iTunes stores. Could we be looking potentially at iWear or iWardrobe scenarios where we download different styles, patterns, textures and colours, for example, to load onto our standard garment? Secondly, this would have significant impact on the way in which we think about fashion design and would mean a significant change in the way in which designers are educated, the way in which they practice, are employed and even sell their designs. In relation to our example, the best part about this idea from the perspective of fashion sustainability is that when this gown has been worn for the theatre or for a school formal (or any other rare occasion), the 'hardware', in this case our standard garment, can be reformatted and used for another purpose, without ending up in the developing world or in landfill after being worn only two or three times.

8.6   The Potential of a UniComp Solution

A key question for sustainability in fashion and textiles is how to inform customers to make more sustainable choices. One approach has been to encourage greater transparency in the supply chain. Labels that feature information about the fabric and where a garment has been made are, of course, one way, but not the only one. In the future another method would be to fingerprint fibres using nanotechnology, so that they have a unique code that can be identified, perhaps with a scanner. This would allow retailers to have greater control of their supply chain, adding value to the brands of those companies who are able to communicate to their customers their own trustworthiness in this respect. Consumers should then be able to access this information, which would be downloadable to an app on a mobile phone (see Fig. 8.5).

The advantage of the systems outlined above is that consumers who are interested in obtaining the information are able to do so. However, what is more likely is that consumers will begin to trust companies that offer the technology as being suppliers of a sustainable product. In our opinion, the choice of whether to buy sustainably or not should remain with the consumer, the role as designers, manufacturers or retailers should be to ensure that they have enough accurate information to make informed choices.

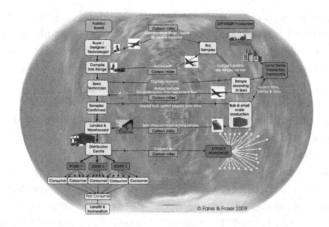

Fig. 8.5   World map globalisation of the fashion and textile typical supply chain.

This raises the issue of whether or not, as consumers, do we actually want to know? Not that we do not want to buy more sustainable products, but do we need to know the myriad details of how and why a product is sustainably produced? Those of us already suffering from digital information overload would rather not. The downside of UniComp in *This Perfect Day* was that the citizens were offered no choice; in our society the problem often appears to be too much choice (increasing the scope to make the choice), or worse, the illusion of choice. Therefore, and even in the novel for that matter, the majority of us seem quite happy to simply be told 'good' or 'bad', particularly if we trust the information source or brand. Many consumers would also like to have garments pre-selected for them based on expressed preferences, rather than having to search for them. Therefore, could a contemporary version of UniComp be the viable solution to serve our needs as consumers in the future?

Would it be possible to develop an information system to support consumers by providing them with an 'information bubble', similar to that proposed in theory and early developments around the idea of the semantic web (Berners-Lee *et al.*, 2001) and cloud computing? We imagine that such a system would have the ability to access thousands of times more data than the current capabilities of engines such as Google; and rather than provide us with 'results' or specific information, would simply provide us with a recommendation based on implicit information. The answer then would not be to buy or not to buy, but perhaps would be a numerical rating or coloured stripe from green to red, indicating that the product is closer to sustainable or not sustainable and leaving the final decision to the buyer.

The next question will of course be how this cloud computing version of UniComp would be programmed and how and where it would gather data? The question should also include what sort of data would it use to make recommendations? At present the amount and kind of data available to us via the Internet is exhausting, and constantly growing. There is so much data available to us that it has become almost impossible for it to be of any use in decision making, even for the expert. The additional data, while perhaps useful in smaller more intimate quantities, has become useless in being of assistance in making an informed decision.

One of the fears played on in *This Perfect Day* is the idea of a uniform and homogeneous citizenry, compelled to conform by an uncompromising and unchanging state. As in the book, the truth of any social reality is that both the citizens and the state are dynamic, and shaped by conflicting social movements, interacting to secure their interests or make a society more progressive. Retailers and consumers can be seen roughly as two such movements (the reality is more complex: consumers are ultimately multiple movements) and, given the high volatility of social networking and its ability to influence consumer behaviour, retailers will have to work hard to stay in place. One way they can keep pace with the game is to become actively involved in the informal social networks that inform consumer behaviour. In this way they will avoid the trap of being merely reactive – they will become collaborative. Access to and analysis of this type of reflective and interactive data should definitely be a consideration for the designers of our new version of UniComp.

An information cloud would therefore have to be supplied with accurate, traceable, but limited, amounts of data that can be navigated on multiple levels and provide reliable results. The advantage of our modern fibres, particularly the development of nano-fibres, could allow the history and future of each particular component of a garment to be known. A scanner, such as in the earlier example, built into a mobile phone could then be skimmed over the surface and read each signature. The data would then be sent out into the information cloud, which would evaluate the combination of the components, potentially with personal data about the user such as size, age and lifestyle (for example) and recommend the purchase as sustainable or not sustainable.

A limitation of the information cloud concept is, of course, the trust involved in relying on this system. For the concept to work effectively, the consumer is required to rely on the recommendations made by a system and method that they are ignorant of and that makes decisions on information that they do not have access to. Of course, we do this already, every single day, when we purchase goods that have brands that we 'trust'. Brands such as Marks & Spencer PLC (UK) and Prada Ltd (Italy) who have had to earn the trust of their customers over long periods of time are now considered to be trustworthy brands. Small manufacturers however, and newer players in the market, do not have these advantages and therefore would have much to gain by being able to be recommended as trustworthy by such a system. The problems of lack of information could be overcome with functionality that allowed consumers who were interested to download a full dataset for their consideration.

8.7 The Potential of 'Source Local, Make Local, Sell Local'

In *This Perfect Day*, there are two societies depicted: the dystopian one in which the majority of the population lived, which was structured, seemingly well-ordered and compassionate; while, in contrast, the small minority (the 'incurables') lived in the old ways, with a more capitalist economic system, and instantly recognisable as a 1970s industrial society, with money, mining, gambling, discrimination, an 'army', a 'Pope', and so on. The former, with its careful husbandry of the planet's materials, is of course supposed to compare favourably with the latter, where we are told there are 'shortages of food and space and resources' (*This Perfect Day*, p.217).

Curiously, though, their treatment of clothing suggests that the more sustainable of the two versions of society in the novel is, in fact, the low technology 'uncivilised' island nations that had not been subsumed into the larger whole. (In one sense, this should not be so surprising: small, rural and/or tribal communities seem to be – and those in closed environments like islands *need* to be – much more effective at managing and sustaining resources than high-tech globalisation.) The 'coveralls' in the novel are worn once and put 'into the chute' for an invisible cleaning, recycling or perhaps for disposal, whereas in another passage, on the island, Lilac is described as mending their clothes. It is quite clear which is the more environmentally-friendly and sustainable approach.

This should cause us to reflect on the fact that in the late 1960s the importance of what happens to our clothes after they are finished with was not a consideration. In a similar way, people at the time would have been putting used clothing in the dustbin and not seeing or thinking about them again. As we now know, this was a luxury that we no longer have as users and consumers. This raises the concept that, rather than thinking about the issues of sustainability as a remote global issue, with global remote problems and solutions, we should be starting to think about the potential of more small scale and local solutions to reuse and recycle.

In the real world, smaller non-industrialised centres have less choice about incorporating sustainable practices into their everyday existence. Not because they are forced to do so, but because to do otherwise would create ongoing problems for societies, especially in regard to minimising landfill and streamlining waste disposal. The nature of our large scale urban environments (latest figures show that 50% of the world's population now live in cities) is that they have a myriad systems specifically designed to make the disposal of waste products as invisible and smooth running as possible to the inhabitants. For example, extensive systems of sewerage, mains water and power and garbage collection appear seamless. The problem for inhabitants is, of course, a disconnection between the realities of the volume of waste that we produce. There are also other problems, including the export of textiles waste to developing nations for disposal. Perhaps, if we were forced to dispose of this waste ourselves, as is the case on the fictional island of Liberty, we might be more conscious of how much we consumed and what we did with it when its usefulness had been exhausted, such as composting, recycling, upcycling and energy recovery.

The increase in the corporatisation of the fashion textile industry, away from the previous smaller scale, patriarchal organisations, also contributes to unsustainable consumerism. The consequent emphasis on shareholder value and maximisation of profits to the exclusion of other values that were previously dominant – such as localising production and a 'job for life' approach – means that companies tend to define themselves (to themselves rather than to the market) almost solely in terms of profits. Each year, managers feel heavier pressures to achieve greater cost efficiencies in order to realise greater profits. Growth is everything. But this growth exacerbates the amount of waste created and the number of people working in poor conditions in sweatshops.

Conscience clothing is the conceptual term first coined in 2003 for the exhibition *Fashion and Modernity*, to refer to clothes that not only have good environmental credentials but which also communicate these credentials to the consumer. To give an example, tracking the clothing worn by five university students in New Zealand revealed that, in one case, the minimum distance travelled by the clothing prior to being purchased was 3,296 miles, while the maximum was 43,765 miles. The combined carbon footprint of the five students was 50.98 tons of carbon emissions in transport alone from the last point of production (the real carbon footprint would have been immeasurably more, see Fig. 8.6). This highlights the benefits, in carbon terms alone, of close-to-market design and manufacturing. So, a greater localisation of the fashion textile chain would have immediate ecological benefits. If this information was included in the label, consumers would be able to vote with their wallets and the result would be that greater localisation would very likely be achieved (cf. Farrer and Fraser (2009)).

Fig. 8.6   Conscience clothing shoot, showing garment miles to New Zealand and related carbon footprint.

8.8   Most Sustainable Long Term Solution

From a point of view of sustainable fashion and textiles in the future, the best possible solution would seem to be the adoption of a standard garment, combined with cutting edge intelligent fabrication and integrated technologies that have the ability to change its behaviour, look and feel. In tandem with this development, new ways of promoting, manufacturing and wearing fashion will need to be explored and developed. These garments have the potential to be investment pieces, the same way that computer hardware is an investment, and could be a way to address the disposable nature of fashion available in the high street. The exploration of these new forms may provide the market with an element of excitement and creativity in design, similar to that seen in the 20th century with the introduction of a raft of new technical man-made fibres.

8.8.1   *Textiles, fibres and sustainability*

The increasing human population, and in particular the burgeoning numbers of people with substantial disposable incomes, means that more and more textiles need to be produced, and this is increasingly being recognised as having ecological impacts that are not, in the long-term, sustainable. How many more sheep can we breed to provide wool (with the associated issues of animal welfare), or how many square miles of cotton fields (notoriously heavy users of water) can we plant? It was this last problem that Ira Levin foresaw: one entrance bears the gold-lettered legend 'The Earth is Our Heritage. We Use It Wisely and Without Waste' (*This Perfect Day*, p. 126). In relation to the fashion textile industry, we have not yet fully understood the need to adapt our behaviours to attain this objective.

An advantage of the new developments in the textiles arena, such as the light emitting textiles and shape changing fibres, is that they are man-made. Traditionally, natural fibres have been associated with being eco-friendly and green, if grown without pesticides such as organic cotton. However, research has since shown that although this might be the perception of consumers, man-made fibres offer many advantages over natural fibres, particularly in terms of closed loop manufacture, where the chemical compounds and processing take place from raw materials in a sealed factory, where pollution is virtually non-existent and fibre, thread or fabric is the end product. Man-made fibres such as polyester and nylon can be upcycled. Man-made fibres should not be confused with synthetic fibres and are often made from renewable resources such as wood and corn. These fibres have developed in appearance, functionality and wearability to a point where they are often preferred to natural fibres, such as wool, which can be expensive, heavy and irritating to the skin.

8.8.2   *Disposal and upcycling*

Most people think that recycling is the answer to retail waste, but there is a strong argument for viewing recycling as a failure of proper waste management along the production chain, such as the right first time concept, which with careful planning there is no waste. Today, Ira Levin's world of no waste is a mirage. Waste has to be dealt with but the current situation, where most of the clothing that is deposited in recycling bins finds its way to developing world countries (where it is sold as a general trade good in street markets, so impeding the development of local textile industries who cannot compete against this very low cost product) is not satisfactory. Instead of recycling, we would be better off thinking in terms of upcycling.

Upcycling (McDonough and Braungart, 2002) is a new paradigm, where what you re-create from waste has more intrinsic value than the original parts. In relation to fashion, if you think of discarded men's trousers dismantled into its component parts and then those materials being used to re-create another item, perhaps a contemporary cocktail dress, this epitomises the upcycling concept (Farrer, 2011). Unfortunately, blended fabrics cannot be upcycled in this way and the best that we can do at present is to incinerate it for its energy potential. This would create the additional problem of what to do with the toxic ash residue. The solution, therefore, is that good waste disposal processes need to be factored in at the 'start of pipe' production stage. However, it is not unreasonable to imagine that the different fibres in blended fabrics may one day be separable by technological means, such as embedded smart dust, to enable fibre recognition (Farrer, 2010).

8.8.3 *Advantages of the standard garment solution*

The main advantages of a standardised garment, as mentioned in Levins description of coveralls, are the production methods which remove the need for throw away disposal, through upcycling of the raw materials used to make the garment. In terms of cut and construction, working from a standardised shape has benefits for manufacturing costs that would mean significant savings for consumers and increased profits for manufacturers. Over time, many production processes could be automated. The advantage of man-made fibres such as organic plastics and polyesters is that they are long wearing and highly durable when compared with their counterparts in nature. The development of such fibres for production is considerably less harmful to the environment. The fibres themselves are also quite suited to disassembly and reuse. The use of a single production system, a limited set of man-made fibres, fabrics, patterns and construction methods, combined with a single method of disposal for upcycling means that the necessity to provide a transparent supply chain in order to guarantee that a sustainable product would not become obsolete.

8.8.4 *Limitations of the standard garment solution*

Although we describe here that there are many advantages and exciting design possibilities for sustainable technological smart textile solutions, there is a key concern that should be raised because, at present, research and development of these new textile products are not a priority for the industry. The key limitation of the fibres is that they are currently being developed to be quick to market for a series of available products that are designed to do specific tasks, and are made from similar materials. For our idea of the standard garment solution to be effective, it would require a combined inter-industrial effort to develop a single product that would be enabled with multiple functionalities. We propose that this could be possible based on the current technical know-how, using simple examples from weave constructions such as tartan, reversible and triple cloth fabrics.

The significance of having specially designed knits and weaves to increase functionality within a single piece of cloth is not only to enable a larger quantity and quality of virtual garment design possibilities, but also to allow a constant of materiality for the purpose of the efficient and safe recycling and upcycling of the product. As discussed, the ability to separate the fibres by expedient methods is currently an advantage of man-made fibres that would need to be ensured for this system to be most effective.

8.9   Conclusion

There have been amazing technological advancements in parallel to an accelerating environmental degradation, which has occurred in the 40 years since the visionary publication of *This Perfect Day*. Ira Levin's future, fictional concepts now illustrate the great potential that the use of pervasive and ubiquitous technology and intelligent textiles and fashion can have in achieving innovative engagement with, and solutions for, the core issues of sustainability.

Ironically, at no point in the book does Ira Levin mention the word sustainability, yet the whole novel is underpinned by its core concepts and the associated problems with regard to achieving a more sustainable world. The issues which are subliminally embedded and openly referred to in the book remain today. However, we are now much more overtly aware of global warming, population explosion, resource management and so on, than were our contemporaries in the late 1960s, which was a time well before the plethora of scholarly scientific, social and environmental reports had been published. Unfortunately, the emphasis of smart textile technologies and computing has moved more towards developing intelligent materials and applications for innovative uses such as the games market or defence. Whereas, by focusing on smart and intelligent materials, combined with burgeoning ubiquitous computing innovation, we could begin to solve the more pressing issues of wellbeing and resource management, so that we would ensure that we can continue the journey towards an equitable, healthy, expanding human population in a way that does not imperil the world in which we all have to live together.

Chapter 9

Wires and Wearables

Janis Jefferies

Goldsmiths, University of London

> *"Look at them," Papa Jan said ... "Exactly the same! Isn't it marvellous? Hair the same, eyes the same, skin the same, shape the same; boys, girls, all the same. Like peas in a pod. Isn't it fine? Isn't it top speed?"*
>
> THIS PERFECT DAY, P. 20

9.1 Introduction

Much has been made in European Union research programmes, and elsewhere, of the metaphors of 'the disappearing computer', 'ambient intelligence', 'territory as interface', 'internet of things' and indeed 'pervasive adaptation'. The underlying idea, of course, is that it is no longer the desktop computer or the handheld device that provides the interface to the computing and network infrastructure; the entire environment is the interface. The aim of *wearable computing* is to include clothing in these metaphors: all someone's garments provide interfaces and affordances for explicit interaction, implicit interaction (see Ferscha, Chapter 2) and affective interaction (see Šerbedžija, Chapter 5).

However, using garments for computing interfaces is both complicated and enriched by the fact that clothing is also a vehicle for fashion, and as such offers an opportunity for expressions of personal identity, group identification, culture, and so on. The question then becomes: if the convergence of technology and fashion changes culture, and culture is a set of shared norms and values, then how is society and culture affected when an individual's behaviour and mindset are both side-effected by wearable computing, which itself is both interface and outerwear?

In fact, cultural critics know how technology is taken up in and influences broader culture, as well as how cultural background can encourage the development of certain forms of technology and utopian discourse at the expense of others. If we know cultural pressure points, then, in the development of new technology, we also have the possibilities to generate new practices and critiques, which can help us understand how we engage in a rich set of interactions in the everyday world. This chapter explores this argument from the perspective of wearable computing or wired garments, i.e. clothing saturated with sensors, actuators and displays (and see also Farrer, Chapter 8).

9.2 Wearable Computing

In *Science Daily* (2008) it was announced that:

> *Garments that can measure a wearer's body temperature or trace their heart activity are just entering the market, but the European project BIOTEX weaves new functions into smart textiles. Miniaturised biosensors in a textile patch can now analyse body fluids, even a tiny drop of sweat, and provide a much better assessment of someone's health* (Science Daily, 2008)

At the same time, Philips Research produced a range of promotional jackets featuring its innovative Lumalive technology. Lumalive textiles carry dynamic advertisements, graphics and constantly changing colour surfaces. Indeed, smart fabrics promise to revolutionise clothing by incorporating sensors into cloth for health, lifestyle and business applications. In the long term, they could consist of circuits and sensors that provide all of the typical electronics we carry around today, like mobile phones and PDAs (personal digital assistants).

Drawing on McLuhan's (1964) observation that the garment is an inter-face to the exterior mediated through digital technology, Seymour (2008) writes that '... the electric age ushers us into a world in which we live and breathe and listen through the entire epidermis'. She argues that technolo-gies enrich the cognitive characteristics of our human epidermis and stimuli of our senses, whether they are based in biotechnology, digital technology or nanotechnology, or even materials like conductive textiles, coatings or electronics plastics on the surface of a garment. Fashionable technology be-come amplifiers of fantasy with technically enhanced functionalities. What do fashionable wearables communicate and what is the context of use? How do they amplify one's fantasy? Do they reveal new forms of social interac-tion? If McLuhan thought the 'Medium was the Message', then the body is that medium. We now have digital-display dresses and remote control couture, there is an ecosystem of accessories, from iPod white wires to in-tegrated ear bud clothing. There is a way of interacting with gadgets that appear and appeal as more 'natural'. These gadgets go beyond single areas of evolutionary improvement. In other words, spreading the functions over a number of cooperating parts, providing more value as a coordinated whole and can be supported by high bandwidth, short-range wireless technologies.

Fig. 9.1 *Wearable Absence* (used with kind permission of Barbara Layne and Hesam Khoshneviss).

Figure 9.1 shows an image taken from the *Wearable Absence* project (2006–2010), a collaboration between Concordia University, Montreal and Goldsmiths, University of London. The project combined innovations with interactive textiles and the idea of archiving an individual's life to provide a new way to activate personal memory. The system uses a PDA or smartphone (normally carried in the pocket) to connect to the Internet. This same device also communicates with the garment wirelessly through Bluetooth. To start the system, the device is engaged by selecting the character that the user wants to 'channel' throughout the day. The garments are a sophisticated sensing device that can download and playback multimedia files. Sensors embedded in the garment take four readings from the body: heart rate, temperature, rate of respiration and galvanic skin response (moisture of the skin). These readings determine the emotional state of the wearer and trigger the downloading and presentation of an archived memory.

All files, (texts, photographs, videos or sound) have been uploaded to a database prior to use by the wearer. Videos and photographs are presented on the PDA or smartphone that is carried in the pocket. The sound plays through small, high quality speakers embedded in the hood (in the case of the female garment) or in the shoulders (of the male garment).

Figure 9.1 also shows how texts scroll through a handwoven LED display embedded in the cuff of the sleeve of the female garment, but uses a different text display for the male: a liquid crystal display (LCD). The system uses two mobile phone batteries that can be removed and recharged.

Some 30 years after the first personal computers appeared, neuroscientists, cultural/cyber theorists, and cognitive psychologists, amongst others, are still concerned with how we live in a world mediated by flickering screens, multimedia/multi-modal integration and interactive programming; a world in which, following Seymour (2008), contemporary fashion mobilises the garment as a mediator of information and communication, a medium that incorporates technological elements that transform the environment itself into an interactive interface.

Quinn (2002, p. 388) makes the point that something like Hussein Chalayan's *Remote Control Dress* references a cyborg: 'a hybrid of machine and organism, a creature of social reality, as well as a creature of fiction', when a human's nervous system '[operates] in direct connection with the artificial intelligence of a machine'. However, as Haraway (1991) challenges, the cyborg is a creature in a post-gender world; it has no truck with bisexuality, pre-oedipal symbiosis, unalienated labour, or other seductions to organic wholeness through a final appropriation of all the powers of the parts into a higher unity.

There is not so much talk about cyborgs these days, at least not in the way there has periodically been since the 1970s, when the sensationalist possibilities of science seemed too good not to be true: a body free of disease, free of ageing, free of its most limiting appendages, and so on. All of these enticing prospects fell in some fuzzy space between science and fiction and never really materialised.

However, in downtown Montreal, and at the Hexagram Institute, cyborg fashion and the androgyny of the future stand in perfect view. For example, Joanna Berzowska's XS Labs, based in Hexagram at Concordia University, Montreal, Canada, is a design research studio with a focus on innovation in the fields of electronic textiles and reactive garments: 'second skins' that can enable computationally-mediated interactions with the environment and the individual. The work is inspired by the technical and cultural history of how textiles have been made for generations (weaving, stitching, embroidery, knitting, beading and quilting) and by new and emerging materials with different electro-mechanical properties. This enables them to construct complex textile-based surfaces, substrates, and structures with 'transitive' properties.

SKORPIONS (see Fig. 9.2) are a set of kinetic electronic garments that move, pulse and change with the body in slow, organic motions. The Eneleon dress is made of heavy handmade felt and creamy leather; its seductive slits pulsate open to reveal a mirrored lamé layer. They have anthropomorphic qualities and can be imagined as parasites that inhabit the skin of the host. They breathe and pulse, controlled by their own internal programming. They are not 'interactive' artefacts, insofar as their programming does not respond to simplistic sensor data. They have intentionality; they are programmed to live, to exist and to subsist. They are living behavioural kinetic sculptures that exploit characteristics such as control, anticipation and unpredictability. They have their own personalities, their own fears and desires.

As designers of wearable technologies, XS Labs asks what wearers (i.e. users, in the traditional terminology of human–computer interaction) want of electronic garments. What kind of information processing do we want to carry out on our bodies? What kind of functionality do we want to enable inside our clothes? The clothing and electronic industries are looking for the killer application, the next big thing that will introduce wearable computing to a mass market. One application of reactive fashion is to enable the idea of changing our skin, our identity and our cultural context. *SKORPIONS* integrate electronic fabrics, the shape-memory alloy Nitinol, mechanical actuators such as magnets, soft electronic circuits, and traditional textile construction techniques such as sculptural folds and drapes of fabric across the body.

Fig. 9.2   *SKORPIONS* from XS Labs (used with kind permission of Joanna Berzowska).

9.3   Cultural Implications

But do 'people of the screen', performativity of the dressed, networked performance or live coding think fundamentally differently to 'people of the book', catwalk fashion, musical improvisation or of traditional theatre? Do here-and-now, let yourself go, ecstasy of communication, fast-paced sensory experiences change how future generations see themselves, and what will interactive electronic media mean for personal identity and society during our lifetimes? For example, as neurochip technology becomes more widely available, tiny devices will take advantage of the discovery that nerve cells and silicon chips can happily co-exist, allowing an interface between the electronic world and the human body. This is demonstrated by the development of cochlear implants, devices that convert sound waves into electronic impulses and enable the deaf to hear (Vaerenberg *et al.*, 2011). In the other direction, a skull-mounted microchip that converts neural activity into spoken words has been proposed – a fantasy perhaps, but part of a futurology that is obsessed with device evolution research?

Incorporation of devices into garments is not as straightforward as is perhaps thought. For example, there is a trade-off between signal loss and antenna size when low-permittivity materials are used for the antenna substrate (Harris, 2008). Furthermore there is a requirement for stretchable and flexible circuitry (Lacour *et al.*, 2006) to make antennas which can be sewn into clothing, ironed or printed directly onto the fabric. In this way it might be possible for the technology to be incorporated in garments that people might eventually wear naturally and without discomfort.

But what if devices were connected to a wireless network? Would we have arrived at a similar point to which science fiction writers have been getting excited about for years? Such device parts could be worn on and in the body: earrings will be speakers, necklaces will be microphones and cameras will become sleeves as screens. Fashion, its theories and histories often focus on the analysis of the detail of a garment or an accessory frequently ignoring the social aspects of everyday dress. Garments themselves are not meaningful. It is the wearer and the viewer, the performer and the audience that attach meaning, but how we 'perform' the techno body in role play is central to identity formation, how we re-fashion ourselves influences the social space and vice versa.

Gestures may be sensed by the clothing we wear and used to control some applications. Progress is already being made in understanding signals from the brain, e.g. controlling artificial limbs (see Chavarriaga and Millán, Chapter 3), so it is not such a leap forward to think about what other devices do and for them to be able to respond. In the shorter term, earrings and necklaces are the examples given, but in the longer term materials must provide instant snap-on wireless connectivity since wiring oneself up each time one dresses is not the most convenient or practical way of getting ready to go out.

9.4   Technological Provocation

Taking a neurscientific perspective, Susan Greenfield wonders what the brain will physically look like in future generations. Her central anxieties are that galloping technological advances and the social changes that they bring will not only transform our sense of who and what we are, but might alter our identity to the point where we may no longer have the capacity to be fully developed people (Greenfield, 2008a). Her prediction is that interaction with technology, from mobile phones to video games, might produce a brain as a first-person perspective of identity that is stuck in what she terms 'infancy immediacy'. Twenty-first century technologies may bend our brains, and hence erode our identities, she argues, but in ways previous generations could not have envisaged.

Greenfield argues that sensation has replaced cognition, process has replaced content and movement has replaced thought. In response to a question on a BBC Radio 3 programme, *Nightwaves* (Greenfield, 2008b), about how interaction with technology is responsible for this, Greenfield took up the theme of ecstasy, which in Greek means 'to stand outside of yourself', to explore the tension between letting go on one hand, and on the other achieving things and having a sense of personal identity, time and space. Anxiety over the stripping of cognitive content in the wake of flashing lights and sweaty bodies, loud music and abstract patterns, propels Greenfield's anxiety that the brain connections will be so messed up, by sensory overload in the moment, to cause a schizophrenia of the perpetual present. This is not dissimilar to the ideas expressed by Jameson (1991).

But Greenfield's point is that, when the individual lets go, the emphasis is on living in the present and all that matters is sensation. Interestingly, the International Society of Electronic Arts (ISEA) 2004 Fashion Show took place in a club setting, the Club Bon Bon in Tallinn, Estonia, rather than on a traditional catwalk. It presented a mix of conceptual electronic clothing that incorporated illumination, wire, sensors, cameras and sound, a great deal of sound. As Michael and Michael discuss in Chapter 10, incorporating radio-frequency identification (RFID) or other tracking technologies into clothing (or even implanting it in the body) could be a mixed blessing. On one hand, such technologies might enable different kinds of personal filtering (perhaps singles at a cocktail party might want to access profiles of other available potential partners while moving through a physical space, or bloggers might want to hear a chime as they approach another blogger to compare notes, all sorts of things are possible), but there is an Orwellian flipside to this transparency, as the power of depicting one's identity and status to the outside world (one typical function of clothing) is increasingly given over to a pervasive network. There are several clear divisions in the world of wearable fashion. The fashion show in Tallinn suggested that technology is a fetish as much as it is an application. Much of the work shown seemed to be more about the idea of technology rather than about actually using it. Waifish models, in the spirit of androgyny, performed a kind of improvisation of a person who clearly did not fit into the typical gender roles ascribed in society. As androgens in velcro suits, sticking together and twitching around, the sensation of performing is reminiscent of the actress Elsa Lanchester, who played the part of the bride in *The Bride of Frankenstein* (1935). The sight of electrocuted, short-circuited bodies in cyber-clothes for the 21st century, were both chilling and full of thrill-bombardment and sensory overload. This could be what Greenfield sees as an identity-dismantling intoxication in a sensory driven rather than cognitively driven world.

Johnson (2005) argues from a different perspective. He has developed a concept called the 'Sleeper Curve', which he thinks reveals the increasing sophistication of modern popular culture, especially amongst the born 'digital natives', which is anyone born post-1980. Johnson finds in this generation a cocktail of reward and exploration, born of a desire to play some kinds of video game that are active, highly personal, sociable and creative. The complexity of some of theses games offers a virtual satisfaction via the richness of the worlds that the players inhabit, with others offering social gaming embedded within social networks (e.g. Playfish), which create new forms of social interaction and social emotions. (Though for some critics, like UK *The Guardian* newspaper's Steven Poole, Johnson's work is 'most interesting as an example of a particular philistine current in computer-age thinking' (Poole, 2005).)

If Greenfield fears that a child habituated to a strong sensationalist present will become addicted to thrill-bombardment, and that, instead of becoming Someone, the future human brain will remain No-One – just a collection of 'inputs' – then the current prognosis is gloomy and rooted in a fear of the present. Following this line of thinking, cyberspace kids and teenagers, blitzed with information from anywhere and everywhere, may never acquire the capacity to see things in context; they may never get beyond the stage of literally taking the world at face value. Does Greenfield reduce humanity to the physicochemical context of the brain itself? We are straying her into territory covered in another Ira Levin book, *The Stepford Wives* (1972). In this book, the women are replaced by robots created by their husbands, in order to conform to their demands for a compliant, manipulable and willing partner, in a manner similar to being atomised and senseless.

Here, Greenfield is at one with other leading neuroscientists. Rose (2008) cites comments by Kandel and Crick that identify a person with the brain itself, but suggests that the problem with such reductionism is to equate a part with the whole. Indeed, the brain is not a problem-solving machine but an evolved organ, adapted to enhance the survival chances of the organisms it inhabits. How does the brain assess current situations? How does it compare them with past experiences? How are appropriate actions generated? It is this evolutionary imperative that has resulted in our large and complex brains. We don't have a comprehensive brain theory that lets us bridge the gaps between molecules, cells and systems to enable us to begin to answer the questions: how do we experience and how do we remember what we wore when we were four years old? What images and sounds are meaningful to us over our lifetimes? These get confused according to the stories we want to tell about ourselves. It is possible to stimulate particular brain regions to evoke sensations, memories, even emotions, but does this mean that a particular memory can be located in that region or is it that the activity in that region is a correlate to the memory? The best anyone can do, according to Greenfield (2008a), is to match biochemical processes to reports of how people feel, and deduce rough correlations.

9.5   Conclusions

The uses of technology in performative textiles or performance in general does not merely add a new tool to an old discipline, but rather challenges some of our most basic assumptions about the disciplines themselves. Indeed, digital, networked, virtual and technological performance challenges the very distinction between 'liveness' and media, sensation and cognition, interaction and intra-action. These methodologies reactivate the relationship between performers and audiences to create new hybrid practices. We can now share the same physical space, a space of becoming, a space of interaction and integration with others. We will be able to take the electronic element in our garments for granted, whether they generate electricity from our movements, provide gaming opportunities through our sleeves or monitor our health. However, we might just keep headphones out of our way as we dance on the street, communicating and collaborating with one another at the same time as calling up our ancestors in a flurry of memory-triggered screens, memory ribbons and sampler sounds.

Sherry Turkle has been called the 'Margaret Mead of digital culture' in her analysis of how young people navigate the emotional undercurrents in today's technological world (Turkle, 2011). As an anthropologist, Mead had been trained to think in terms of the interconnection of all aspects of human life, so that the production of food cannot be separated from ritual and belief, and politics cannot be separated from childrearing or art. This holistic understanding of human adaptation allowed Mead to speak out on a very wide range of issues, and in particular the relationship between generations (Mead, 1978). While she wrote of a global culture made possible by mass media, her words actually foresaw fundamental changes made by computer communication networks that were just beginning. Mead believed that in the past, culture was transmitted from an older to a younger generation through social rituals and an exploration of what might be shared experience in the process of full attention face to face. Turkle argues that new technologies – including e-mail messages, Facebook postings, Skype exchanges, role-playing games, Internet bulletin boards and robots – have broken this tie. The more networked and wired society becomes, the more we are seduced and addicted to an 'autistic' world, where we expect more from technology and less from each other. Turkle is not just concerned with the problem of online identity, she is disquieted by the banalities of electronic interaction, as a younger generation of Americans' range of expression is constrained by gadgets and platforms, a networked life of loneliness and failed solitude. This implies an even greater separation between generations and cultures than ever before and raises new questions about subjective identity and objective identification.

Indeed, culture clashes are alive and living well in the hands of Embroiderers' Guild and YouTube. What we need to think through are the ideas proposed by Suchman (2007, p. 176), in which situated interaction is characterised as 'lively, moment-by-moment assessment of the significance of particular circumstances' through the electronics of our clothing and in the sensation of our performative gestures. In her terms, interaction is a name for ongoing, contingent co-production of the socio-material world, an engaged participation that cannot be stipulated in advance. Feminist scholar Karen Barad's quantum physics-inspired posthumanism redeems the concept of performativity from a techno-scientific standpoint. She argues that science, as a knowledge-based endeavour, is inherently 'performative' – science 'performs' in experiments, in laboratories, with specialised instruments, with human agents, etc. She observes that:

> *the move towards performative alternatives to representationalism shifts the focus from questions of correspondence between descriptions and reality (e.g., do they mirror nature or culture?) to matters of practices/doings/actions.*
> (Barad, 2003, p. 802)

Fashion and wearable technology have, as their departure point, the ability to act as second skin interfaces to a world in which we live and breathe and listen through the entire epidermis, as Sabine Seymour describes at the beginning of the chapter. Wearables, as a technology, cohabitate with the body and 'perform' stories of amplification. These are stories of science fiction and fantasy and are beginning to be played out in new and unexpected ways. The 'Look at me, I'm electric!' appeal of wearable technology has entered celebrity status with Lady Gaga performing in a living, kinetic dress with moving parts. She is almost transformed into the bride of Frankenstein herself.

Chapter 10

Implementing 'Namebers' Using Microchip Implants: The Black Box Beneath The Skin

Katina Michael and M.G. Michael

University of Wollongong

> *But they weren't a mighty Family, [Chip]*
> *thought. They were a weak Family, a saddening and*
> *pitiable one, dulled by chemicals and dehumanized by*
> *bracelets.*

THIS PERFECT DAY, P. 97

10.1 Introduction

The use of electronically-based physical access cards to secure premises such as government buildings and large corporate offices has been in operation since the inception of barcode and magnetic stripe cards in the 1970s. Over time, for secure access control, these first generation card technologies, based on optical character recognition (OCR) and magnetic ink character recognition (MICR), were replaced by more sophisticated technologies such as smart cards and biometrics, containing encrypted data and techniques that were more difficult to dupe or to replicate (Michael, 2003a).

An employee today, wanting to gain access to their place of work, typically carries a photo identity card in addition to a contactless smart card based on radio-frequency technology, and may also use one of his/her unique physical characteristics (e.g. fingerprint, palmprint, iris or face) for verification. Generally, the more information-sensitive the public or private enterprise, the greater the security measures introduced to safeguard against fraudulent activities. Card technologies, nonetheless, which are items carried by personnel, can also be lost or stolen, and photograph identity badges can also be falsely replicated. This has led some innovators to consider the potential of radio-frequency identification (RFID) or implantable devices for employee identification, with the added possibility of using wireless networks to undertake location fixes on employees in large premises (e.g. open cut mines or manufacturing plants). Automatic identification devices have the added capability of providing access to militarised zones, based on roles and privileges as defined by administrator access control matrices.

RFID implantables are, theoretically, not transferable and thus ensure a better level of security than traditional techniques. They are injected into the human body, in the same way that implants are injected into animals. Microchip implants come in the form of tags or transponders which contain an integrated circuit (see Fig. 10.1). Animals have been implanted using this technology from the early 1990s to curb against disease outbreaks and, more recently, for total farm management (Trevarthen and Michael, 2007, 2008). Registering your cat or dog by having it permanently microchipped for easy pet identification is now law in some countries (see, for example, the Companions Animal Act 1998 in the State of New South Wales in Australia).

Masters and Michael (2007) define three types of application areas for human implantable microchips. These are implants for control purposes (e.g. access control), implants for convenience-oriented solutions (e.g. e-payment), and implants for care-related applications (e.g. accessing electronic health records remotely). A control-related human-centric application of RFID is any human use of an implanted RFID transponder that allows an implantee to have power over an aspect of their lives, or that allows a third party to have power over an implantee. A convenience-related human-centric application of RFID is any human use of an implanted RFID transponder that increases the ease with which tasks are performed. A care-related human-centric application of RFID is any human use of an implanted RFID transponder where the functionality is associated with medicine, health or wellbeing (Michael and Masters, 2004).

Mann (1998, 2001) plotted a graph for wearable devices based on their existentiality against their wearability, distinguishing between the degree of user control on the one hand versus the portability on the other. On

Fig. 10.1   Cyborg 1.0: The silicon transponder that was implanted into Professor Kevin Warwick's forearm to allow a computer to monitor him as he moved through halls and offices of the Department of Cybernetics at the University of Reading. Courtesy of Kevin Warwick.

the existentiality axis, he then distinguished between implants which were owned and operated by the wearer (e.g. toothcam implants), implants that are controlled by the issuer, and implants that are not removable by the bearer. He thus identified the potential for varying levels of control, but without alluding to newer forms of implantables for drug delivery or access control. Clarke (1994) predicted very early on that it was only a matter of time before implantables in animals found themselves a use in humans. Situated at the bottom of Mann's existentiality axis, close to the point where the bearer has no control, Clarke wrote of implants: 'In order to discourage uncooperative subjects from removing or disabling them, it may be necessary for them to be installed in some delicate location, such as beside the heart or inside the gums'.

RFID bracelets have been used since the mid-1980s for home detention, extended supervision orders, prison inmate tracking and monitoring. Implantables are considered to have the added advantage of being discrete, in that they are not visible in outward bodily appearance. For example, parolees on extended supervision orders who might be implanted would be given the opportunity to undergo rehabilitation without the added stigmatisation from observers for past felonies or misdemeanours (Michael *et al.*, 2009). Similarly, people who have been charged with a crime but not yet tried or convicted could be granted bail and monitored electronically via the use of implantables, remaining innocent until proven guilty. In the same light, it is argued that if employees are implanted they may be less of a target for professional thieves, given that they cannot be identified as linked to corporation X or Y. For example, the theft of corporate laptops was highly prevalent around the peak of the *dot.com* bubble, as professional thieves aimed to obtain and then selling on competitive intelligence on the black market. Those individuals well versed in the art of social engineering need only know the make-up of an identification badge to break through layers of physical protection to obtain company secrets, or to steal pieces of valuable equipment from the company premises. Even wearing corporately branded coveralls was not advised by regional security officers, especially while traveling abroad, for it distinguished employees as belonging to particular corporations, making them identifiable targets.

10.2 Background

To date, RFID bracelets have been used in closed campus facilities such as prisons (to track inmates, security guards and visitors, providing access to particular zones), and also for hospitals (to track patients, medical staff, and visitors through 'contact and trace' programmes such as during the SARS epidemic) (Michael and Masters, 2006). This technology ensures that people have access to specific rooms in a building, or, conversely, ensures that they do not venture (willingly or otherwise) outside certain perimeters (e.g. to protect newborn babies from being stolen from post-natal wards). Beyond tracking people, corporate assets are also being tagged to guard against theft or loss (Huber and Michael, 2007; Michael and McCathie, 2005). Assets can then be linked to employees who may loan the equipment or are responsible for the safe-keeping of the equipment.

The potential to use RFID implantable devices for employee identification has been demonstrated in a commercial context in two well-known cases: the *Baja Beach Club* in Barcelona in Spain (2004–2009) and *City-Watcher.com* in Cincinatti, Ohio (2006–2008). In the case of the Baja Beach Club, both employees and club patrons were given the opportunity to receive implants. The employees used the implants to gain access to restricted areas in the Club (e.g. IT systems and administration records), and the club patrons used the implants for e-payment and to gain access to very important 'patron' (VIP) lounge areas within the Club. With respect to the CityWatcher.com implementation, all employees of the small business were given an opportunity to get an implant for access control, and a total of four employees were implanted. It should be noted that in both instances, implantation was not mandatory. What the cases did demonstrate, however, is that implantable devices can work just as well as contactless proximity cards for physical access control to premises. Both programmes have now been discontinued and there have been no official documents identifying the major and minor outcomes of the deployments.

10.3   The Human Chip Implant Controversy

Some of the challenges that were prevalent in the organisational deployments mentioned above had more to do with overcoming usability issues than with social, ethical or legal concerns, since both commercial programmes were on an opt-in basis (Clarke, 2010; Kargl *et al.*, 2008; Kumar, 2007; Michael and Michael, 2007; Michael *et al.*, 2008; Wang and Loui, 2009). Ironically, the CityWatcher.com implant project preceded the State of Ohio's anti-chipping legislation for the enforced microchipping of employees, but was in accordance with the law, given the practice was entirely voluntary to staff of the organisation (Friggieri *et al.*, 2009). The three biggest hurdles had to do with the actual location of the implantable device in the human body, as designated by the vendor (at the back of the triceps of the upper right arm); the location of the RFID readers (too high for some members of the population, such as those with wheelchair access requirements or short people); and the complexity of getting the implants implanted into willing participants, as it required a number of personnel to be engaged in the end-to-end procedure (IT manager, nurse or doctor, end user, management for witnessing consent, etc.).

When interviewed and explicitly asked about social, ethical or legal dilemmas and the risks related to the implantation of humans, representatives from both cases, Baja Beach Club and CityWatcher.com, stated that there were no risks or risks that were of a very limited nature. Both representatives of the companies touted the benefits, the convenience, the rewards and the future prospects above and beyond any perceived risks. Additionally, both representatives were passionate about the possibility that one day all humans might indeed never have to worry about carrying wallets, that credit card fraud would diminish, and that identity fraud would be eradicated. When asked about some of the major challenges, such as the cloning of implants, electronic viruses on implants (Gasson, 2010), the need for continual upgrades, dysfunctional implants, and members of the community who did not wish to opt-in, both interviewees seemed untroubled by the problems these might pose. In all instances, dissent by members of the community over implantables for citizens or employee ID was seen to be generally limited to either Christian fundamentalists who harboured concerns over the infamous 'number of the beast', those who (genuinely) had 'something to hide', or those that would raise complaints against just about anything. Indeed, according to the interviewees, all risks were simply considered to be teething problems of an emerging technology and would be overcome in the very short-term, similar to the security controls introduced since the inception of the Internet. The *risk* versus *reward* question was not a point of contention – the rewards would outweigh any plausible risks, according to the two key informant interviewees.

The implant controversy has to do with the potential for all human beings to be implanted with what seems a liberating technology (i.e. you do not need to carry wallets or cards or proof of ID). However, microchip implants are in reality a technology of controls, limits and rights. The controversy will become especially rife if the majority of society enjoys the perceived benefits of using implants, with the minority deciding to live 'off the grid'. There is a great deal of literature on the digital divide, but the divide that might eventuate as a result of implants is particularly radical and has not been commensurately addressed. The introduction of potentially culture-shifting techniques is invariably surrounded by controversies in clashes of policy, law, society, and philosophical and religious beliefs. In this instance, we have seen the enactment of anti-chipping laws in the United States (Friggieri *et al.*, 2009), to guard against the possible abuse and/or misuse of embedded technologies within various relationship contexts: parent–child, employer–employee, doctor–patient, state–citizen etc. In fact, the State of Ohio declared enforced implantation of employees to be an illegal practice in *SB 349 A Bill To Prohibit an Employer from Requiring an Employee of the Employer to Insert into the Employee's Body a Radio Frequency Identification Tag*. Section 4113.81 reads: 'no employer shall require an employee of the employer to have inserted into the employee's body a radio frequency identification tag. Any employer who violates this section shall be subject to a fine of not more than one hundred fifty dollars per violation'.

The five major problems are: their permanency (depending on the site and length of implantation); the requirement for a third party to enact removal upon request; the bearer's capacity to understand how the device may be interacting with the space around them, with or without their consent; the device's insecurity; and enforceability when considering the implantation of minors or people suffering from cognitive disorders or Alzheimer's, for safety reasons, and others in dependable relationships (Michael and Michael, 2009). Early signs of the controversy and of its significance were indicated by reactive responses to legislation, and minority groups who voice public concerns at the implications of instituting a given technique. Today, online bloggers use the Internet as a vehicle to voice their concerns, and marketers can study perceptions, beliefs and attitudes towards particular technology adoption and diffusion by studying blogger behaviour (e.g. *uberVU*, a real-time social media analytics platform). Invariably, what follows after such activity of heightened concern by an advocacy-based non-government organisation (NGO) or grass-roots community lobby group is a slow period in product adoption. It is at this time that an invention will either be completely rejected or, after a stabilising period, be adopted with even more stealth. Despite a technology's acceptance by users, after widespread adoption, court cases attempting to settle disputes between consumers and commercial entities invariably follow. These cases set precedences, as they identify particular consequences of new innovations, but they do not and cannot halt a technology's proliferation. At this very moment we are at that fork in the road with respect to the human implant controversy.

10.4   Where Have We Been?

The first known person to be implanted with a transponder for the purposes of demonstrating identification was Eduardo Kac in 1997 (Michael, 2003a). Kac, a multimedia, communications and biological artist, produced a work entitled *Time Capsule*, which depicted him self-injecting an implant into his ankle, 'web-scanning' the transponder, and then proceeding to log on to the Internet to register himself on an animal database (see Fig. 10.2).

In the following year, Kevin Warwick's 1998 experiment *Cyborg 1.0* had a profound impact on what could be achieved using implantable technologies (Warwick, 2002). Warwick was the first person to be implanted with a functional transponder for non-medical research purposes. This experiment allowed a computer to monitor Warwick as he moved through halls and offices at his workplace, using a unique identifying signal emitted by the implanted chip. He could operate doors, lights, heaters and other computers without physical interaction (Michael and Michael, 2009). Warwick's

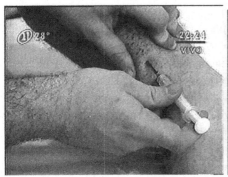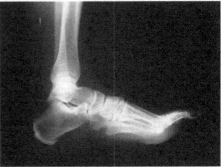

Fig. 10.2 Eduardo Kac, *Time Capsule* (detail), 1997, microchip implant, X-ray of the implant, dimensions variable. Courtesy of Eduardo Kac.

experiments, including that of *Cyborg 2.0*, demonstrated the potential for RFID implants to be used in convenience, care and control oriented applications (see Fig. 10.3).

Fig. 10.3 Cyborg 2.0 Project: The micro-electrode array that was inserted into Kevin Warwick's wrist, and fired into the median nerve fibres below his elbow joint. The implant was able to measure transmitted nerve signals as well as create artificial sensation. Courtesy of Kevin Warwick.

While Warwick was demonstrating the many uses of implantables that exist today, Kac was pointing to the ethical dilemmas and what he called 'trauma' in the creation of technology. According to Kac (1997), the 'physical trauma ... amplifies the psychological shock generated by ever-faster cycles of technological invention, development, and obsolescence'. Thus, Eduardo Kac preempted philosophical debate on the question of implants with his *Time Capsule* work and Kevin Warwick demonstrated the implant as an identity and location finding capability, propelling further debate on the impending possibilities. Kac and Warwick saw into the future, years before its enactment.

Three years after Warwick's Cyborg 1.0 experiment in Britain in 1998 came the unrelated establishment of the *VeriChip Corporation* in the United States. Scott Silverman, the CEO of VeriChip, was often quoted describing the need for implants, especially for first responders, given the tragic way so many fire fighters lost their lives in the Twin Towers. He and Richard Seelig, the Vice President of Medical Applications at VeriChip, were implanted in early 2002, before the VeriChip implantable RFID had received US Food and Drug Administration (FDA) approval. VeriChip was a subsidiary of *Applied Digital Solutions*, a commercial entity who became a reseller in the pioneering human implantable space, after acquiring an animal ID transponder implant company. Having tested the RFID implants in animals for so many years with generally beneficial outcomes in farm operations, Applied Digital Solutions embarked on human implantables through its subsidiary.

In 2002, the Jacobs family volunteered to be the first consumers to receive a VeriChip, and their chipping procedure was broadcast live on American television (BBC, 2002). VeriChip then chose to implant some high profile people including Rafael Macedo de la Concha (Mexico's Attorney General) and a number of his staff, citing security purposes (Gardner, 2004). The company also drew support from political figures like Tommy Thompson, US Secretary of Health and Human Services (2001–2005) and candidate for the 2008 US presidential election, who ultimately also served a two year directorship on the board of VeriChip (Albrecht and McIntyre, 2005). In 2004 and 2006, Baja Beach Club and CityWatcher.com, respectively, were engaged in human implantable programmes on their company premises, and a host of private 'Veri-chippings' were conducted with members of the public. The private cases included implanting Alzheimer's patients and people suffering from medical conditions and allergies. Doctor John Halamka, Harvard Medical School Chief Information Officer, and others in the medical fraternity at the time, were convinced at the value proposition of human implantables.

In 2005, Amal Graafstra was implanted with his first radio-frequency identification tag (see Fig. 10.4). Graafstra (2007), and others like him (e.g. Mikey Sklar and Jonathan Oxer), pioneered human implantables of a noncommercial nature for custom built home applications, being dubbed *do-it-yourselfer* RFID implantees by observers. For Graafstra, the VeriChip transponder, sold to the public within a commercial setting, represented completely different privacy challenges than the glass tags being embedded in his own body. In fact, he was clearly not in favour of getting an implant that possessed anti-migration coating and that was under the control of a third party, injected so deep into the body (Graafstra *et al.*, 2010). Graafstra's *RFID Toys* (2006) was aimed at 'tech-heads' who wanted to adapt their social living spaces for their own convenient interactivity.

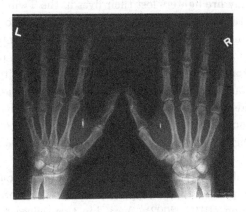

Fig. 10.4   Amal Graafstra has two RFID implants, one in each hand, as shown by this X-ray. His left hand contains a 3 mm by 13 mm EM4102 glass RFID tag that was implanted by a cosmetic surgeon using a scalpel to make a very small cut, into which the implant was placed. His right hand contains a 2 mm by 12 mm Philips HITAG 2048 S implant with crypto-security features and 255 bytes of read/write memory storage space. It was implanted by a family doctor using an *Avid Injector Kit* similar to the ones used on pets. He can access his front door, car door, and log into his computer using his implants. Courtesy of Amal Graafstra.

However, living people are not the only ones who could be chipped; other human-centric cases have been documented by the media. For example, Dishneau reported in 2005: 'as body counts mounted and missing-person reports multiplied in the days after Hurricane Katrina, some morgue workers began using a new technology to keep track of unidentified remains'. Due to the sporadic nature of news reports on the chipping of the deceased during disasters and times of crisis, it is unknown whether or not the chippings were done by VeriChip or other vendors. Perhaps one of the few things left to be done, at least in a commercial setting, is to inter-relate all the different components of subject and object types, in effect making the link between things that are 'lifeless', and things which are 'living' within a Web of Things and People (WoTaP) (Michael *et al.*, 2010).

10.5 The VeriChip Implantable Device

This section discusses the VeriChip Corporation, which is now known as *Positive ID*, and which was formerly a subsidiary of Applied Digital Solutions (itself now known as the Digital Angel Corporation). Despite the birth of the human-centric microchip implant for control and convenience solutions coming before the establishment of the VeriChip Corporation, the authors felt that it was important to document how the innovation came about in a commercial setting. By understanding where we have come from we can gain insights into where we are heading and at what velocity. Today, consumers are becoming increasingly aware of body-wearable technologies, yet the vast majority of people are still oblivious to the fact that there existed implantable solutions for non-medical related applications, such as access control, as far back as 2003. Even until recently, when the authors presented their research findings on the legal implications of microchip implants in the United States, engineers were, firstly, largely unaware of the existence of such a commercial innovation, and, secondly, that some states had already passed laws governing their usability. The point of the company case study is to demonstrate the high degree of complexity that companies who play in this space must contend with – issues to do with information assurance such as risk, accountability, social responsibility, data storage, access and disclosure, transferability and much more.

The reader must also gain the ability to contrast between the various motivations for microchipping people – e.g. the performance artist who implants to evoke a response from the public, the researcher who seeks to engineer breakthrough technologies, the do-it-yourselfer hobbyist implantee who wishes to make life more convenient through customisation, and the company that wishes to provide services to consumers. It is the latter category which is intriguing from the perspective that profit maximisation is the essential goal of every corporation, and yet this element is absent from the performance artist who wishes to be remembered for their 'work', the researcher who wishes to be remembered for 'daring to go where no one has ventured before', and the hobbyist implantee who just wishes to make life 'easier' for themselves. The VeriChip organisation probably had a technology that the global market was not ready for back in 2002. This is not to say that the market has not evolved since that time and that today people are more willing to ponder the question of getting 'chipped'.

Given the VeriChip Corporation was the first company to market microchip implants for humans, under the parent company Applied Digital

Solutions, and enjoyed 100% of the market share in the time of its existence, it is valuable to document how it came into existence, what commercial solutions it created, and where and how it was used by real customers. Following this, two detailed cases of VeriChip customers are presented, showing the implementation of the implantable system at the Baja Beach Club and CityWatcher.com. The dominant source data presented in the main body of this chapter stem from primary interviews conducted with employees of the companies, considered to be key informants of the cases by the very nature of their involvement in the human implantable programs. The IT Manager of the former Baja Beach Club, Serafin Vilaplana, was interviewed in person in Barcelona, Spain, by Katina Michael in June 2009. Gary Retherford, of Six Sigma Security, who previously consulted for CityWatcher.com, was interviewed by telephone in June 2009 by Katina and M.G. Michael. Retherford is currently a business developer at LogicWorks Inc. and is an advocate for RFID product tagging and human-centric microchips.

10.5.1　*Applied Digital Solutions and the VeriChip*

The organisation that developed the implantable chip for humans was the VeriChip Corporation (once known as 'CHIP' on the NASDAQ). At the time (2001), VeriChip was a subsidiary of an advanced technology company, Applied Digital Solutions, which owned several companies and was well-known for its innovative Digital Angel application. This application featured a 'wander, fall down, alert back to base' function, using an RFID device in concert with global positioning systems (GPS) technology. This was still in its developmental infancy in 2002 but was marketed on the Internet as an end-to-end turnkey solution. Despite the potential of the application, especially in the context of Alzheimer's patients, the product was discontinued, at least to the knowledge of the consumer market.

The two companies that Digital Angel Corporation still own today are *Signature Industries* and *Destron Fearing*. Destron Fearing had been specialising in implantable radio-frequency identification tags for animals since the 1980s. Many believe that the Destron Fearing company, which already had an implantable tag for animals approved by the FDA, was acquired for the sole purpose of developing a human implantable device. Despite Destron Fearing denying this on numerous occasions early on in the acquisition, it did ultimately play a role in that development, at least in being able to convey its experiences from its animal ID chip business in location tracking and transportation monitoring.

The investment relationship between Applied Digital Corporation and VeriChip changed in 2004, although it is still not apparent exactly what happened in terms of legal ownership. The VeriChip Corporation launched its own brand in 2004 and then purportedly cut business ties with Applied Digital Corporation, which withdrew from the public eye for about two years. In 2009, VeriChip merged with *Steel Vault Corporation* and rebranded to Positive ID Corporation. Positive ID now has two main divisions: HealthID and ID Security. On the health side, for example, Positive ID and *Receptors LLC* joined forces to develop the H1N1 (bird flu) prototype implantable chip, which uses an onboard virus triage detection system. In the ID security space, Positive ID is marketing novel ID theft protection applications such as www.nationalcreditreport.com, and enabling web-based electronic medical records in such applications as *Health Link*. As a matter of course, one can only assume that all of Positive ID's marketed products would somehow be linked to the application of a unique microchip implant.

In summary, three points needs to be emphasised. Firstly, the way the innovation has been diffused and obscured behind a range of companies, including both developers and resellers. Secondly, that there are marketable solutions for micro-chipping people that have changed in guise over time. Thirdly, this development began with a parent company that said they would never go into microchipping people, who then bought out a livestock ID company, and then went in for micro-chipping people when the political landscape changed after the September 11 attacks.

10.5.2 *The VeriChip: phase I*

Marketing plans for the VeriChip began in the beginning of 2002, less than six months after the September 11, 2001 terrorist attacks (Richter and Frappaolo, 2002). One of the patent applications in the area of implantables for living creatures was filed by Mejia and Casey (2007) on the passive integrated transponder tag, comprising of an integrated circuit and a unitary core (US patent: 20020154065). VeriChip received clearance from the FDA to distribute its RFID transponder as a medical device in 2004 (Kahan, 2004), despite the fact that a family had already been chipped in Florida, in 2002 (Scheeres, 2002). A reclassification request to a device of type class II was made by the owner of the VeriChip product so there could be a reasonable assurance of safety and effectiveness of the device (Gantt, 2004). Yet, while the US FDA provided permission for the VeriChip to be fit for use as a device for electronic health monitoring, little is known about the commensurate jurisdictional authorisation gained in the European Union and South America at the time the product was rolled out for club patronage and security access control.

10.5.3 *The 2003 'Get Chipped' campaign*

The campaign to 'Get Chipped' was launched in early 2003. There were a number of Veri centres where the procedure could take place in the United States. There was even a high-tech *ChipMobile* bus fully equipped to perform the implant procedure 'on the road'. About the size of a grain of rice, the VeriChip was the world's first subdermal RFID microchip for humans. In theory, an implantee could be identified in a Wi-Fi network, such as in a workplace or university campus. Whereas GPS has known limitations with in-building locations, RFID thrives in a local area network (LAN) setting, allowing walkways and door entries to act as reader devices. Radio-frequency energy from the reader triggers the dormant VeriChip and in turn sends out a signal containing the unique ID number. The exchange of data is transparent and seamless in the case of RFID; there is no need to physically stop to verify a biometric feature – the network is ubiquitous. Dependent on the application, a log may be retained or the implantee's location updated. At present, it is up to the proprietary systems and vendors how this data is further used, as global standards have not yet been developed. In another scenario, an individual could be identified by the RFID implant, giving emergency services access to the implantee's medical data and history, which could be potentially life saving. The VeriChip is not only 'always on', ready to communicate and transact, but also 'ever present' inside the body of the subscriber, taking ubiquitous commerce to the next level. And, unlike physical biometric attributes, the VeriChip is inconspicuous to the naked eye.

10.5.4 *The original VeriChip cornerstone applications*

When VeriChip first launched their product range, they had four cornerstone application contexts: VeriPay, VeriMed, VeriGuard and Corrections (see Fig. 10.5). The *VeriPay* system allowed end users the capability to perform cash and credit transactions with the embedded implant. In effect, VeriPay was a payment technology that a merchant could implement for utilisation by their customer base. Either VeriChip themselves could do the 'chipping' of the end users or the merchant could do the chipping with the relevant personnel on site. *VeriMed* was a user-driven healthcare information portal whereby consumers (i.e. patients) could enter their own medical details online. Hospital staff and emergency services personnel could then access that information to get patient history, as well as allergic reactions to drugs and more. The *VeriGuard* application was considered to be a versatile secure access technology, which let in authorised people and blocked out unauthorised people. VeriGuard could be used in a government agency or business setting where sensitive information resided, or highly priced items were stored. Finally, VeriChip's *Corrections* product had to do with chipping people who had committed a crime, were on parole or probation, or were awaiting trial. It was this application, which monitored offenders, that was considered to gain the most public acceptance from the very beginning. In a 100 person survey conducted in Australia in June 2005, the proposed chipping of criminals was shown to be more acceptable than the chipping of all citizens for the purposes of national security (Johnson *et al.*, 2007). In a similar survey in the United States, with respect to RFID implants, Perakslis and Wolk (2006) state that less than half the participants of their sample were unwilling, whereas one third of the respondents were willing to have a chip implanted.

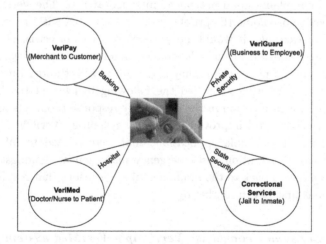

Fig. 10.5   VeriChip's four main product solutions when it was still a subsidiary of Applied Digital Solutions in 2003/04.

There was little information on the Applied Digital Solutions website in 2004 about the pricing of the VeriChip, however it was stated that the global

VeriChip subscriber (GVS) registry monthly subscription fee was US$9.95. There was a cost for the implant medical procedure as well, although this was not provided. In 2002, the first 100 pre-registered people were granted a US$50 discount on the chipping procedure (Pilato, 2003), and thereafter the cost of purchasing the implant was US$200. The pricing for the new VeriPay and VeriGuard services had yet to be published, probably given the business-to-business-to-consumer (B2B2C) detail that made generic pricing difficult. The *Trusted Traveller* and residential security programs (i.e., prisoners who were serving their sentence from home) are two examples of VeriGuard applications that could be used to conduct some level of location tracking (Business Wire, 2003).

10.5.5   *VeriChip corporation: phase II*

It is estimated that there were over 2,000 recipients of the VeriChip with many more thousands having been sent to distributors of the technology (Lewan, 2007). The implantable VeriChip was used for the VeriMed application, namely patient identification. As of 2008, there were over 900 registered medical facilities in the United States that were equipped with VeriChip readers, although admittedly the vast majority of these were not scanning for implants upon patient admittance/arrival. The VeriMed system claimed to overcome the problems often associated with 'at-risk' individuals. For example, it would aid patients in times of crisis, i.e. if they had collapsed, suffered memory loss, were unable to communicate, or had a complex medical history that they could not recollect under duress.

Corporate marketing identified the following benefits of the VeriMed system: rapid identification in the emergency response room, instant medical record access, and improved emergency response. VeriChip has also developed non-implantable applications that were related to infant protection, wander prevention and emergency management, amongst others, which was a return back to the fundamental applications that Applied Digital Solutions first began marketing.

10.5.6   *Consumer concerns: VeriChip's VeriMed system*

One of the major concerns of the VeriChip, despite its FDA approval, is that the actual chip consists of a tissue-bonding cap that is designed to prevent the chip from moving around once it has been implanted inside the body. A series of veterinary and toxicology studies have found that chip implants, similar to the VeriChip, have caused malignant tumours in animals, but the interpretation of these results differs widely (Albrecht, 2010). In 2008, the CEO of the VeriChip Corporation denied the claims of the potential for tumours in humans caused by the VeriChip, stating that the technology had been used for more than 15 years, and that the company had received no complaints from VeriMed subscribers about the FDA approved anti-migration caps (Associated Press, 2007). To date, a single formal adverse event report has been submitted to the FDA, in 2007, pertaining to the removal of the chip after the bearer experienced discomfort at the point of implantation some hours after the initial insertion (FDA, 2007).

RFID 'do-it-yourselfer' implantees, like Amal Graafstra, have indicated that the problem with the VeriChip is the depth of the implantation, and the fact that a given individual cannot remove the device without causing bodily harm (Graafstra *et al.*, 2010). Graafstra indicated the problem with the VeriChip is the propensity for it to become engrained in tissue and muscle, and to become one with the body over a short period of time. Professor Kevin Warwick also discussed this problem, after his Cyborg 1.0 experiment, which lasted only nine days. Others, like the not-for-profit *MedicAlert* information service, claim that it is unnecessary for an individual to embed a device when less-expensive non-invasive techniques abound. The argument posed by many is if you can wear it, why put it in the body?

This leads to the ethical questions surrounding the technology (McGee and Maguire, 2007), and the potential for the technology to be used outside medical applications. Is it ethical to embed an individual with a device they cannot remove themselves, even if they are voluntarily subscribing to commercial services at a given point in time (Foster and Jaeger, 2007)? What happens when an individual decides to opt-out of a VeriMed subscription after 12 months? Is the procedure painless or even possible? Who gets to decide who gets chipped, especially in the case of minors or those suffering from mental illness? And what of the potential for RFID, promoted as purely an identification device, when it is coupled with cellular or other satellite tracking network capabilities like GPS as recombined hybrid technologies? There are a great number of unanswered questions here which cannot be tied down to 'trial and error'. It is important to remember that, historically, scientific endeavour has shown us, time and time again, that if a technique is possible, it is inevitable. It is here where the precautionary principle (Weckert and Moor, 2006) would be most effective, although it too is not without its critics.

While the VeriChip Corporation had documented an explicit privacy policy on its website, pertaining to implantable chips in humans, a privacy policy does not truly address the total question of ethics (Ermann and Shauf, 1997). The company claims that 'privacy is our ethical responsibility', and while the authors of this chapter do not refute the organisation's intent, it should be pointed out that privacy is merely one aspect of ethics. The VeriChip system, like any technology, is not foolproof. Human error is ever present, and errors in data entry on the GVS registry service may even have a detrimental effect on an incapacitated individual, even if the errors have been entered by the implantee themselves. And the VeriChip system is rendered useless if emergency services or hospitals are not adequately fitted with the right technology to read unique identification numbers. It is possible that, in the future, implantees might have their ID tattooed onto the surface of the implant zone for ease of identification (and if reverting back to manual processes is required), just like mice are tattooed in Somark Innovation's Labstamp product. There are also the all too common network disruptions, power failures and other technical issues that could render the implantable technology completely ineffective.

Again, this is not to say that the technology cannot save lives but, in its present form, there are evident problems, many of which are bound to legislative concerns. The long-standing debate over biometrics as unique identifiers have subsided recently, as legislators have ruled that given the low level of physical intrusiveness of biometric reader devices (i.e., they do not break or penetrate the skin), it is permissible for human biometric features or characteristic data to be collected for the purposes of national security (Michael and Michael, 2006). The human implantable system for non-medical applications has even greater challenges confronting it, even though some contend that biometrics data collection is a more intrusive procedure than getting an implant.

One of the underlying issues of the VeriMed system was the control aspect. In VeriChip's privacy policy it is outlined that 'the content of the database itself [health records] and eligibility for access to the database are under the control of the VeriMed patient'. Control, however, is a separate matter to consent. The patient would ideally be in control of data entry typographic errors and their particulars on records but would certainly not be in total control of too much else. The organisation also claims that the VeriMed is tamper-proof and loss-proof. This may be the case with the actual database, but the actual chip implanted in the subscriber is not without risk of tampering and loss. There have already been numerous

RFID trials, for instance, that expose how a subscriber attack can render an RFID chip useless (e.g. ePassport). Even during seemingly harmless information technology trade fairs, repeated warnings are noted to delegates who have pacemakers or cochlear implants not to approach certain exhibits.

Today we have verified accounts of the VeriChip system being used for law enforcement personnel identification, VIP club lounge entry, as an anti-kidnapping technology, and even for employee physical secure access. Though these cases are limited, the potential for widespread use of microchip implants in humans is real and possible. The following section provides two detailed case studies of VeriChip implementations within two businesses – the Baja Beach Club and CityWatcher.com.

10.6   Case Study 1: Baja Beach Club (2004)

In May 2004, news broke in the United States of a club in Barcelona that was implanting patrons with 'electronic credit cards' under the skin (Maney, 2004). Put simply, an RFID transponder was being inserted into the body of a consenting club patron, a unique ID number identifying the individual, which could then be used for electronic payment and as an access control mechanism to special VIP-only areas. The Baja Beach Club in Barcelona, Spain, was one of two clubs (both carrying the same name) to conduct the RFID implant deployments. The other was the Baja Beach Club located in Rotterdam, the Netherlands.

10.6.1   *Chipping club patrons*

The Baja Beach Club implementation of RFID transponder acted to allow club patrons to pay for items purchased with a wave of their hand (e-payment solution), and also to allow implantees to access VIP zones within the club. The implant service for patrons was launched in August 2004, with only 12 people adopting the solution by year end (Baja Source, 2004), with implantation occurring on Tuesday evenings. Although widely cited in the secondary online data that becoming a VIP patron by being implanted cost about 100 euros, the IT manager stated in a primary interview with K. Michael that participants in the service were not charged to be implanted, given they would often spend a great deal of money at the club anyway, and so charging extra for implantation hardly made sense.

The decision to deploy RFID transponder implants to patrons came from the former young manager of the club, Conrad Chase, who had previously visited the United States and heard about the use of implants in the medical field, especially for the elderly and sick (mainly for identification purposes). He considered the possibility of implanting club patrons in Spain and believed the idea would be of commercial value, even if all it did was to generate discussion via word of mouth between patrons and tourists visiting the area, thus creating an aura around the brand, and acting to generate revenue by drawing larger crowds. The implants were also used by staff at the club to provide access control to various sections of the club, thus ensuring additional security and the ability to do away with keys (see Fig. 10.6).

Fig. 10.6   The Baja Beach Club VIP Access application interface for club patrons. This screenshot shows that *Steve* does not have access to the VIP zone in the club. Courtesy of Drew Hemment of Lancaster University.

10.6.2   *Access control and the patron e-payment solution*

The Baja Beach Club implant scheme was all about convenience for club patrons. Given the location of the club, patrons could enjoy the natural setting of the beach, come into the club in the late afternoon/evening and not worry about carrying precious valuables such as a purse or identification badges. If patrons had gone through the necessary ID checks during the process of implantation, then being implanted implied that the club knew their identity and knew they were of the legal age to enter the club and therefore also eligible to drink alcoholic beverages. For those 100 people who opted into the programme, not a single implanted patron ever complained about the customised Baja Beach Club application. In interview, the former IT Manager said that everyone who opted in to being implanted was positive about the application, often touting its benefits.

The implant did not merely act as an ID device. The IT Manager proudly explained:

> *what I did was to create a whole purchasing programme that had a back-end database with patron details. On the chip itself all that was stored was an ID number. I built a system that would read the ID number at the point of sale, and when the implantee purchased a drink or any other services, the total amount would be deducted from their stored value. They could top up their balance at any time they wished. It was really easy. We never had anything go wrong with that, ever. I had readers positioned all over the place, in strategic entry/exit points and also on all the doors, and areas leading into and out of VIP areas and of course at point of sale. I made sure to build the database on sound principles.*

It is interesting to note that, for the Baja Beach implantable system, the VeriPay product of VeriChip was not used, but rather a custom-built application.

In describing the effect of the application he had built for Baja Beach Club, the IT Manager said:

> *our implanted patrons would have access to special VIP areas, and when they walked into the club, their name would automatically flash up on a big screen and a loud beep could be heard echoing throughout the club. The reaction by the other clubbers was always 'Oh, look, so and so is here and he is bearing an implant in his body', or 'Ah! Here comes that person again, he is special'. It was quite interesting to sit back and watch people's reactions, it was at times quite amusing really, but the implantee patrons really loved the extra attention, and people would instantly go up to them and talk to them and strike up a conversation about anything. They were no longer anonymous but were very approachable because people knew their name.*

The IT Manager considered by far the best feature of the implant system was the fact that it kept out unwanted people from restricted areas in the club, intended for either VIPs or senior staff alone:

> *access control was really the best outcome of the pro-*
> *gramme. For instance, we are now conducting this inter-*
> *view in the office deep underground, and even these doors*
> *were secured so no one could snoop around where we keep*
> *all our files and computer equipment. No one could get*
> *into this nerve centre to steal important documentation.*
> *You can use access control to exclude and include depen-*
> *dent on the identity of the person.*

The IT Manager went on to explain the importance of access control matrices denoting people as 'types'. For example, a person could have the role of VIP patron, employee, manager or even administrator. Each role either enabled or disabled access privileges. Caution was required not to wrongly register someone in a database, e.g. granting a VIP patron accidental access to the management area instead of the VIP zone. David Lyon (2003, p. 2) has warned: 'to consider surveillance as social sorting is to focus on the social and economic categories and the computer codes by which personal data is organised with a view to influencing and managing people and populations'.

Inspiration for the way the system was built was instinctive to the IT Manager, although he also stated he had done a great deal of research on the Internet, including looking at military applications. The IT Manager commented:

> *have you heard about the way that some countries are think-*
> *ing to integrate RFID implants for gun control? That is,*
> *the gun can only be fired when the right person, bearing*
> *the right ID tries to fire the gun. If anyone other than the*
> *soldier picks it up to fire, they would be unable to*

Beyond gun control, K. Michael shared other applications linked to the law enforcement sector with the interviewee, commenting that a lot of the potential market applications have been born out of science fiction.

When asked whether or not he was aware of any other implant trials (e.g. CityWatcher.com) incorporating consumers or employees linked to the implant programme, the IT Manager answered no. He was also very clear that employees at Baja Beach Club had the freedom to join the programmes and that no one was ever forced into the implant programme. He emphasised the point by insisting that government programmes that mandated that the whole population should be implanted with microchips simply would not work because one's freedom would be curtailed.

> *I must underscore here – consent is of utmost importance.*
> *If people want it [the implant] they can adopt it, if they*
> *don't want it, then that's that. The decision must be with*
> *the consumer and not with the system creator. We never*
> *told anyone at the club – look, now you are under our pa-*
> *tronage you must take this technology. No, never! And for*
> *the patrons, I must stress again, it was always up to them.*

About the only limitation of the RFID implant was that the enrolment process was very messy, in that it required all these people to come together so that just one patron could be registered. According to the IT Manager:

> *it was very time consuming and very disruptive to add a*
> *new patron to the programme. You needed a doctor, you*
> *needed a club employee who had been trained in the process*
> *of registration (and most of the time it was me needing to*
> *be available to do the data entry and make sure it was all*
> *working as it should be), you needed the patron to make*
> *sure they wanted to participate in the trial, and that some*
> *kind of light anaesthetic would be applied so the person*
> *would not feel any pain. So for me, the main problem was*
> *that you just needed too many people to be involved in the*
> *whole registration process. It is just not viable as a business*
> *process, as there are too many set-up costs involved.*

A few teething problems had to do with the site of implantation on the human body. Baja Beach Club was directed by the reseller to implant people in the back of the arm at first, but the IT Manager soon realised that that was not the most convenient location, so then began to implant people in the wrist:

> *this is the site that gives the individual maximum mobility*
> *and is user friendly. We injected so far as the implant*
> *could lodge itself in the muscle of the person and would not*
> *go moving around inside the body to render the programme*
> *useless.*

After the closure of the Baja Beach Club, the system was disabled, despite the fact that none of the implantees had officially had their implant removed. To the best of the IT Manager's knowledge, the implant is 'just sitting in their body, [and] it cannot do them any harm'. About the potential risks associated with the large-scale deployment of RFID implants, the IT Manager responded plainly: 'No. Frankly I can only see positive benefits. There are no negatives'.

10.7   Case Study 2: CityWatcher.com (2006)

Located in Cincinnati, Ohio, CityWatcher.com was a small government contractor specialising in equipment and surveillance related projects. In February 2006, two of its employees had glass encapsulated microchips with miniature antennas embedded in their forearms. The microchips acted just like RFID proxy cards, save for the fact they were beneath the skin. The embedded microchips were used by the employees to gain access to a restricted area, which contained vaults of sensitive data and images related to policing (e.g. Cincinnati Police Department) and private business (Sieberg, 2006). In fact, the small business had contracts with six cities to provide cameras with Internet monitoring capabilities. CityWatcher.com mainly stored on its premises CCTV video surveillance of public streets in Cincinnati (World Net Daily, 2006). The CEO of the company, Sean Darks, considered the implants to be more sophisticated than keycards and touted their usability and affordability when compared to biometric systems (Sidener, 2006). Darks was quoted on several occasions as saying that the solution was very convenient. It should be noted that the company ceased operations in 2008 for reasons that were unrelated to the implanting of employees (see Fig. 10.7).

10.7.1   *Chipping employees*

The adoption of microchip implants by CityWatcher.com employees was entirely voluntary. It was claimed by the CEO of the company that implanting the employees had less to do with media attention and more to do with overcoming limitations of the handheld contactless card. At first, two people agreed to be implanted, and later a third, although the network administrator, Khary Williams, chose not to receive an implant. The employees who opted out of being implanted received instead a key chain with a transparent plastic heart-shaped mould containing a transponder (World Net Daily, 2006). One of these employees discussed it with his parents and thought the idea of getting an implant was a little weird, the

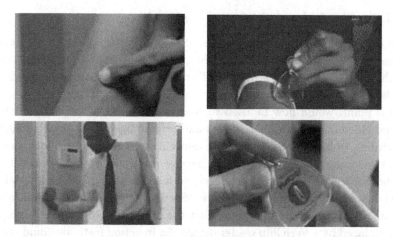

Fig. 10.7 Left: Sean Darks, former CEO of CityWatcher.com in Cincinnati, Ohio, 2006, points to his implant site in his forearm, waves his forearm close to a VeriChip reader to grant him access to the secure server room. Right: The alternative to an implant was opting into a heart-shaped plastic moulded key ring which contained an RFID transponder. Courtesy of Gary Retherford of Six Sigma Consulting.

other employee was not convinced on safety/health issues but later agreed to be implanted, and the third simply did not wish to be implanted. A senior consultant from *Six Sigma Security*, Gary Retherford, also received an implant, spearheading the systems integration effort of the VeriChip technology at CityWatcher.com. He believed that the implant was a move towards an additional layer of security, complementing the existing access control practices of the small organisation. Retherford also noted that the implants did not suffer the limitations of the alternate proxy card, namely that of transferability and lost or stolen cards. This is despite a *Gartner Research Report* by Martin Reynolds in July 2004 which stated clearly 'not [to] implement surgically implanted microchips as a security mechanism' and that, when preparing for a new access control system, a contactless smart card was to be preferred instead. By contrast, Retherford has said, on numerous occasions, that embedded technology like the VeriChip is 'always with you', and that contactless cards are not. Reynolds (2004, p. 2) however disagrees:

> *Implanted devices are highly unsuitable for virtually all security purposes. Only the body part containing the implant, not the entire employee, is required for access permission, so this approach will not work against people willing to commit bodily harm.*

10.7.2 *Physical access control application*

The chip used to implant the employees was a VeriChip, which only contained a 16-digit identification number, with additional data being stored on the VeriGuard database system. The VeriGuard technology suite, which worked just like a proximity card system with a fixed reader outside the access point, would now be used to control entry to the server room that stored video images of public streets and private businesses (see Fig. 10.8). According to Retherford, there were four entry doors, two perimeter doors and two interior doors that were on access control using a swipe card. One of those interior doors provided access to a server room that had a higher level of security and was only really accessed by three of the six employees. It was to that special server room that the old proxy reader was taken off and replaced by a VeriChip reader device. So in actual fact, you could enter the building if you had a card, but you could only enter the server room if you had either the chip implant or the transponder on a key ring.

Fig. 10.8 Employees at the former CityWatcher.com small business going about their daily tasks. Employees gaining access to the secure server room which contained surveillance footage of public streets in Ohio, USA, could only do so if a successful read was registered against the VeriChip reader and the RFID transponder carried by the employee. Courtesy of Gary Retherford of Six Sigma Consulting.

When an employee decided to leave CityWatcher.com, the database would be updated, rendering the ID chip useless at the company's premises. It would be up to the individual, as a private citizen, to decide whether they would like to retain or remove the implant. However, according to some experts, removing the VeriChip from the body is not as straightforward as removing a splinter. The capsule's anti-migration coating renders it buried deep in the arm which might even require a sensor X-ray and monitors to locate the chip, and a plastic surgeon to cut away scar tissue that might have formed around the chip (Albrecht, 2010; Lewan, 2007). It is for this reason that some hobbyist RFID implantees would never get implanted with a commercial VeriChip (Graafstra *et al.*, 2010).

10.7.3   *To get implanted or not to get implanted – that is the question!*

The network administrator of CityWatcher.com, who actually took care of the server equipment, chose not to be implanted and instead was given a key ring with a chip inside. His reason for not participating had nothing to do with religious reasons, said Gary Retherford, but rather that this particular employee could not get past the uneasiness of having something implanted into his body. It was not because he thought he would be tracked with the RFID and it had nothing to do with conspiracy for him – 'he just did not like the idea of having this item implanted inside of him', said Retherford. When asked whether the network administrator felt 'left out', Retherford responded that there were other employees who had decided to opt out, at least another two or three. Retherford, who is very much a practical and forward thinking executive, saw this VeriChip implementation at CityWatcher.com as a mini trial: '[we] put it out there as an option because at this point we were kind of more interested in seeing what the feedback was going to be like'.

In another instance, a young man who worked at CityWatcher.com stated that his decision not to get implanted was heavily influenced by the advice of his parents who 'felt that it was too much of an intrusion in his personal life.' For this individual, it was not so much the creepiness factor but 'it was more of a feeling of "Big Brother" tracking – even though you could not track.' Retherford recounts the difficulty of educating people of the fact that one cannot track another just because they have an RFID chip implanted, although it all depends on what you mean by tracking (e.g. real-time and continuous versus historical log data and discrete time stamping). The young employee clearly had opted out of the implant programme because of the perceived problems linked to privacy, civil liberties and human rights.

There was also a female employee who had originally stated that she did not wish to get implanted but then changed her mind after the others were implanted. After talking to several companies about having employees 'get chipped', and getting general feedback, Retherford came to realise that once the 'chipping' began in the company, people who had initially said 'no' would later say 'yes'. He would later comment with some humour about the employees who had initially opted out: 'when they saw that the other guys' arm didn't fall off they realised that, well, if I do this, I'm not going to end up like a drone.' Accordingly, these types of employees finally realise how convenient the solution is and commit, saying: 'Well OK, I guess I will do it'. It has mostly to do with the fact that people no longer need to remember to carry a card with them. For Retherford, Pareto's *80/20 principle* should be noted. Analogously, he said that 20% of people would probably say 'yes' to a company implant on the spot and that 80% would initially say 'no'. But he believed that within a few months of an implant programme being initiated, possibly there would be 80% of people who would end up saying 'yes I want an implant' and only 20% who would maintain their 'no'. Some would see Retherford's prediction as alarming, but it has yet to be tested in a large scale implementation and across cultural boundaries (Rogers, 1995).

There was no doubt that the novelty of what was occurring at City-Watcher.com was apparent to the employees, as the phones rang off the hook with requests for interviews for days after the implantation. It culminated in CNBC doing a special documentary called *Big Brother, Big Business*. However, after only a month, when the interviews slowed down, there was a feeling from those who had opted in to the implant that it was business as usual and no different than any other aspect of their job. Employees mainly felt reassured that they had received the implant. The only problem with VeriChip's official direction on the actual implantation site, i.e. 'the upper [right] arm in the back, of that fatty tissue area', was that it was somewhat awkward to use given the reader height and the variable height of the users. Retherford elaborates:

> *Well, we mounted the readers at CityWatcher where we had our original card readers. Typically, this is about the height of your belt buckle. So when we went to have everybody chipped, we said 'where should we put the chip'? And it became obvious that you had to put it in a part of the body that was going to make sense relative to where the reader was. So the chip was too big to put in my hand, so we had to find the closest fatty part of the arm, and typically in the right arm, where you could still put the chip in and not see it. So that ended up becoming in the front part of the forearm, below the elbow, ... like down in the front part of the arm.*

It is interesting to note that the Baja Beach Club also found the location of the VeriChip implantation to be awkward. Despite VeriChip's call to implant only in the specified implantation site that had been approved by the Food and Drug Administration, both Baja Beach Club and City-

Watcher.com defied the advice. VeriChip told CityWatcher.com that they should have simply moved the reader to an individual's standard upper arm height. But Retherford said that would not concur with state legislation which required equity for people in wheelchairs, etc.

Retherford still believes if VeriChip manufactured a better access control reader that employee implants in select corporations and job functions would have by now become commonplace. He observed that:

> but VeriChip did not have its own capabilities. They were not willing to make a commitment to invest in a better fixed reader to make it smaller and more cost-effective. The question of interoperability again becomes a key factor and could ultimately prove to be one of this technology's principal weaknesses. The reader that they manufactured for access control was approximately eleven inches high by five inches wide. So that's a big monster thing to put on somebody's door, when most readers today using a card are significantly smaller in dimensions.

The potential for secure identity access control mechanisms for employees continues to be emphasised by organisations like *HID Global*. On the company's blog, Kathleen Carroll (2009) has stated that:

> Some legislation would ban the use of the [RFID-based] technology in such applications as access control systems. In other cases, the legislation would require employers to label each access control badge with a warning that the badge contains RFID technology. Some state legislation even goes so far as to give employees the right to refuse to carry an access control badge that uses RFID.

The main point that Carroll makes is that the most onerous legislation has not been passed, and thus we can postulate that it is possible that, in the future, employees will have the option of opting in to a chip implant or wearable implant system if they so wish.

10.8 The Technological Trajectory

George Orwell's *Nineteen Eighty-Four* (Orwell, 1949) may well have been published in 1949, introducing the world to the notion of 'Big Brother', but had Orwell lived beyond 1950, one can only ponder what he would have made of 'Two Thousand and Four' and the potential for 'thoughtcrimes' to be controlled using implantable devices. Would Orwell have predicted the Big Brother 'on the inside looking out' (Michael and Michael, 2010)? It is equally instructive to ask ourselves what would philosophers with the critical foresight of Heidegger (1954), Marcuse (1964), McLuhan (1964), Ellul (1964) and Illich (1973) have made of this technological trajectory. These thinkers asked the big philosophical questions of technology and were already arguing along the lines that we ourselves were in danger of becoming 'the raw materials in the technical process'. And what kind of cinematic expression, for instance, to ubiquitous surveillance would Fritz Lang, the director of the futuristic and dystopic *Metropolis* (1927), conjure up for us today? And what new slants could we give to *Kafkaesque*, for example as we find in the work of Brin (1998) and Solove (2004)?

When the IT Manager of Baja Beach Club was asked where the technology was ultimately heading, he responded that it was his hope that one day he did not have to carry cards at all. Serafin Vilaplana is not the only implantee to have made such a remark, indeed most implantees feel a sense of freedom and control with not having to carry cards with them, or something external to the body. With evident anticipation, Vilaplana hopes that in the future everything will be stored on centralised databases, and that his ID will be an implant so he does not have to carry around cumbersome wallets:

> *I would feel very relieved as a consumer if all this would happen. I just want to be free of extras that are a nuisance. I just want people to be able to check my records, so I can go about my daily business without any hassles. It will save so much time. Today we carry so many, many cards, what is the point? I cannot wait for this revolution to take place one day.*

Despite the fact that RFID is one of the most insecure automatic identification technologies, Vilaplana touts the insecurity as a purposeful characteristic, which allows for easy identification to systems, and is rather cavalier about the fact that RFID implants simply store an ID number and that is it. His vision of the future is secure database driven. He adds:

> *you would require a great deal of validation to be going on in the system, but with today's processing speeds [it] is achievable. So you need to check the databases, validate, and synchronise with each transaction.*

For Gary Retherford, the consultant who worked to integrate the VeriChip with existing CityWatcher.com practices, the picture of the future is a little different. Retherford does not see a future that is RFID implant compliant only, but rather a world where there are a combination of automatic identification technologies working in concert. This coincides with the findings of K. Michael's thesis investigation of 2003, which concluded that supplementary and complementary automatic identification technologies would be co-existing and that migration, integration and convergence of automatic identification technology would be an ongoing industry trend (Michael, 2003b). For Retherford it is not a question of the 'future' of RFID implants and societal acceptance of the emerging technology. He is adamant that as far as the RFID implant revolution goes, 'we're already there, society accepted it'. For him it is not an question of shutting down something which may not concur with some of the dissenting voices. Retherford affirms:

> *It's an argument that says we're already there really, even though it may not be. I guess in some respects you could apply it to almost anything. I'm kind of past the argument of saying, 'well, this is implanted inside you.' I think that's a moot point. I think there is enough acceptance in the general population and there are a lot of people that are just waiting for it to happen.*

10.8.1 *Waiting for the train*

For the last five years, Retherford has been gauging consumer sentiment through every day conversations he has had with different groups of people, both offline and online. Between 2005 and 2007, when he was very focused on a business proposition surrounding the chipping of people, he literally talked to hundreds of people. He was categorical with the consumer response being positive or at least acknowledging the future trajectory:

> *Every single time, I mean, it was literally 99%, there was agreement. Even when people said, 'well, I do like it' or 'I don't like it', they all said: 'oh, but I know it's coming.*

For Retherford, innovation and societal acceptance go hand in hand, after all it is members of society that are doing the innovating. He perceives that society is now on board with the idea of implanting:

> *So, society has accepted it. I mean, they've basically said*
> *flat-out: 'I know it's coming'. So, it's like you're waiting*
> *for the train, you know it's coming. So it was really inter-*
> *esting, that they just resigned to the whole idea, and that I*
> *probably am not going to have a choice and so therefore I*
> *have mentally accepted the whole notion that at some point*
> *in my lifetime, you know, relative I guess to how old one is*
> *and how long one thinks they're going to live, they'll be re-*
> *ceiving an implantable microchip for a variety of potential*
> *reasons, typically medical or security.*

The crux of the argument is *choice*. Perhaps in this age of high-tech gad-
getry and the wireless Internet, people might feel so much anxiety about
'missing the train' that they are on a perpetual platform waiting for the
next train to take them to some place new. The perceived usefulness of a
technology probably no longer matters, what is more important is whether
or not one remains connected to the 'Network' (or the 'grid', 'cloud', 'matrix' or whatever term is used for the future Internet). For Retherford,
society has become receptive to change and is generally more tolerant of
government intervention or of corporate intervention into their lives. He
believes it is merely the 'vocal minority' who reject implants (Renegar and
Michael, 2009; Trocchia and Ainscough, 2006).

Convincing employers and senior management that there was a value
proposition in RFID implants for their companies was not difficult, according to Retherford, 'that wasn't the hard part at all'. Although Retherford
did not get 100% buy in, he had enough people who said they wanted to
have a microchip, as opposed to carrying a card, that he felt implanting
employees for access control purposes would be a very successful business
venture. He continued: 'In fact, sometimes they were saying they wanted
to do it and there was really no logical reason why. They just said, "well,
oh, I just want to get chipped".' While Retherford does not believe that
the introduction of implantable technologies for secure identification would
come in one massive wave, given there is bound to be some kind of revolt
in such sweeping change, the revolt for all intents and purposes will be
short-lived. Retherford does not doubt the end point – that humans will be
implanted *en masse* – he is only unsure of how rapid the adoption might
be and whether or not it would follow a traditional diffusion curve. At
the time the interview was conducted, the only bottleneck for continuing

to deploy implantables was that VeriChip was temporarily not selling any more chips.

10.8.2   *In an age of Überveillance*

For those of us working in the domain of implantables for medical and non-medical applications, the message is clear: implantables will be the next 'big thing'. At first, it will be 'hip to get a chip'. The extreme novelty of the microchip implant will mean that early adopters will race to see how far they can push the limits of the new technology or to even 'blueprint' it in their own homes (which brings a whole new set of questions to the table). Convenience solutions will abound – a bit like the proliferation of applications for the iPhone. Implantees will not be able to get enough of the new product, and the benefits of the technology will be touted to consumers in a myriad ways, although these perceived benefits will not always be realised. The technology will probably be first tested where there will be the least resistance from the community at large, that is, on prison inmates (Best, 2004) or those serving an extended supervision order, then those suffering from Alzheimer's disease or who have medical dependencies (e.g. insulin delivery for diabetics), and in military and emergency services personnel. From there it will not take long for it to be used in children and on those suffering from cognitive disorders or even mild depression.

The functionality of the implants will range from passive ID-only to active multi-application, and most invasive will be the medical devices that can, upon request or algorithmic reasoning, release drugs into the body for mental and physical stability. There will also be a segment of the consumer and business markets who will adopt the technology for no clear reason and without too much thought, save for the fact that the technology is new and seems to be the way advanced societies are heading. This segment will probably not be overly concerned with any discernible abridgement of their human rights nor the small print 'terms and conditions agreement' they have signed, but will take an implant on the promise that they will have greater connectivity to the Internet, and to online services and bonus loyalty schemes more generally. There will certainly be a honeymoon period where consumers will feel free of wires and liberated of the artefacts they have had to hold onto to prove their identity, whether it be at their front door, their work office, government and social security agencies, financial institutions, or at public venues, for example. These consumers will thrive on ambient intelligence, context-aware pervasive applications and an augmented reality

– ubiquity in every sense – they will feel on top of the world at the height
of the implant bubble.

But it is certain that the new technology will also have consequences
far greater than what we can presently conceive. The neutrality of technology is an immaterial point in this new 'plugged-in' order of existence.
For Brin (1998, p. 334), the question ultimately has to do with the choice
between 'privacy' and 'freedom'. He concludes: 'this is one of the most
vile dichotomies of all. And yet, in struggling to maintain some beloved
fantasies about the former, we might willingly, even eagerly, cast the latter
away.' And thus there are two possibilities, just as Brin writes of 'the tale of
two cities' in his discerning book, *The Transparent Society*. Either implants
embedded in humans with the required infrastructure will create a utopia
where there is built-in intelligence for every thing and everyone in every
place; or implants embedded in humans will create a cacotopia which will
be destructive and will diminish one's freedom of choice, individuality, and
finally that indefinable essence which is at the core of making one feel 'human'. A third possibility, the middle way between these two alternatives,
would seem highly unlikely excepting for the 'off the grid' dissenter. Recently, Yarney (2010) describes this class of people as *SÜbers* in his thriller
The Banjo Player. Yarney writes:

> *SÜber! It's short for Super Überveillance. Living above
> Überveillance. Living above the all-encompassing, om-
> nipresent electronic surveillance that we humans are now
> subject to and will most probably experience at a new level
> when we have some chip implant inserted somewhere in
> our bodies in the next few years as the technology develops.
> A SÜber can live above all that ...*

10.8.3   *The touted potential benefits*

Bearing a unique implant will make the individual feel extra special and
add worth to the importance of the 'self', though most will possess an
implant that will be marketed on the basis of 'uniqueness'. Each person
will have one implant that will coordinate hundreds of smaller nanodevices,
but each nanodevice will have the capacity to act on its own accord, a little
like the eight tentacles on an octopus, which are commandeered by the one
brain, yet work independently. The philosophy espoused will be one of legal
protection – 'I bear an implant and thus you cannot give false witness on any

of my goings on, and given I have *nothing to hide*, all will be well.' It will feel safe to have an implant because emergency services will be able to rapidly respond to a call for help or any unforeseen signals that automatically log problems to do with your health. Emergency service organisations will always go to the aid of 'an implantee' before 'an outmode' (i.e. a non-implantee), due to the increased probability of being able to save their life by getting there first. Implantees, no matter how devastating the accident, will automatically be able to provide emergency services practitioners with their up-to-the-second condition, and historical medical records accessed via a remote database which will ensure the correct operating procedures are taken.

Fewer errors are also likely to happen if you have an implant, especially with financial systems, even if you live in the same house and bear the same name as your next of kin. Businesses will experience a rise in productivity, as they will understand precisely how their business operates to the nearest minute and centimetre, and companies will be able to introduce efficiencies which will come about because employees will be where they are supposed to be at all times, and doing what they are supposed to be doing, and driving the company car by company rules via the shortest path route. Losses in back-end operations, such as the effects of product shrinkage, will diminish, as goods will be followed down the supply chain from their source to their destination customer, through the distribution centre and retailer. People will be linked with things and things with places and organisations and households in a *Web of Things and People*. There will be no need to simulate society at work, there will be the capacity to take cross-sectional snapshots of real-time operations for modelling purposes – of people moving around as units of family, friends, employees or citizens, or of livestock being reared and what they are fed for reasons of traceability, of cars and public transport on roads and railways, of goods in trucks and shipping containers – all within an instantaneous 'global-to-ant-view'. This is the way that disease will be contained (or even in certain instances unleashed).

Automatic Teller Machines (ATMs) and passwords will be an annoyance of the past with all financial transactions. There will be a transparency about things that will potentially enable a type of oneness of mind and spirit, like how the world works, how government works, how companies work, and how people work. In relationships, everyone will be seemingly honest and getting to 'know' the other would come down to minutes and not years. People will marry their perfect match based on their genetic makeup, geolocation data, qualifications and medical history, all of which will be securely linked to the chip implant that stores one's DNA as the unique identifier. There will be little if any crime, bribing would be eliminated, and counterfeit paper money would be a thing of the past. But the transparency, or lack thereof, will largely depend on whether you are part of the scientific elite developing the technology and the supporting infrastructure, on the government which institutes the chip for law and order, on an implantee who uses the chip to gain even greater rewards and search for upgrades on his/her way to becoming 'the Above-Human', or on an outmode who does not bear an implant and who does not seek to become an *Electrophorus* (Michael and Michael, 2005, 2007). There will be varying levels of control, even for the proponents of the new technology. There will be an 'axis of access' into the system, which will determine who knows what and who can do what. But the perennial problem remains: *Quis custodiet ipsos custodes?* Who will guard the guards themselves?

It will take some years for the infrastructure supporting implants to grow and thrive with a substantial consumer base. The *function creep* will not become apparent until well after the early majority have adopted implants and downloaded and used a number of core applications to do with health, banking and transport. New innovations will allow for a hybrid device and supplementary infrastructure to grow so powerful that living without automated tracking, location finding and condition monitoring will be very difficult initially, and almost impossible afterwards. Part of the problem will be the divide between old and new media and those people in particular who exercise their right to hang on to their mobile handset v1.0, which can only receive, call out and SMS (short message service) and does not contain a GPS chipset. There will be a disconnect between what we understand as traditional automatic identification technology and radical implantable ID that will contain vital information, such as one's DNA, remotely linked to a database containing all manner of highly charged information. Initially, the insurance company will want your DNA on the chip implant, in the event that it is required for forensic or medical purposes.

The chip, which is location-enabled, taking logs of speed, distance, time and altitude measures as well as physiological characteristics like temperature, pulse, heartbeats and sugar levels, will also let the insurance company know whether you are walking 30 minutes a day, sleeping eight hours, and attempting to procreate at the designated time of the month, etc. Together with the DNA profile, they will also be able to estimate when you might die and in what manner. Individuals will have a 'choice' to know this information, and for some this very knowledge will be all too much or all too dangerous. Governments too, for example, will be able to know which of their citizens are behind on their taxes, who is engaging in white-collar crime, which groups have been immunised against the latest viral outbreaks and which are carriers of potential fatal viruses, who has not exercised his/her democratic right to vote, the fine detail of how and what a citizen uses, in terms of online facilities such as keywords used on search engines, and whether or not someone might be planning a terrorist attack.

10.8.4   *The real exposure fallout*

It will also take some years for the negative fallout to be exposed; for the greater part it will be hidden. UniComp's brand image will be similar to that of the *World State's* motto in Aldous Huxley's classic anti-utopian novel, *Brave New World* (Huxley, 1932): 'Community, Identity, Stability'. At first only the victims of the fallout will speak out through formal exception reports, but these will not be highlighted by government regulatory agencies, as it will not be in the best interest of the largest UniComp-style companies. Because of this fallout, some of the aggravated implantees who wish to opt out will form a resistance movement that will specialise in the removal of deeply embedded devices, and begin both mental and physical rehabilitation to help people return to basic pre-embed functioning, or in other cases, educate implantees on how to live 'off the grid'. The electronic detoxification process will be very nearly unbearable. People will have come to rely on the embedded microchip so much, that without it, they will feel utterly desolate, without a future, and by common consent they will be considered untrustworthy. Those who wish to live off the grid will be considered the 'e-homeless' and will find employment almost impossible (Ip *et al.*, 2008). There will also likely be a group of implantees who will go back to a basic ID-only implant for fundamental transactions that allows them purchases of the most basic kind, something like a food coupon system; potentially these will be implants with a finite physical lifetime.

The technical problems associated with implants will pertain to maintenance, updates, viruses, cloning, hacking, radiation shielding and onboard battery problems. But the greater problems will be the impact on the physiology and mental health of the individual: new manifestations of paranoia and severe depression leading to an increase in suicide rates and obsessive compulsive disorders, such as continually wanting reassurance about one's implant functioning correctly or that they are 'clean' of any virus, and that their personal database is error free. There will also be the desire to conduct continual online searches, in a quest for more and more knowledge towards 'upgrades' to becoming the perfect being, 'the Above-Human'. Despite this, those who believe in the 'implant singularity' will continue to stack up points and rewards and add to their social network, choosing rather to ignore the warnings of the ultimate technological trajectory of mind control and geoslavery (Dobson and Fischer, 2003). It will have little to do with survival of the fittest at this point, although most people will be sold (and believe) the notion of an evolutionary path towards the *Homo Electricus* (Michael and Michael, 2008).

The health risks associated with implants will only surface after a number of years. Some, however, will be susceptible much earlier but will put it down to other causes, such as an unhealthy lifestyle, driven by the need to 'work' or to 'play' almost without ceasing, using wearable computing devices. But it will later become apparent that one's health would have deteriorated as a direct result of the UniComp mother implant, whether by *intention* or *design*. Some will suspect that they are battling with sophisticated electronic viruses. For some, it will mean that they cannot bear any offspring as the implant will find too many faults with their genetic makeup. For others, it may result in isolated amputation as they request a removal of the locative media from their bodies, given the cancer caused by the radiation or the anti-migration coating on the implant and other secondary infections. Of course, removal will depend on the length of time that the implant has been in the body and whether or not it has migrated inside the transdermal layer of the skin. Some of the more advanced implants will be able to capture and validate location-based data, alongside recordings (visual and audio capture). The ability to conduct Überveillance via the implant will be linked to a type of *blackbox recorder* in a cockpit (Michael and Michael, 2009). Only, in this case, the 'cockpit' will be the human body, and the recorder will be embedded just beneath the translucent layer of the skin that will be used for dispute resolution (Michael and Michael, 2009). Outwardly ensuring that people are telling the full story at all times, there will be no lies or claims to poor memory. But truth and memory itself, similarly to stored data, will be subject to the manifold degrees of manipulation by UniComp.

Much of this scenario is predicted to materialise within two generations (Haggerty, 2006). All those born before the mainstream proliferation of government ID cards will be dead and those born after the boom of the Internet will be nearing their early thirties. Getting an implant in '2025' will be very much like buying an iPhone, iPad or iPod today, only this new media will be the 'iPlant' (i.e. Internet implant) . It will just be another phase of development towards the expectation of UniComp's singularity (Millikan, 2010) – the lowest common denominator node – the heralding in of 'Person View' systems, satisfying visions way beyond Google Street View. What the person sees, records, does, 'sousveillance', a moving map of his or her own world, will be available for public download via *Über View*, giving the ability to not only see dwellings in Street View, but being able to zoom right down to the individual within the home and being able to see what they see and to listen to their private conversations. Privacy will be dead because the world will only be made out of public places.

The freedom or not to believe in a 'Higher Being' will be overridden with 'faith' in UniComp transnational companies and subsidiaries. And while UniComp will claim that they are the only 'all-seeing eye' with the sense of omnipresence, they will never have the true capability of omniscience which will be the ongoing cause of its mistrust and its visions for even deeper levels of depth-charged surveillance. Not surprisingly, the apparently infallible Überveillance will ironically herald in the *misinformation, misinterpretation and manipulation of information.* As Ayer (1987) has written:

> *Even if we were aware of what was going on in people's*
> *central nervous systems, it is unlikely that we should cease*
> *to find a use for explaining their behaviour in terms of their*
> *conscious thoughts or feelings.*

UniComp will deceive the masses into believing they have the complete transparency and visibility, it will encroach on private and inner space and sell the 'everything should be public' mantra for the sake of national se-curity, personal safety and relationship building. A new comprehensive philosophical system and language will evolve to support and legitimise the ground-breaking technological trajectory, the scientific infrastructures, and its affiliate political ideologies. Religions will also hurry to revise and up-date their respective apocalypses as they have done during any of the huge cultural shifts of the past, and, paradoxically perhaps, the personality cult will thrive in these uncertain but awe-inspiring times. At the same time, interpreters of *Revelation 13*, with its reference to 'the mark *[charagma]* of the beast' will in the era of nanotechnology be challenged as to one 'mark' or many 'marks', or even of the potentially hundreds (if not thousands) of nanoimplants (Michael, 2010).

There will be no living space for those who do not wish to take an implant and participate in the UniComp solution to the world's political, economic and environmental problems. At first, people will have been given the choice; some years later, living without the implant will be difficult, as it will be needed to be eligible for most social services, and finally the implant will be made compulsory by UniComp, which is working closely with its support players and nested affiliates towards a totalitarian state. No one needs reminding as to what sort of political systems are obsessed with surveillance and with the accumulation and storing of private information. Outmodes will continue to exist but their lifespan will be compromised due to the lack of accessibility to services, most of the outmodes will be unemployed, and as a minority they will endeavour to build some resistance. Living without an implant will be an almost hopeless task. Believing in anything outside the UniComp lifestyle will be regarded as backward and detrimental to one's future on earth or in cyberspace. The key to UniComp's success will be its ability to interfere with the mind of all those who have been 'marked' with the implant. Initially touted as one of the great wonders of the technological age, it will give UniComp a hitherto unforeseen facility to directly influence, and eventually to alter, the way people *live, believe and behave*.

The insightful words of Queisser (1990, p. 185), written towards the close of our last century, have taken on an additional urgency and importance in the context of what has thus far preceded:

> By mastering the atoms in the silicon crystal lattice, man has uncovered a promising microcosm – though one that is full of uncertainties. In the Middle Ages man saw himself as a microcosm. As we approach the end of the twentieth century we no longer find 'the heavens' mysterious, sometimes frightening ruling power. Instead, we find ourselves part of a mechanistically determined cosmos. The atom, the new microcosm, now decides our definition of the world and our destiny in that world. We now look to plutonium nuclei, silicon, and other atoms for the secrets of creation and destruction, as well as harmony and symmetry. Now the macrocosm of society seeks the harmony of the microcosm of the atom. The quest for reconciliation of the parts with the whole has assumed a new character. We cannot look at the world with just one eye.

10.9 Conclusion

While implantable microchips would serve an important purpose in securing access to physical premises, and suitable readers are being built specifically for this type of application, by far the biggest prospects of implantables is in healthcare, which, for the greater part, is welcome. Beyond the potential for electronic health records (EHRs) to be implemented using microchip implants, already there are patents that have been awarded for swallowable implantables (e.g. drug delivery) (Laurance, 2010) and pandemic virus protection alerts, among many others. Of interest, say in jurisdictions like the United States, is the conflict between some of the enacted and pending legislation and regulation, and seemingly opposed state laws which render some forms of chipping (by the state, employers, hospitals, parents or guardians) illegal. Indeed, the human implantable trials in the United States were seen by many to be 'testing the waters', so that some sort of debate, regulation or legislation could be instigated, ultimately legitimising or heralding in an innovation that was not in breach of any deliberated enactments. In the case of the European Union, the multiple Baja Beach cases in Barcelona and Rotterdam aided to preempt an *Opinion* on the topic of ICT implantable devices (Rodota and Capurro, 2005), which took a critical look at some of the future possibilities and vetted some of the possible harms to a society governed by such invasive technology.

Gary Retherford, the Six Sigma security consultant, expects that people will soon be fed up with identity theft and credit card fraud, seeking an alternative ID measure. He ponders about RFID implants as being the alternative, despite the fact that the technology will certainly introduce other new risks. Retherford defends those new risks as being 'relative' and to those who say the chip will never happen he replies:

> *yeah it will, and the reason it will is because human nature says that it has to, not me or somebody else, but human nature demands that we go into this technology and that's because we've been told you can't go. As long as there's the possibility you know, it's like 'Why did he climb Mt. Everest? Because it was there.*

Despite the belief that our innately curious human nature might be demanding that we enter the human chip implant domain, the question remains: what if it all goes horribly wrong? The real issue is, as Retherford himself put it: 'we can't go in reverse, we can't stop where we are, we always have to go onto the next level'.

With each new level, we will be entering a new world of unknowns from which there is no rewind. It is not a matter of denying the pioneering human spirit, nor the marvellous wonders of technology, but rather the stark realisation that we are entering into *irreversible* territory, literally, and that this will bring with it its own everlasting consequences, both very good and very bad. We are not giving ourselves an analogous time to test, to reflect and to speak to each other on the long term possibilities of these innovations. As Joy (2000), the former chief scientist at Sun Microsystems once attested:

> *We are being propelled into this new century with no plan, no control, no brakes. Have we already gone too far down the path to alter course? I don't believe so, but we aren't trying yet, and the last chance to assert control – the fail-safe point – is rapidly approaching.*

Today, the only way for leading organisations to succeed, and even survive in the global market, is to continually invent new methods that allow them to deploy their new technologies, products, processes and systems at even faster rates of 'rapid-speed' (Wheelwright and Clark, 1992). Software companies are typical of this trend, where open beta programs are released 'live' to consumers for testing over the Internet, so that bugs and system errors can be identified and addressed in the commercial release of the application at a later date.

The problem with this mode of delivery is that some bugs just never get ironed out and the beta version is so widely adopted that it becomes the commercial release by default. Some Web 2.0 applications are in what is now known as 'perpetual beta' (Glotzbach, 2009), and this has major implications for liability claims by end users, should they arise. Another problem with this type of 'web-speed delivery' is that features and functionality of the software have not always come directly from user requirements, but from what software developers perceive user requirements to be. This type of accelerated stage-gate approach is very different to the way software was once built in the 1980s (Cooper, 1993).

Creating market demand is normally a high risk enterprise; smart entrepreneurs know that the safest way to go about initial product placement is market segment identification. One of the more remarkable details within the 'implantables' industry is the subtle but detectable shift towards the creation of market demand. That is, if we are to exclude the biomedical research area, which has more to do with prognosis and healing rather than unambiguous 'enhancement' (Banbury, 1997), the prime driver behind this unbridled rush to put microchip implants into our bodies is the corporate sector, also known as industrial developers. This manifest rush, given the permanency of the product, is highly reckless, for it is at the expense of an equal measure of practical reason. It is what will in essence give rise to the technological singularity as postulated by Kurzweil (2005) and others before him – technological change so rapid and profound that it will cause a 'big bang' of sorts in human history.

For now, anyone questioning the direction of future technological developments in this specific domain is by and large considered backward, a *bio-Luddite*, and not with the times. But long gone are the days when discussion of the potential for every citizen to be implanted with a unique lifetime identifier (ULI) for the conduct of almost *every* transaction is considered to be a near impossibility (Michael and Michael, 2006). Most local area councils now demand that household pets are implanted or penalties ensue. But still, some citizens (probably most) cannot comprehend that such ID schemes for humans could be rolled out within their lifetime as simply as ATMs were rolled out across the world in the 1980s. In the early period of ATM deployment, banks were distributing 'keycards' to ten year olds through school banking programmes, despite the fact that most children banked 'cents' and not 'dollars' and that ATMs were incapable of allowing people to withdraw coins. Consider a school banking program based on a microchip implant 'rewards' system.

The introduction of human implantable ID systems, like most ICT systems today, requires a complex value chain of stakeholders to come together to offer a complete product. These stakeholders include: the technology providers (those involved in the manufacture and system and software development related to the device); the service providers (those responsible for issuing the technology and branding the device); and the end user (such as merchants, who accept the technology just like they accept EFTPOS, and every day consumers who are implanted). The interaction between these stakeholders will determine whether the human implantable device will succeed or fail. But it is time for individual members of society to also think about what they would do – and this question is increasingly likely to be posed, should we follow the trail of evidence and believe professionals like Retherford – if they were asked, in the not too distant future, would they accept an implant that they could carry for employee or citizen ID? The danger in this instance is not if, but when the implant starts to become a function of every day life; to open bank accounts, receive medical benefits, be eligible for government services, and even to catch public transport. It would be wise in this instance to not only remember that famous Latin phrase *caveat emptor*, but also its counterpart, the less often cited but probably more pertinent *caveat venditor*.

Chapter 11

Robot Companions: Technology for Humans

Serge Kernbach

University of Stuttgart

> *[Chip] had been teasing a scanner somewhere, putting his bracelet to it again and again, and he was being taught not to. That winking red no was the first in his life for a claim that mattered to him, not just for starting into the wrong classroom or coming to the medicenter on the wrong day; it hurt and saddened him.*
>
> THIS PERFECT DAY, P. 20

11.1 Introduction

Creation of devices and mechanisms which help people has a long history. Their inventors always targeted practical goals such as irrigation, harvesting, devices for construction sites, measurement, and, last but not least, military tasks for different mechanical, and later mechatronic, systems. Development of such assisting mechanisms dates back to Greek engineering, came through Middle Ages and led finally, in the 19th and 20th centuries, to autonomous devices which today we call *Robots* (Craig, 2005).

Robot embodies three essential principles: mechanical strength due to utilisation of an independent energy source; programmable actuation through perception and information processing; and autonomy of behaviour. All these principles can be implemented in different ways, for instance Japan's karakuri ningyo, mechanical automata from the 18th and 19th centuries, used mechanical energy and specific wood gears (Law, 1997), see Fig. 11.1(a). Industrialisation replaced water and mechanical tension energy with steam, chemical and electrical energy; this resulted in a new generation of mechanisms. The term *robot* first appeared in the 1920s, and reflected a public discussion of that time related to development of such assisting devices.

Modern robotics has had almost 100 years of development from the first mechatronic devices of the 20th century. It now includes such branches as industrial, service, entertainment and educational robotics; differentiated into humanoid (see Fig. 11.1(b)), field and collective systems (see Fig. 11.1(c)); covers water, surface, air and space domains; it is represented in nano-, micro-, mini- and macro-worlds, from 10^{-7} m to 10^2 m sizes (Kernbach, 2011; Siciliano and Khatib, 2008). Robotic technology advanced into micro-mechatronics, genetic engineering, bottom-up chemistry and bacterial (see Fig. 11.1(d)) areas. Currently, robotics is integrated not only into human society but also exists as mixed robot-animal systems and even raises the question of independent robot cultures (Winfield and Griffiths., 2010).

Human–robot interaction is one of the critical issues of modern robotics. It comes back to the origin as an assisting device for humans and requires re-consideration of the old dilemmas: do we need a 'friend', an 'assistant' or a 'butler' (Dautenhahn *et al.*, 2005)? Is a robot companion aimed only at elderly people (Cesta *et al.*, 2005)? Can a robot be a mate? Robot companions for humans require a re-thinking of human aspects in human–robot interactions and an estimation of a boundary for our acceptance of technology. Are we ready to accept a synthetic life or do we need only an assisting device? This chapter is intended to overview the technological transition *autonomous device* → *humanoid assistant* → *social robots*, which robotics is now undergoing, and to focus on *social* and *self-driven* developmental aspects of robot technologies.

This chapter is structured in the following way. Section 11.2 briefly introduces different state-of-the-art robot technologies in hardware and software areas. Section 11.3 is devoted to future technologies, which are potentially applicable in robotics in the next few years, and Section 11.4 overviews a large field of collective systems. Section 11.5 discusses social aspects of robot companions and the driving forces of modern robotic de-

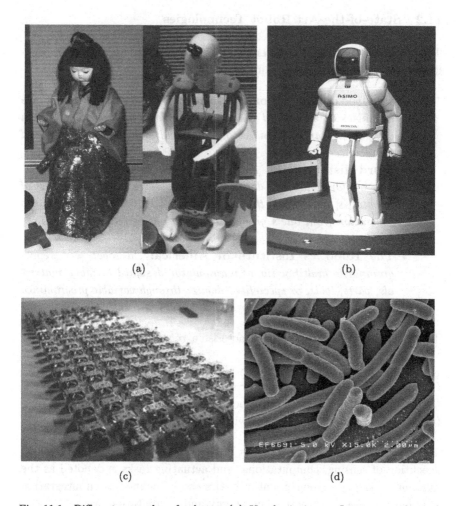

Fig. 11.1 Different examples of robots. (a) Karakuri ningyo, Japanese mechanical automata from the 18th and 19th centuries (image source: Wikimedia Commons). (b) Humanoid robot ASIMO created by Honda (image source: Wikimedia Commons). (c) Collective robotics, swarm robots Jasmine. (d) Bacterial robotics: scanning electron micrograph of *Escherichia coli*, grown in culture and adhered to a cover slip (image source: Wikimedia Commons).

velopment. Finally, Section 11.6 returns back to the topic of *This Perfect Day*, as described in Chapter 1, polemises self-driven trends in robotics and concludes this chapter.

11.2   State-of-the-Art Robot Technologies

To make an overview of different robot technologies, we look first for a definition of *robot*, which is commonly defined as:

- **The free online dictionary:** '*a mechanical device that sometimes resembles a human and is capable of performing a variety of often complex human tasks either on command or by being programmed in advance.*'
- **Word History:** '*robot*' *comes from Czech* '*robota*', *meaning* '*servitude or* '*forced labour*', *derived from rab,* '*slave*'*. The Slavic root of* '*robota*' *is* '*orb-*', *from the Indo-European root* *orbh-, *referring to separation from one's group or passing out of one sphere of ownership into another.*
- **The Robotics Institute of America:**   '*a robot is a reprogrammable multifunctional manipulator designed to move materials, parts, tools, or specialised devices through variable programmed motions, for the performance of a variety of tasks*'.

To generalise further, we may characterise a *robot* as a system capable of:

(1) on-board sensing;
(2) on- or off-board autonomous or semi-autonomous data processing;
(3) on-board energy supply or on-board energy transformation;
(4) actuation and/or interactions with its environment.

The dependence between (1)–(4) is briefly sketched in Fig. 11.2. Cyclical execution of sensing, computational and actuating tasks is denoted as the *autonomy cycle*. To some extent, robotics can be defined as an integration of science over sensing, actuation, energy and computation areas.

However, robotics not only follows and builds on technological developments from other domains. Due to the autonomy cycle and the independent energy source, robotics includes *autonomous and behavioural aspects*. These are important features and both lead to an appearance of *cognitive functionality*. Further, a combination of these three properties and the involvement of different learning approaches contributes to *evolutionary and developmental features*. Thus, four interacting hardware elements (sensing, actuation, energy and computation) enable five 'soft features' (autonomy, behaviour, adaption, cognition, and development): all of them determine modern mechatronic robotics.

```
┌─────────────────────────────────────┐
│           energy source             │
└─────────────────────────────────────┘
                  │
                  ▼
        ┌───────────────────┐
   ┌───▶│    computation    │───┐
   │    └───────────────────┘   │
   │         ┌─────────┐        │
┌──┴─────┐   │ autonomy│   ┌────▼────┐
│sensing │   │  cycle  │   │actuation│
└────────┘   └─────────┘   └─────────┘
     ▲                          │
environment                environment
```

Fig. 11.2 General dependence between sensing, actuation, energy and computation parts. Cyclical execution of sensing, computational and actuating tasks is denoted as the autonomy cycle.

There are several robot taxonomies (Siciliano and Khatib, 2008), based on such criteria as size, available onboard energy and on-board computational power. We can roughly define seven classes of robot platforms, as shown in Fig. 11.3. In the following, we make a short overview of robot technologies for these classes of robots.

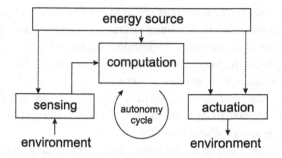

Branche of robotics	outdoor/ field	service	mini-	large micro-	small micro-	MEMS	colloid/pacticle
Typical size	2-50m³	0,5-2m³	0,1-0,5m³	0,01-0,1m³	10^{-4}-10^{-3} m³	10^{-5}-10^{-4} m³	10^{-7}-10^{-6} m³
Typical energy	a few kWh	50-500Wh	1-50Wh	typ.1Wh	typ.1mWh	—	—
Typical comput. power	>50k MIPS	5k-50k MIPS	1k-5k MIPS	10-1k MIPS	2-10 MIPS	—	—
Typical memory	a few GB	a few GB	100MB	100kB	10kB	—	—
Typical OS	PC OS	PC/Mobile OS	Embedded OS	—	—	—	—

Fig. 11.3 Seven robot classes based on the dependency between available on-board energy, computational power and size of robots. Typical values/examples of size, available on-board energy (Wh), computational power (MIPS), memory and operating systems (OS) are shown for different classes of mobile robot platforms.

Energy. On-board energy supply is one of the most challenging problems in mobile robotics. Generally, a dependency between the size of a mobile system and available energy defines robot classes, shown in Fig. 11.3. With the reduction of a system's size, the energy consumption is reduced; however, the available space for energy is also reduced. For the large field platforms, combustion engines are used, whereas smaller platforms use mostly rechargeable electrical energy sources, such as lithium-polymer accumulators. Due to autonomous recharging capabilities, autonomous work in almost all platforms varies between a few hours and a few days. There are several projects which explore alternative energy sources, for example Microbian fuel cell (Aaron *et al.*, 2010) or Hydrogen fuel cell (Patil *et al.*, 2004) sources, as well as the utilisation of energy harvesting (Priya and Inman, 2008); also see Mitcheson, Chapter 13.

Actuation. Actuation is the most energy-consuming operation, typically 70%–80% of on-board energy is spent for actuation. Therefore, actuating capabilities are closely related to the available energy for each class of robot systems from Fig. 11.3. Generally, there are only a few types of actuators used in robotics: magnetic/electrostatic actuators; DC, AC and piezzo-motors; and pneumo- and hydraulic-actuators. Their capabilities also vary from 'very strong' in field devices to 'very weak' in microsystems. Actuation and sensing are closely related to each other: when sensing enables a robot to perceive the environment, due to actuation, a robot can modify the environment. Both are used for direct and indirect communication, for example trophallaxis and stigmergy.

Information processing. Available energy and size constrain the computational capabilities of robots: from several on-board PCs with several thousands MIPS down to tiny embedded systems with only a few MIPS in 8 bit microcontrollers. Due to the development of micro-electronics and smart mobile devices, on-board information processing rapidly advanced in the last few years, in all classes of robot. Primarily, this technology is related to microcontollers, memory, peripheral control and buses. The level of current integration in Programmable Systems on Chip provides all the necessary functionalities in one chip, which allows for a flexible reconfiguration of components.

Sensing. Sensing technologies in robotics follow general trends from industrial sensor development. They use common optical, sonar or electromagnetic approaches with transmissive and reflective techniques (Kornienko *et al.*, 2005). Application of vision-based methods for navigation and localisation is also well established. The sensing range varies between 'very large' in field robotics down to 'very small' in micro-systems. Normally, sensor data requires preliminary processing, such as noise reduction or linearisation and final data processing, where data are matched with the model to understand the meaning of the current sensor information. These capabilities in turn depend on the available computational power.

Autonomy and Behaviour. As mentioned above, through a cyclic execution of sensing, computational and actuating tasks, a robot exhibits a phenomenon that we call autonomous behaviour. Autonomy is a very basic property; we say that *autonomy in robotics is a capability to act independently as a self-determining closed system.* The degree of robot autonomy caused a large discussion in the robotic, multi-agent and human–robot interaction communities (Goodrich *et al.*, 2007). The concept of autonomy can be applied separately to sensing, computation and actuation, so that two principally different viewpoints on autonomy can be encountered. Firstly, a robot keeps its autonomy; in other words, it performs sensing, data processing and actuating autonomously. We call this a *strong autonomy.* Secondly, sensing, actuation and computation can be shared among different robots. One or several processes can be performed on the level of the whole system or even on a host-computer. Robots still retain some degree of autonomy, however they depend on other agents in decision making. We denote this autonomy as a soft or *weak autonomy.*

Autonomy enables a robot to behave as an *independent unit.* Since robots operate in environments, they interact with other robots and also with environments. These interactions introduce behavioural aspects into robotics. Depending on the level of central or decentralised coordination and the degree of autonomy, the interactions between robots can demonstrate several kinetic relationships (Kernbach *et al.*, 2009), geometrical and spatio-temporal dependencies, energetic balance with the environment, and coevolution with each other and with the environment (Futuyma and Slatkin, 1983). For example, some behavioural aspects of swarm systems are similar to the behaviour of gas molecules and multi-particle systems, and these similarities have stimulated several macroscopic probabilistic approaches to modelling (Martinoli *et al.*, 1999). Robotic systems are often used to model and to investigate different biological systems (Schmickl and Crailsheim, 2008).

Adaptation, Cognition and Development. These three concepts are high-level issues in robotics. Adaptability is closely related to environmental changes, the ability of a system to react to these changes, and the capability of the designer to forecast the reaction of the environment to the system's response. Therefore, adaptability is defined in terms of the triple-relationship: *environmental changes → system response → environmental reaction.* In general, adaptability is the ability of a system to achieve desired environmental reactions in accordance with *a priori* defined criteria by changing its structure, functionality or behaviour. Adaptive technical systems are expected to have some degree of freedom, so they may adapt to their environment. In this context, adaptivity is closely related to three issues: developmental plasticity, capability to detect changes and, finally, mechanisms allowing reaction to changes by utilising plasticity. Since adaptive systems are approached from several independent directions, the understanding of these underlying mechanisms differs from research community to research community.

Cognition is a general term that implies a perception, processing of information, building and changing of knowledge and their expressions in behaviour (Indiveri *et al.*, 2009). When the notion of cognition was first originated in psychology, the development of autonomous behavioural systems led to a transfer of these principles to robotics (Clark and Grush, 1999). Since cognition unifies other notions such as autonomy, behaviour or adaptation, robotics is undergoing a 're-thinking process' as embodied cognitive science.

Development is the highest notion and has its origin in biological systems as an ontogenetic development of an organism, i.e. from one cell to a multi-cellular adult system (Spencer *et al.*, 2008). The development in this context is related to epigenetic systems, which 'explain how phenotypic characteristics arise during development through a complex series of interactions between genetic program and environment' (Brauth *et al.*, 1991). Plasticity of development is related to cause–effect sequences by which information is read out in genotype in the presence of environmental stimuli. Artificial developmental systems, in particular developmental (epigenetic) robotics (Lungarella *et al.*, 2003), are new emerging fields across several research areas – neuroscience, developmental psychology, biological disciplines such as embryogenetics, evolutionary biology or ecology, and engineering sciences such as mechatronics, on-chip-reconfigurable systems or cognitive robotics (Asada *et al.*, 2009). We can say that the development is the bounded or unbounded process of functional, structural and regulatory changes undertaken by the system itself, related to its specific understanding of itself (expressed by so-called self-concept). Normally, the development or self-development is initiated by differences between the self-concept and endogenous or environmental factors, and may be unlimited in time and complexity.

The five 'soft components' of modern robotics mentioned above have different expressions in the seven classes of robot platforms. First of all, the high-level functionality requires a lot of computational resources, which are not available on small platforms. Secondly, the operating environment has an essential impact on the needs of higher cognitive capabilities: requirements in unstructured outdoor environments are much harder than those in domestic and laboratory conditions. In this way, we observe two different trends: working with minimalistic capabilities, for example minimally cognitive systems (Dale and Husbands, 2010), and a full scale approach with extended sensing and actuation.

11.3 Bio-, Chemo- and Neuro-Hybrid Robotics

Classical mechatronic devices, as reviewed in the previous section, represent only a part of robotics. We face new developments from synthetic biology, molecular (Balzani *et al.*, 2003), bacterial (Martel *et al.*, 2009), colloidal (Hunter, 1989), bio-hybrid (Novellino *et al.*, 2007) and cultured neural (Reger *et al.*, 2000) systems, artificial chemistry and self-replication (Hutton, 2009). It seems that robotics should be defined in a broader way, without emphasising the mechatronic point of view. Overviewing the state of art in hybrid systems, we can currently differentiate four mainstreams in development of hybrid systems: bio-techno artefacts, neuro-hybrid, chemo-hybrid and bio-hybrid systems.

Hybrid robotics addresses several important questions. One of these is an attempt to interact with biological systems by means of technological artefacts. Examples can be given by robotic prostheses, e.g. Fig. 11.4(a), controlling mixed societies of robot and insects (Caprari *et al.*, 2005), autonomous management of grazing cattle over large areas (Schwager *et al.*, 2008), or by social communication between robots and chickens (Gribovskiy and Mondada, 2009). A similar approach is related to the integration of different robot technologies into human societies, for example the management of urban hygiene based on a network of autonomous and cooperating robots (Mazzolai *et al.*, 2008).

Interactions between neuroscience and robotics represent another interesting research area in hybrid systems. This is primarily related to a combination of cultured (living) neurons and mobile robots (Novellino *et al.*, 2007) to investigate the dynamical and adaptive properties of neural systems (Reger *et al.*, 2000). This work is also related to the understanding of how information is encoded (Cozzi *et al.*, 2006) and processed, within a living neural network. For instance, the Hybrot project (DeMarse *et al.*, 2001), see Fig. 11.4(b) and the NeuroBit project (Martinoia *et al.*, 2004) addressed the problem of the control of autonomous robots by living neurons.

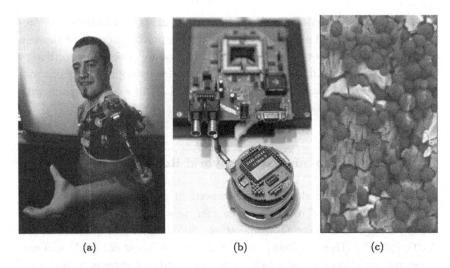

(a)   (b)   (c)

Fig. 11.4 **(a)** Christian Kandlbauer lost both arms in an electrical accident in 2005 but was able to live a largely normal life thanks to a mind-controlled robotic prosthetic left arm and a normal prosthesis in place of his right arm (with permission, AP Photo/Ronald Zak). **(b)** Hybrot, a 'hybrid robot' (DeMarse *et al.*, 2001), a robot controlled through electronics and biological neurons (source: Wikimedia Commons). **(c)** Prototypes of chemical robots ('chobots') (source: BBC News; credit Frantisek Stepanek).

This hybrid technology can be used for neuro-robotic interfaces, different applications of *in vitro* neural networks (Miranda *et al.*, 2009), or for bi-directional interaction between the brain and the external environment.

Another approach in hybrid systems is inspired by artificial chemistry (Dittrich *et al.*, 2001), self-replicating systems (Hutton, 2009) using bio-chemical mechanisms for, for example, cognition (Dale and Husbands, 2010) or the well-known quasispecies (Eigen, 1971). In several works, this approach is denoted as swarm chemistry (Sayama, 2009), see Fig. 11.4(c). Researchers hope that such chemistry-based systems will give answers to questions related to developmental models (Astor and Adami, 2000), chemical computation (Berry and Boudol, 1992), self-assembly, self-replication, and simple chemistry-based ecologies (Breyer *et al.*, 1997) of prebiotic life.

The bio-hybrid approach is represented by synthetic biology and the integration of real bio-chemical and microbiological systems into technological developments; for example using bacterial cellular mechanisms as sensors (Wood, 1999), the development of bacterial bio-hybrid materials, the molecular synthesis of polymers (Pasparakis *et al.*, 2010) and biofuels (Alper and Stephanopoulos, 2009), genome engineering (Carr and Church, 2009) and more general fields and challenges of synthetic biology (Alterovitz *et al.*, 2010). Here, bio-hybrid and pure bio-synthetic systems overlap in several applications; we expect that both areas will be developed in parallel.

Bio-, chemo- and neuro-hybrid systems raise new technological challenges in robotics: the integration of bio-chemistry, micro-biology, synthetic biology and robotics will be a vital challenge in coming years and promises several radical breakthroughs regarding the adaptive and developmental properties of artificial systems. Currently, there are only a few real applications for them (such as robotic prostheses); however, we expect that in the future this field will be one of the dominant areas of robotics as an assistive technology for humans.

11.4   Collective Robotics

There are two reasons why collective robotics should be mentioned as a separate area of research. First of all, collective robotics, in many aspects, overlaps with a larger domain of collective systems, which include many biological, bio-chemical or sociological examples, see Fig. 11.5(a) and Fig. 11.5(b). Problems appearing in such populations can be modelled and analysed with robots (Kernbach *et al.*, 2009). Secondly, one of the most common features of collective systems is the idea that by working together, such systems achieve results that are not attainable by individuals alone. Generally, collective systems consist of many interacting *individuals*, such as molecules, insects, animals, robots, software agents, or even humans. Through their *interactions*, the individuals of a collective system are able to achieve behaviours, functionality, structures and other properties that are not achievable by these individuals alone. Such synergetic effects are of essential interest in many other disciplines (Haken, 1977) that do not touch robotics directly.

Collective robotics represents a relatively new area of artificial systems. The earliest references go back to the late 1980s and early 1990s (Fukuda *et al.*, 1989). Collective robotic systems appear when sensing, data processing and actuation are distributed among many different robots. We know 'the system is more than the sum of its parts' (Aristotle, 1989). This 'more' – often referred as the common organisational principle – is the most important issue when designing collective autonomous systems. The common organisational principle can be understood as a common goal, common strategy or something that makes the system focused on one. This defines how the sensing and computational processes are distributed among different 'pieces of hardware and software':

> *Given some task specified by a designer, a multiple robot system displays cooperative behaviour if, due to some underlying mechanism for example the 'mechanism of cooperation', there is an increase in the total utility of the system.* (Cao et al., 1997)

Fig. 11.5 Examples of collective systems. **(a)** Termites (source: Wikimedia Commons). **(b)** Human crowd (source: Wikimedia Commons). **(c)** Automatic guided vehicles, courtesy of psb intralogistics GmbH. **(d)** Swarm robots.

Thus, collective robotics is an intentionally designed system of interacting autonomous or semi-autonomous robots, which distribute or share sensing, computation, energy supply or actuation. These robots can be of technological, bio-synthetic, or any other origin, and with a common organisational principle such as a common goal, intention or strategy underlying the whole system. In most cases, a collective robot system consists of many independent autonomous individual robots, each of which is capable of sensing, computation and actuation. Sometimes, these robots can be autonomous in actuation, although they may share computational and sensing resources, as do those in the cooperative KUKA's 'RoboTeam' robots (Vasilash, 2006). In some cases, robots are not fully autonomous, but are still distributed in actuation, such as automatic guided vehicles (AGV) (Watanabe *et al.*, 2001), see Fig. 11.5(c). Recently, collections of a large number of relatively simple robots have come to represent so-called swarm robotics, see Fig. 11.5(d), which is historically situated in observation of the natural world, in particular social insects.

The concept of collective systems provides several essential advantages (Kernbach, 2008). First, systems consisting of many independent autonomous elements are very reliable. Second, collective systems have many degrees of freedom and are much more flexible than centralised ones. Such flexibility can be used for adaptation (Kornienko *et al.*, 2004), or for developmental processes. Third, due to the decentralisation of regulative and functional strictures, collective systems are scalable in a wide range of structural, diverse and dynamic conditions (Constantinescu *et al.*, 2004).

11.5 Social Aspects of Robotics and Robot Companions

11.5.1 *Robots as assistive technology*

Various technologies, as briefly mentioned in the previous sections, define many facets of modern robotics. However, following the original idea of a robot as an assistive technology for humans, we need to investigate another side of this problem – the need of the human for assistance in the first place. The bridge between the current capabilities of robots and this need for assistance is addressed within the area of human–robot interactions and design of sociable robots (Breazeal, 2002). Considering Fig. 11.3, we can say that different classes of robots are capable of performing different tasks, and, first of all, we need to clarify a potential usage of these classes. Table 11.1 summarises several of these classes, their main characteristics and possible applications.

Based on this table, we can identify several key drivers of robotics as the technology for human assistance. However, it is necessary to keep separate: potentially interesting developments, which may have an essential role in future; various academic research programmes, with development prospects; and industrial applications with commercial prospects.

Table 11.1   Classes of robot platforms and applications

Class of platforms	Several Characteristics	Potential Usage
Field robotics	general class of large outdoor robots of 2–50 m^3 and >1 kWh onboard energy; operation in unstructured and dynamic environments.	construction, forestry, agriculture, mining, sea and underwater, search and rescue, military, and space.
Outdoor robotics	primarily mobile systems from field- and service-class platforms and intelligent vehicles, targeting specific challenges of outdoor environments.	different outdoor applications, autonomous transportation of people and goods.
Service robotics	general class of indoor and outdoor robots used in different service areas, ranging between 0.5–2 m^3 size and 50–500 Wh on-board energy.	large application domain related to human companions, e.g. a guide in museum, hospitals, different assisting tasks.
Domestic robotics	part of service robotics, related to '@home applications'; dynamic home-like indoor environments with fixed structure.	assistance at home, different sorts of cleaning, intelligent refrigerators, ironing and similar (see also Ferscha, Chapter 2).
Medical and Healthcare robotics	various systems, such as manipulators, preprogrammed or teleoperated robots, operating in medical environments.	surgery, orthopaedics, endoscopic and micro-surgery, rehabilitation tasks, physical therapy and training.
Mini-robotics	general class of small indoor robots. Size varies typically between 0.1-0.5 m^3 and 1–50 Wh on-board power.	domestic and educational applications, different service tasks in small areas.
Micro-robotics	general class of very small robots. Size varies typically between 0.0001–0.1 m^3 and 0.001–1 Wh on-board power.	several medical applications, education, micro- and nano-manipulation, fluidic systems, factories on the table.
Colloidal and Particle systems	new class of robots with programmable properties. It consists of several different systems of biological, chemical or material science origin.	programmable bio-chemical and hybrid systems, drug design and discovery, applications in molecular manufacturing.

This progress from (a) to (c) is challenging and obviously not all results can be transferred. However, what is clearly indicated is a development from initial 'toy scenarios' to real products with concrete applications. Below we discuss in turn four such application areas.

Industrial Needs. This is one of the main current drives in many different areas of automatisation and robotics, and is primarily related to handling, processing, assembling or transportation. To some small extent, the toy industry also stimulates development of robot technologies. New industrial applications in such areas as drug discovery and drug design involve robotics. Potentially interesting for industrial applications are micro- and nano-technological systems, dealing with micro-actuation, micro-cleaning, structuration of material and similar tasks. Here we can also mention the automotive industry and attempts to create an autonomous intelligent vehicle, as well as different military applications of this technology. Space robotics for autonomous space missions or space manufacturing can also be located in the sector.

Future computation, surveillance, S&R, sensor networks. These are today's applications, where small- and middle-size groups of robots perform tasks of inspecting or monitoring technological processes, checking availability of specific/dangerous substances, tracking objects/people. Depending on the number of robots and their degree of autonomy, these applications vary between mobile computing devices (these devices can represent a next generation of computers) and autonomous self-maintaining sensor networks. Such sensor networks are closely related to autonomous underwater systems and cooperative micro-unmanned aerial vehicles. This application domain is very attractive for collective systems (especially swarm robotics), due to the capabilities of converging large areas, fast reactions in case of accidence in monitored areas, lower power consumption, and self-deployment. Search and rescue scenarios can be also included here.

Medical and biological applications. Medical and healthcare robotics, as well as robot companions for elderly people, is a growing technological area. In many aspects, such systems overlap with service applications. However, due to specific requirements, they are driven by different social and political forces. Biological applications are closely related to the medial domain, for example exploiting living bacteria for such activities as drug delivery or micro-actuation inside of human body. More generally, there are two approaches, which are actively developing here: making robots smaller, and making robot actuation more accurate and precise for nano-manipulation, whereas the robot itself remains large. This is a large and promising area, which has many potential applications.

Service applications. This field represents flexible robotic systems in warehouses, autonomous cleaning in large areas, diverse tasks in hospitals, guidance in museums, and various domestic and '@home' tasks (Iossifidis *et al.*, 2005). To some extent, these applications are a direct spin-off from the RoboCup initiative. Since these systems operate in unstructured environments and involve communication and interactions with humans, a large amount of research is still required for successful applications. Furthermore, one of the main requirements in the service area is the adaptivity and flexibility of robots, so there is a particular interest for collective reconfigurable and self-developing robotics. In the following section we review this field in more detail.

11.5.2 *Service area and robot companions*

Service area is directly related to interactions with humans and to the idea of robot companions. Surveying the literature on human–robot interactions, e.g. (Dautenhahn *et al.*, 2005; Oestreicher and Severinson Eklundh, 2006; Wilkes *et al.*, 1998), we can make several conclusions about the expectations of humans on robot assistance. For instance, 'in general it turned out that people were positive towards having robot assistance in their homes, ... between 30 and 50% of the informants said that they were positive to have a robot support' (Oestreicher and Severinson Eklundh, 2006). Moreover, in this work several household tasks are identified, such as dish washing (43%), window polishing (39%), dusting and other similar cleaning tasks (44%), wet cleaning (of floors, etc.), washing clothes (37%). Thus, the expectation is primarily related to robots from the service-class platforms which are not fully autonomous.

Khan (1998) states that:

> the tasks that received most 'NO's [to robot assistance] were in order of frequency: baby sitting, reading aloud, watching cat/dog, acting as a butler, cooking food and taking care of kitchen goods. The tasks that received the most 'YES's meaning that a person actually wants a robot to help or conduct these tasks were in order of frequency: polishing windows, cleaning ceilings and walls, cleaning, wet cleaning, moving heavy things and wiping surfaces clean.

Related to the appearance of robot platform (i.e. the class of robot platforms), the responses were 22% neutral, 57% machine-like and 19% human-like design. However 71% of subjects in Dautenhahn *et al.* (2005) prefer to communicate with a robot in human-like manner. As we can see, the relevance of humanoid platforms for service tasks is limited.

Dautenhahn *et al.* (2005) collected further data, with similar results: for example about 40% of subjects liked having a robot companion at home. We reproduce two images related to preferred tasks for a robot companion in the home and desired roles for a future robot companion from this work in Fig. 11.6. The authors came mainly to the conclusion that 'The finding

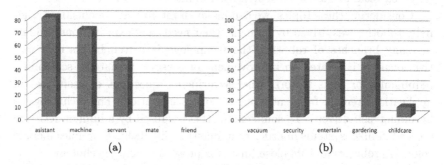

Fig. 11.6 **(a)** Desired roles for a future robot companion and **(b)** preferred tasks for robot companion in the home (data from Dautenhahn *et al.* (2005)).

that people frequently cited that they would like a future robot to perform the role of a servant is maybe similar to the human "butler" role'. As we can see, understanding the main facets of "@home applications" and the role of robot assistances has not essentially changed during the last ten years. To some extent it also reflects a human desire for servants, which we can observe in all cultures and epochs.

11.6   Conclusion

The previous sections of this chapter are devoted to the different spectacular areas of modern robotics. We shortly overviewed key software and hardware technologies, as well as considering the fields of mechatronic, hybrid and collective robotics. We introduced robotics as a tool to assist humans and then made a revision of modern human expectations towards such assistance. It turned out that robotics is driven by four main forces: industry, networked computing, service and bio-medical applications, whereas the primary human expectation remains to have a robot as a servant.

Unfortunately, many relevant points of robotics remained outside of this consideration. For example, cognitive aspects: sensing by different robots and problems of sensor-fusion, world modelling and collective localisation. Another issue is learning: team- and group-based learning, collective and learning, and so on. We did not consider such points as mechanical and electrical engineering and design, which are very relevant for embodiment and, finally, for success in applications. Many different research projects are addressing these issues, and they, due to complexity and amount of collected results, cannot be represented in one overview.

Considering these topics, we can make an interesting conclusion. Originally robotics was driven by humans, their needs and expectations. Today, in many branches of robotics, the technology is driven by its own motivations. It is related to improvement of sensors, actuators, scalability, redundancy or costs factors, whereas principal questions of usefulness in applications remain frequently outside of consideration. The technology is becoming 'self-driven'. To some extent this is caused by a human desire to create 'life-like' systems in order to understand life itself. Examples include cognitive robotics and its close link to neuroscience and psychology.

These 'self-driven' trends in robotics lead to so-called self-issues: self-adaptation, self-repairing, self-replication, self-reflection and so on. These self-issues are related in many aspects to adaptability and evolve-ability, to emergence of behaviour and to controllability of long-term developmental processes. Currently, little effort is invested in understanding predictability of self-processes, principles of making purposeful self-developmental systems and consequences of a long-term independency and autonomy. We are facing, even now, an appearance of independent self-development of robots, e.g. in the area of evolutionary robotics; in the future these processes will be much larger and more intensive. We should be ready for the emergence of artificial robot cultures and start to realise their meaning and the potential consequences for humankind.

Chapter 12

When the Battlefield Robots Come Home From War

Ken Wahren and Jeremy Pitt

Blue Bear Systems Research Ltd./Imperial College London

> *Soon after, they heard a copter's hum; it passed and repassed above them*
>
> THIS PERFECT DAY, P. 180

12.1 Introduction

There is no shortage of science fiction cautioning against the combination of autonomy and armament. This theme is commonplace in popular culture, witness the films *The Terminator*, *The Matrix* and *Red Planet*, to name but a few; the *Watchbird* story mentioned in Chapter 1; or *Computer One* (Collins, 1993). In *This Perfect Day*, the supercomputer UniComp, although not armed *per se*, does hold the power of life and death over humans. It is perhaps the ubiquity of this theme, an autonomous non-human intelligence with the power to take our lives, which causes people to interpret reports of battlefield robots as the realisation of a long-held fear.

Indeed, almost any account of the most recent conflicts in Iraq and Afghanistan contains references to the terms 'drone', 'Unmanned Aerial Vehicle' (UAV), 'Unmanned Ground Vehicle' and 'robot'. If 1991's Desert Storm was the war of GPS and smart bombs (from a technological standpoint, at least), then the distinguishing technological feature of these later conflicts could well be the use of robots to provide 'battlefield superiority' in the context of asymmetric warfare.

For many people though, the idea of a battlefield robot is frightening; after all, the concept of a relentless machine with eagle vision and the ability to attack silently from a vast stand-off range is particularly disturbing, and redolent of Paul Bäumer's description of mechanised warfare in *All Quiet on the Western Front*:

> *Tanks, which used to be objects of ridicule, have become a major weapon. They come rolling forward in a long line, heavily armoured, and they embody the horror of war for us more than anything else. ... the oncoming waves of enemy attackers are human being just like we are — but tanks are machines, and their caterpillar tracks run on as endlessly as the war itself.*

> Erich Maria Remarque (1929, pp. 198–199)

While 'tank' at least has innocuous connotations, names like Predator (see Fig. 12.1) and Reaper don't necessarily offer much in the way of disguising intent or offering reassurance, either.

Fig. 12.1   An armed Predator UAV (source: Wikimedia Commons).

However, the public anxiety that this technology will make the transition from military to civilian application, as this chapter will try to explain, is at present largely misplaced. Instead of the confluence of autonomy and armament, though, there is another concern, derived from the confluence of remote operation and imaging equipment together with the transition of this technology from military to civilian applications.

There is within most liberal societies a strong resistance to intrusion into an individual's privacy – by other individuals, by collectives such as corporations and, most importantly, by the state. These fears are most noticeable when technology is deployed in a way that compromises privacy, and when that technology is very visible. For example, the installation of additional CCTV cameras in parts of Birmingham provoked an outrage in 2010, and the cameras were subsequently withdrawn (Brant, 2010). Similarly, the deployment of Google's Street View vehicles has provoked community protest and legal action (BBC, 2009). This last example is particularly relevant since, as will be explained, one of the key potential civilian applications for the current generation of robots (particularly flying robots) is mobile, remote surveillance.

Fears about the potential of UAVs with imaging equipment to encroach on personal privacy need to be addressed seriously. Successfully addressing this concern would open up a number of applications for the current and near-future generation of robots, particularly flying robots (i.e. UAVs), which could be adapted from battlefield applications to serve a broad range of peaceful applications, from law enforcement and security, to emergency services, to civil engineering and social scientific research (Nonami, 2007). As will be discussed, it is either the unthinking or unprincipled application of the technology which provokes an 'auto-immune response' from society's safety mechanisms, rather than limitations of the technology, which are preventing the robots coming home from the war just yet.

12.2 Battlefield Robots Today

Although 'drone strikes' receive much media attention (in part because they capture the public's imagination, or their horror), most battlefield robots exist to do the 'dull, dirty and dangerous' jobs previously performed by soldiers, airmen and sailors – so much so that the phrase 'dull, dirty and dangerous' has become a cliché in the industry that produces them. For example, the man-portable Packbot, popular in Iraq and Afghanistan, was developed because a soldier charged with clearing a cave had no option but to enter the cave in person – and suffered the consequences. The idea of a man-portable mobile platform, carrying a camera into dangerous situations as an alternative to personal inspection, soon took off. Variants of this robot, manufactured by iRobot (who also produce the Roomba robotic vacuum cleaner), are used for explosive ordinance disposal (EOD), another task dangerous to service personnel.

In the air, unmanned aerial vehicles (UAVs) have performed at their best as Intelligence, Surveillance, Target Acquisition and Reconnaissance (ISTAR) platforms. With no pilot on board, these vehicles are optimised for performance, both in terms of sensor payloads and communications equipment and their operational longevity, exceeding the endurance of a single flight crew, in the case of larger vehicles. In many ways, the nature of the conflicts in Iraq and Afghanistan, which have been, for the most part, characterised by uncontested airspace, has greatly helped in the uptake of the technology. A level of autonomy that did not require UAVs to handle contested airspace was far easier to achieve, and most modern UAVs do little more than trundle from one human-defined waypoint to the next, or from one human-requested flight pattern to the next. Indeed, some still operate as remotely piloted vehicles, where only the low-level flight functions are automated, but where a remote human pilot still 'aviates' with the benefit of remote sensors.

For the most part, a large UAV's ISTAR function requires a dedicated ground segment to make the UAV's flight, at whatever level of automation, meaningful. A sensor operator typically steers and zooms one or more sensors remotely, in a way similar to the operation of a CCTV camera, providing a targeted sensor feed to the ground, while a colleague coordinates the trajectory of the vehicle itself, and interfaces with other airspace users and controllers. For larger unmanned aerial systems (UAS), this is just the beginning – the process of then analysing and disseminating the data can take more manpower than the operation of the vehicle and sensor itself.

For smaller UAS, operation is somewhat simpler (see Fig. 12.2). Because these systems are typically deployed and operated closer to front lines, it would be a burden to mandate that operators have aviator training. Consequently, these systems typically incorporate a higher degree of autonomy than some of their larger cousins, so the platform trajectory, including take-off and landing, is usually highly automated, and is controlled at a high level, as is sensor pointing (i.e. controlled by commands ('climb to 500 metres'), rather than controlling pitch directly through the elevators).

In addition, limitations in size, range and altitude, and typical operation near the front line, rather than from congested air-bases, mean that smaller systems pose lower risk to other air traffic, and require less coordination in most (but not all) situations. These factors add up to simpler operation, less manpower and a lower training burden.

Fig. 12.2 Blue Bear iSTART® UAS in action (source: ©Blue Bear Systems Research Ltd).

One of the main missions of in-service UAVs, both large and small, is to provide reconnaissance in advance of an operation by ground troops (see Fig. 12.3). UAVs are typically tasked to gather aerial imagery of an area during the planning stage of an operation. This imagery is then used to update the tactical commander's understanding of the area. UAVs can also be used to survey a region of interest, looking for suspicious activity that might indicate the placement of improvised explosive devices (IEDs), or as a means of spotting anything out of the ordinary in the behaviour of residents, like changes to the 'pattern of life' that might indicate the presence of insurgents planning an attack or ambush.

Yet another mission is to find covertly, identify and track human or vehicle targets; a function in high demand in counter-insurgency campaigns such as the one in Afghanistan.

Arming the larger platforms was almost an afterthought, when it was realised that, having identified a target from a UAV, often the closest platform from which to launch an attack before the target disappeared would be

Fig. 12.3   Blue Bear BMAV UAV in action (source: ©Blue Bear Systems Research Ltd).

the UAV itself. Military people call this the 'prosecution of time sensitive targets', and although the missile is launched from an unmanned aircraft, there is very little about this that differs conceptually from an opportunistic strike by a manned patrolling aircraft. No computer is involved in the decision to strike – the computer is simply a tool that funnels data to a human and carries out the human's order, remotely but with very little intelligence by any definition of the word. To counterpoint this benign assessment of current battlefield robots as surveillance platforms, occasionally armed but never attacking of their own volition, and to touch on the theme of a sinister computer that really does decide when people live and die, as in *This Perfect Day*, it is worth considering a counter-example or two.

In 2006 the South Korean company Samsung Techwin announced the development of an armed sentry robot. Using sensitive cameras to identify targets, the system has closed loop fire control – when activated, a computer decides when and where to shoot, based on its sensor information. Designed for use in the Korean demilitarised zone (where any person entering the zone is considered an enemy), the system does not discriminate between friendly and unfriendly targets – when activated, it will attack any target that it sees with ruthless precision and firepower.

Another example comes from the naval battlefield. The Phalanx Close-In Weapon System (CIWS) is a ship-mounted sentry gun designed as a last line of defence against anti-ship missiles (see Fig. 12.4). It is essentially a 20 mm Gatling gun with rapid, automated pan, tilt and fire capability. The system is designed to be very self-contained, so that it can continue to operate even when the ship has taken damage. It includes its own radar and fire controller, and will happily detect and attack threats with no human input. In 1996 a Japanese Phalanx opened fire on, and hit, an American A6 Intruder towing a radar target. The crew ejected to safety, but the subsequent investigation revealed that the Japanese had meant to let their Phalanx engage the target, and not the aircraft, but had activated the system with the American aircraft still too close.

Fig. 12.4   Phalanx Close-In-Weapons System (source: Wikimedia Commons).

While both of these examples are disconcerting, the computer is following instructions, and in neither case has the computer been empowered to 'decide' that a target will be engaged, or even that a human will be killed (which would be a sinister conclusion indeed). The idea of an 'empowered killing machine' is a distraction from the real risks. The real risks – for the moment at least – lie in poor programming and technological complacency, rather than artificially intelligent, 'tooled up', hardware.

For example, although a computer program is definitely part of the closed loop 'kill chain' in the examples provided, there is nothing really 'complex' (in the complex systems sense); complicated perhaps, but still deterministic, unlike complex or adaptive systems, where emergent and unpredicted properties may arise spontaneously in the system. In the examples above, the computer was enacting a set of rules with defined inputs and outputs, one of which happens to engage a weapon. The problem is that such systems often perform well under laboratory conditions, but rather less well in field conditions. However, it is one matter for the Iris Recognition software to give a false positive at the airport, it is another matter if the battlefield weapons systems start acting on false positives.

There is also a potentially pernicious interaction between poor software and interface design and the resulting systems being used in decision support for human operators. For example, the USS Vincennes shot down an Iran Air civilian airliner in 1988, for reasons that some analysts attributed to flaws in the design, implementation, deployment and failure to evaluate the AEGIS decision support system being used (Swartz, 2001). There were errors in the the interface design, one of which was spotted during development and not fixed; failure to consider the operating environment (a darkened room) or the stress in the operating conditions; and a failure to evaluate the system properly. Furthermore, the users trusted the AEGIS system (technological complacency), and in a classic form of 'groupthink' convinced themselves that one set of readings which indicated that the airplane was descending (as if on a bombing run) was correct, while another set of readings which indicated that the airplane was ascending (as indeed it was) was over-ruled.

This indicates that it is important to ensure that battlefield robots are subject to stringent software design, training and regulation regimes. This will become increasingly important as advances in machine learning and complex systems result in forms of artificial intelligence that perform in ways not intended or predicted by their designers and developers. For example, of some concern is the current development of unmanned combat air vehicles (UCAVs). These are UAVs designed specifically to contest airspace, and they are currently being prototyped by a number of defence prime contractors. The degree of autonomy they will be afforded in terms of weapons release is yet to be seen, but this is a serious issue worthy of some considerable attention. Given the expected firepower and autonomy afforded to these systems, the first of Asimov's fictional three Laws of Robotics – 'A robot may not injure a human being or, through inaction, allow a human being to come to harm' (Asimov, 1950) – looks like so much wishful thinking.

12.3   How the Technology has Evolved, and Where it Might Go

The technology of battlefield robotics has evolved over a long period of time. It wasn't long after the dawn of flight, for example, that 'winged bombs' were developed. During the Second World War, guidance systems developed for German V1 and V2 missiles, limited by the technology of the time, were nonetheless effective, and if considered as a UAV, the V1 represented a big technological advancement in its day.

In the post-war years, 'drones' were developed by several nations for surveillance and target practice, but systems were not reliable, nor were they flexible in terms of the range of missions that could be conducted. It took a number of advances, in a number of fields, to enable the capabilities of modern UAVs. These include advances in:

- ICT, particularly increases in computing and communication power.
- Miniaturisation of electronics.
- Sensor technology in a range of modes.
- Guidance, navigation and control methods.
- GPS.
- Materials, especially composite materials.
- Propulsion methods, especially more power dense and efficient wet and electric motors and batteries.
- Rapid prototyping methods.

Although land robots have also benefited from these advancements, and in fact have had to wait for some of them, a major challenge to the degree of autonomy achievable by the land robot remains the land itself. Whereas the air is free of hard obstacles (if not of weather), the ground is often cluttered and difficult to negotiate autonomously. Ground robots have always faced this additional challenge compared to their aerial cousins, and it is only with recent advances in sensing and machine vision that much headway has been made (Durrant-Whyte and Bailey, 2006).

For both air and land robots, miniaturisation, material advances and power train advances have enabled greater capability in smaller packages. For UAVs, this has led to three relatively new widely recognised classes of vehicle: 'Mini' (size of an albatross); 'Micro' (size of a bat); and 'Nano' (size of an insect).

Whilst platforms of the two larger classes typically resemble well-studied aircraft configurations, such as aeroplanes and helicopters, the last has a tendency to more novel bio-inspired configurations, such as flapping-wing configurations (Platzer *et al.*, 2008). In part this has been driven by scientific curiosity, and in part by the need to deal with a very different flight regime at such small scales.

Up to the time of writing, various branches of artificial intelligence (AI) have shown promise in application to battlefield robots, but have perhaps failed to live up to expectations. For example, machine vision has struggled to cope with the real world environments into which these systems are deployed. Often the most critical questions (e.g. 'Is that person armed?') cannot be answered reliably without a human in the loop. A high level of autonomy in motion has been stalled on both the ground and in the air. On the ground, obstacle avoidance has proved a crucial challenge, although huge strides have been made within the past decade. The DARPA Grand Challenge was an excellent barometer of this progress: in 2004, not a single entrant completed the 240 km course for an autonomous land vehicle, the best effort failed to reach the 12 km mark; in 2005 there were five finishers (Thrun and Others, 2006); in 2007 the challenge moved to the urban environment, and six teams finished the course. In the air, the challenge has mostly been about air traffic management. Autonomy of motion must be accompanied by a sense-and-avoid capability, in both military and civilian applications, so as not to risk the lives of human airspace users and people on the ground. For this reason, although autonomy of motion is technically feasible, it has generally not been acceptable at a high level, outside of a research context. Sense-and-avoid capability therefore remains a hot topic of research.

Despite the sometimes seemingly slow progress towards greater autonomy, it can be expected that, concurrent with platform technology advances that will deliver more capability per pound of vehicle, advances in AI will ultimately lead to more service-based human interaction – pervasive systems advanced enough to provide humans with seamless services, as opposed to the current 'operate-it-yourself' paradigm.

12.4   Integration into Civilian Society

There are many potential applications for the current generation of battle-proven UAVs and land robots in the civilian area, and some of these are starting to be realised (although not necessarily with the same platforms as one finds on the battlefield – military applications have, however, been the crucible for much of the technology).

If the function of current CCTV networks is to promote safety by allowing authorities to monitor people and places, then current generations of land robots and UAVs could provide a more flexible alternative that is responsive to crowd movements and events. Some current UAVs have a 'perch and stare' capability that would make them eminently suitable for this task.

The emergency services could also benefit. 'Dull, dirty and dangerous' jobs such as fire-spotting, coastal patrol and traffic monitoring could arguably all be performed more effectively by UAS than by manned aircraft, as could aerial search and rescue. In applications from motorway incident response (where UAVs could be used for quicker damage assessment as well as diversionary route monitoring) to helping fire services plan how they will approach a burning building, UAVs could add significant value. Some of these applications are already being realised: the West Midlands Fire Service, for example, is already using a UAV to assess burnt or burning buildings for safety.

Police forces could benefit from the use of UAVs for intelligence and surveillance missions in advance of operations, or for the purposes of gathering evidence – these applications are closely related to the typical military *modus operandi*. Ground robots already have a place in bomb disposal, and again, this role is familiar to them from the military context.

In the commercial arena, infrastructure monitoring, from that of wind turbines, to bridges, to stadia, to pipelines, as well as monitoring of active construction projects, is an area of great potential application for UAVs. This is particularly true where parts of a structure are difficult to access by any means other than the air, or where the structure itself is in a remote area or on a decommissioned nuclear site inaccessible to humans. Crop monitoring is another commercial application that is being realised on a small scale.

In various earth science communities, UAVs are already being widely employed. Because much of the research that drives the requirements for these UAVs is conducted by universities, some of the systems in actual use have been home-grown (for example, as a collaboration between an earth science department and an engineering department). Remote locations of employment (often abroad, in places such as Antarctica) mean that these systems attract little interest from airspace regulators. Applications include aerial mapping, atmospheric monitoring, volcanology, wildlife surveys and flood monitoring.

Regulation remains an impediment to the wider adoption of robotic technology initially developed for the battlefield, let alone a pervasive deployment in any of the application areas discussed above. Whereas certain properties and modes of operation of these systems are tolerable in a purely military context, they are not acceptable in the civilian arena, and regulators have been reluctant to cede significant ground to manufacturers. One of the main concerns in the context of UAVs is the need to manage the airspace. While sense-and-avoid technology is not considered essential on the battlefield, in crowded civil airspace a collision between a manned aircraft and a UAV is seen as a high risk, which must be mitigated by advances in the technology before widespread acceptance of civil UAV operation can occur. The density of the human population on the ground is also a deciding factor (see below) that is likely to drive redundancy and reliability requirements to a higher standard than is currently accepted for military operations in more sparsely populated regions.

12.5   Likely Social Response

The social response to the introduction of UAVs and land robots is likely to vary widely according to context. Applications that require UAVs to operate far from populated areas are unlikely to raise much concern. Applications that involve operation in populated and urban areas are more likely to provoke a stronger response due to the trade-offs involved, for example finding the right balance between security and safety. Furthermore, if the response to CCTV is anything to go by, civilian UAVs in law enforcement and security applications are likely to get a mixed reception. And detractors may have even more to worry about – after all, having a CCTV camera pan after you is one thing; having a robot companion to look after you is another (see Kernbach, Chapter 11); having an aerial robot following you 'with intent' is yet another.

In the UK, there has been a long-running tension on whether police drivers in pursuit of suspects can (or cannot) be prosecuted for violating traffic laws, especially as the number of people dying in accidents caused by pursuits has increased. We face essentially the same issue with UAVs. For example, in 2010 the Merseyside Police used thermal imaging on a UAV to apprehend a couple of car thieves, only to find they had violated the UK

Civil Aviation Authority's statutory regulations on UAVs. These had been introduced earlier in the year, because of *safety* concerns related not to the use of imaging, but to flying unmanned aircraft in built-up, populated areas, for which a licence was now required. This provoked a public outcry and led to a suspension of the force's UAV operations; and it was not good enough to argue that a desirable outcome had been achieved, whatever the methods used (Lewis, 2010). This case demonstrates the importance of conducting UAV operations in the context of a carefully-drafted regulatory framework, and ensuring that security enforcement shows respect for the rule of law.

In addition to safety concerns, applications that involve active monitoring of the public raise concerns over the balance between security and *privacy*. CCTV is perhaps the best predictor of the social response to widespread use of UAV-borne imaging equipment, used for law enforcement and security. Unsurprisingly perhaps, CCTV and its associated technology has strong detractors and strong advocates. Both sides have a spectrum of arguments, both reasonable and unreasonable. On the one hand, organisations such as the 'No CCTV' campaign (see Fig. 12.5) argue that the proliferation of CCTV cameras, a lack of regulation, and their unprincipled use could lead to invasions of privacy. Moreover, in conjunction with other legislation enacted by a series of UK governments, there are arguments that it could lead to the loss or diminution of civil liberties. There is also a luddite tendency which is just opposed to new technology *per se*. They are balanced on the other hand by those who maintain that CCTV is an essential tool in law enforcement and crime prevention, that it maintains liberties, or assert the well-worn 'if you have nothing to hide, you have nothing to fear' argument.

The personalised version of this latter argument is extremely weak, and although in its generalised form it is more complicated, it can still be refuted (Solove, 2007). For the other two claims, we are moving into much the same territory as was covered by Michael and Michael (Chapter 10) with respect to micro-chip implants, on opt-in versus opt-out, control, and so on. However, as it is with ID cards and implants, so it is with CCTV. The claims that 'CCTV prevents crime' and is popularly supported, is exposed by statistical data to show the case for CCTV is, at best, unproven or of little help (relative to cost) in either crime prevention, detection, or prosecution (Cameron *et al.*, 2008). The temporary illusion of security is consequently dispelled by the new instances of criminal activity, but now citizens have two 'fears': a fear of the original crime and a fear that

Fig. 12.5   The 'No CCTV' campaign champions anti-CCTV protest across the UK
(source: No CCTV, www.no-cctv.org.uk).

their own recorded data, of deliberate or inadvertent behaviour (including
everything they do not do, see Ferscha, Chapter 2) is used in ways they did
not expect or intend.

However, to lose this debate might in turn mean losing to the luddites,
which as a consequence may mean missing out on the real case for civilian
UAVs: a wide range of compelling and potentially beneficial applications for
crowd and traffic safety, short- and long-term planning, disaster response,
and so on. The key requirement is to ensure that people's security, privacy
and civil liberty concerns are properly addressed.

We therefore prefer to rise above this debate. The essential issue is that
it is not the technology itself that is 'right' or 'wrong', 'good' or 'bad', it is
the use to which it is put, especially if unprincipled usage has unexpected
detrimental social impact and we only seek to regulate that usage post hoc.
The use of technology is also particularly problematic when, in the absence
of any evidence or a refusal to accept the available evidence, a policy-maker
mandates that a specific technology solves a problem: for example that ID
cards or biometrics will solve terrorism, illegal immigration, social security
fraud, and so on. They may do no such thing of course. There is just
considerable expense, the original problem is not solved, and now there
are possibly a new set of offences to commit. What is required before

introducing any new technology, as in medicine, is that we should run well-designed randomised controlled trials to get evidence for the efficacity, or otherwise, of the technology, and to anticipate any secondary, tertiary or unexpected consequences.

The conclusion is that the transition between military and civil applications of UAVs should be handled with both forethought and with a regulatory framework in mind during the transition, not appended post hoc as an afterthought. National and international research programmes which pay attention to developing the regulatory framework at the same time as the technology, together with randomised controlled field trials, are essential if we are to reap the real benefits of civilian applications of UAVs carrying sensors and imaging equipment.

12.6 Conclusion: If UniComp Had Today's Battlefield Robots

Today's battlefield robots are highly capable agents in the physical world, even if they are not as autonomous (yet) as some may assume. UniComp would no doubt have made frighteningly effective use of their sensing capabilities for surveillance – Chip and Lilac (the 'they' of the epigraph) would not have remained hidden for long if the 'copter flying over them had been equipped with thermal imaging equipment. As for UniComp controlling UAVs with combat capabilities – with a passive population these would be largely superfluous, but there might have been a requirement in order to 'unify the islands'. In general, though, an artificial omniscience combined with omnipotence supported by the gun and the bomb? Well, that doesn't bear thinking about ...

Chapter 13

Power and Sustainability

Paul D. Mitcheson

Imperial College London

> *Rain in the daytime! Christ and Wei, how strange! And how inconvenient!*
>
> THIS PERFECT DAY, P. 317

13.1 Introduction

This chapter will concentrate on one of the significant difficulties that often restricts the practical use of pervasive sensing – providing a sustainable power supply for all parts of the system. However, unlike many pervasive sensing scenarios that are now beginning to emerge, where sensor networks simply gather data, powering the UniComp system described in Levin's fictional world would be more challenging than just powering very many small devices: there would be significant engineering difficulties in providing power to large systems required to control the Earth's tectonic plates and in being able to control the weather. Such devices are the actuators in Levin's sensor network. Here we will discuss the feasibility of some of these engineering challenges, with a focus on the difficulty of providing the power supply, and show that with today's technology we have actually progressed a surprising way towards achieving some, if not all, of these feats.

In the modern electronic world, we normally do not give a second thought to the supply of power to all our gadgets, whether they are large or small. Home appliances are plugged into the wall; we maintain a power supply for our cars by making occasional trips to the petrol station; and we charge our mobile phones every couple of days. In all of these cases, a specific infrastructure has been put in place to allow us to keep these devices powered. For the car, we have oil pipelines and tankers delivering refined petroleum to stations throughout the world. Electric power is generated in a relatively small number of central power generating plants and transmitted through large distances across countries before being distributed to individual dwellings and commercial buildings, where plugging in is made easy. We power our mobile phones and MP3 players reliably using batteries, and as they start to run low we simply connect them to a mains socket to top them up when it's convenient to do so. Looking at it this way, we already seem to have pretty much solved the problem of supplying power conveniently as and when we need it, in both chemical and electrical forms.

However, one only has to consider the simple example of the need to replace the battery in a smoke alarm to realise that we may not have solved the issue of the provision of power as well as we might, even for today's society, let alone the supply of power in the more technologically driven world described by Levin. Smoke alarms in many homes are battery powered for good reason; the installation of a permanent power supply is too difficult and bothersome for most people and therefore it is common to settle for the trade-off that installation can be achieved easily if, around once a year, people change the alarm's battery. However, UK statistics indicate that people are twice as likely to die in a home fire without a working smoke alarm, and the main reason that smoke alarms do not work is that the battery is flat or missing (Directgov, 2011). Another example of where an important device is powered from a battery, which is more difficult to replace than the one in a smoke alarm, is the heart pacemaker. Even though modern pacemakers have batteries that can last in excess of ten years (Sarma Mallela *et al.*, 2006), many patients must undergo repeat surgery during their life time. Thus, we have identified two clear examples in the early 21st century where running a permanent power supply is difficult or impossible, and replacement of the local power source is undesired.

In Levin's world, each person lives to the age of 62, give or take some months. Whilst ending life at a certain point can be readily achieved in the book using an overdose of the routinely injected chemicals, Uni would also need a mechanism for monitoring the health of each individual in order to be able to schedule medical treatment, to ensure they reach the age of 62. At present, the interest in telehealth and telemedicine is driven, of course, by the desire to improve quality of life (towards a *'eutopia'*?), but in our society the aim is also to reduce the cost of health care. For example, prediction of a heart attack by continuous monitoring of ECG signals, even a short time in advance, can make a significant difference to the survival chances of the patient (Fischell *et al.*, 2001), as well as reducing the cost of the operation and recovery.

Such monitoring requires widespread use of implantable and wearable wireless medical devices. Although the complete control of people's lives as described by Levin does not seem very enticing and would require a very high density of sensors distributed throughout the environment, the electronic monitoring of the health of individuals does seem largely desirable, and this subset of the functionality of Uni alone requires the use of a large number of distributed and implantable sensors. At the same time, if we can develop autonomous self-sustaining wireless sensors they need not be restricted to health and wellbeing applications: they can be used to monitor the health of physical infrastructure (Kim *et al.*, 2007) and help improve the energy efficiency of buildings (Buratti *et al.*, 2010).

Assuming a back end system – some form of UniComp – is in place to receive the data collected by the sensors, the data must somehow be quickly processed and stored. It would appear at first glance that supplying energy at a sufficient rate to some kind of centralised data centre system is not too problematic, as discussed by Pitt in Chapter 1. After all, the present system of centralised generation of power, using reliable transmission and distribution networks, is sufficient to power modern data centres such as the ones run by Google. Although Google is able to perform a very large number of searches very quickly, the kind of computational power required to maintain complete control of Levin's society would present a significant computational challenge. However, if we are more interested in what we can achieve with the scaling of telehealth and telemonitoring, it is interesting to consider whether a system equivalent to Google's would be able to monitor the health of each person on the planet, and, if not how large such a system would have to be and how much power it would consume.

The largest consumer of power and energy in Levin's society might be the several very large systems which control the physical environment. One example from the book of such a large system is one which controls the movement of the Earth's crust in order to be able to stop earthquakes. For total environmental control it is necessary to also be able to modify the weather. Although these two tasks seem very far fetched when stated as plainly as this, present technology is making progress towards these goals, perhaps not through brute force solutions, but in other more subtle ways which we will discuss.

In summary, there are three main types of device that must be powered to create Levin's 'utopian' society, some types of which are in existence or being worked upon by present day researchers. These three classes of device, in likely order of increasing required power level are:

- A data gathering sensor network – a massive number of embedded and distributed sensors obtaining the information necessary to make decisions.
- Centralised intelligence – essentially a massive data centre with exceptional computing power, bandwidth and storage.
- Powerful actuation mechanisms – the means by which large physical environmental systems could be controlled.

In the rest of this chapter we will look in detail at the state of the art of the engineering solutions towards creating such systems and theoretical possibilities in making such a world a reality, from the perspective of providing practical power sources. As we will see, practical engineering and present day research has some surprising parallels with the energy related topics in Levin's book. We will also perform some light-hearted calculations to estimate how much energy some things in Levin's world require when taken more literally than the more subtle solutions which present society has adopted.

13.2 Powering Distributed Sensors

Wireless sensors networks, or WSNs, and body sensors networks, or BSNs, are a growing area of research in both academia and in industrial laboratories. As discussed earlier, providing power to the many individual nodes in these networks can be challenging, especially when devices may be implanted into the human body, as in the case of some BSN devices. However, we may still classify these sensors into two main types, depending on the scenario in which they are used, i.e. those which could theoretically be wired to a fixed supply through conducting wires and those, such as body sensors, which cannot.

13.2.1 *Wired power supply*

Before we review the technological solutions that are currently being investigated and deployed by engineers to provide autonomous power supplies for WSN nodes, we can perform a light-hearted calculation to consider just how impractical complete instrumentation of the environment is, in terms of total monitoring of the population in a way required by Levin, especially if the sensors would have to be wired up. The total land area on earth is approximately 150,000,000 km^2 (Gregory, 2010). If we assume that a requirement for Levin's scenario is some form of sensor is needed for each square metre of land mass then we would need 1.5×10^{14} sensors installed. If each sensor was wired to a power supply over a cable run of average length 10 m using a two core cable, then we would need a total cable length of 3×10^{15} m. Using thin wire of around 0.1 mm diameter we would require a total volume of conductor of approximately 2.4×10^7 m^3. Using copper as the conductor, this is equal to 2×10^8 Tonnes, or 200 million Tonnes of material. To put this in perspective, the estimated accessible world resource of copper is around 1600 million Tonnes (Tilton and Lagos, 2007), so providing power to such a sensor network using copper wires could use around one eighth of the world's total copper resource. Of course, installing this many sensors seems totally unrealistic, but the argument in terms of resource and practicality pushes us to use other forms of power supply for any large sensor network deployment.

13.2.2 *Wireless power supply*

If we are to remove the need to run power to a sensor through a cable, we must either provide a local store of energy or find some other way to deliver energy. Batteries are the most common form of energy storage device for powering portable or remote devices. However, although battery research is a large activity and progress is being made in increasing capacities and reducing their size (Gerasopoulos *et al.*, 2008), batteries will always contain a finite amount of energy and so they will always eventually run out. There is therefore desire to be able to create an effectively infinite energy source to power a device without having to run cables to it, to run, for example, wireless sensors. Current research activity involved with developing these inexhaustible supplies has largely been driven from two application domains (Mitcheson *et al.*, 2008):

- The need to monitor old and ageing infrastructure such as water distribution mains, the electricity grid and large machinery in chemical process plants.
- The desire to provide inexhaustible power supplies for medical implants.

We first need to answer the question of how much power is required in order to run a small sensor node. This is very dependent upon the application, but for simple sensing of temperature and other low bandwidth signals, the practical limits are generally accepted to be between 1 and 100 μW. One of the most energy consuming tasks for a WSN node is probably transmission of video data, and such an application may consume a few hundred mW or more (Kulkarni *et al.*, 2005). Therefore, to make true wireless sensors a reality, we require a power supply capable of delivering somewhere between 1 μW and up to around 1 W in the worst case.

Even though we routinely transmit data wirelessly, which of course corresponds to a transmission of energy, it is still not common to transmit this energy for the purpose of powering remote devices. Transformers are of course wireless, but they link flux between primary and secondary using an iron core, not air, and as such are not in the spirit of what we mean in this context by wireless power transfer. However, success has recently been reported for true wireless power transfer over a distance of a few metres, using resonant magnetic coupling; in effect a coreless transformer. This is not a new concept, but Witricity Corp., a spin out company from Marin Soljacic's work at MIT (Kurs *et al.*, 2007), have been able to make use of advances in electronics and materials to enable the transmission of hundreds of Watts over distances of a few metres. A demonstration system for this technology is shown in Fig. 13.1 and illustrates the typical scenario for such a system: the powering of one, or possibly a small number of devices, over a short distance.

However, such a system uses near-field, or inductive, resonant coupling and aims to reduce the energy radiated into the far field, in order to increase efficiency. This means that the method is not designed for and is not suitable for transferring power over the long distances required for powering very large numbers of distributed sensors. Another possibility is to transmit energy wirelessly over large distances by radiation, for the purposes of powering many sensors at long range. However, the relatively large electric fields required to generate sufficient voltage across the antenna of a small sensor node make this a very challenging task (Yeatman, 2004). So, if wiring up devices is impossible, beaming power wirelessly over large distances is

Fig. 13.1   Resonant magnetic power transfer from Witricity.

impractical, and as batteries require too much maintenance overhead when very many wireless devices are to be deployed, then a different solution has to be sought.

13.2.3   *Energy harvesting*

A possible approach, and one that is being investigated in detail by many research groups, is to provide each sensor with the capacity to generate its own power. This solution is not particularly helpful if a finite fuel supply, such as oil, has to be provided to the sensor to power the generator, but if the generator is able to harvest energy from its natural environment and convert it to electricity, then this is potentially a mechanism for provision of an inexhaustible supply of energy. Possible forms of energy that can be collected are solar, kinetic, thermal and radio frequency (RF).

Early examples of this method of powering devices, called energy harvesting or energy scavenging, are corn-grinding windmills that harvest energy from the wind, and paddle wheels which power textile mills from the kinetic energy of water flowing in rivers. Today we harvest energy from the wind and sun using wind turbines and solar panels in order to provide power to the electricity grid. Thinking on a smaller scale, more in line with powering embedded sensors, the solar powered electronic calculator is also a practical example of a device which is sustainable, because its supply of energy is taken directly from the environment that surrounds it. Another example of a miniature energy harvesting device is something with which

many people will be familiar – the Seiko Kinetic watch. The internals of
the Seiko mechanism are shown in Fig. 13.2.

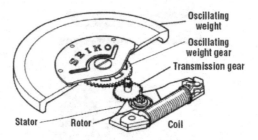

Fig. 13.2   Seiko Kinetic watch power generation mechanism (used with kind permission
of Seiko Watch Corporation).

The basic operating principle of this device is quite simple: as the wearer
moves around, the half-circular mass swings from side to side and turns
a conventional miniature electromagnetic generator through a high ratio
gearbox. The typical power requirement for a wrist watch is around 1 μW,
and so the necessary average output of the generator in this case is quite
modest indeed.

We have identified two main scenarios in which we would like to power
wireless sensor nodes. These are sensors that monitor civil infrastructure
or the environment and ones which are used in body sensor networks with
a primary use in health monitoring. Clearly, the Seiko device is designed to
generate power from the motion of the human body, and whilst the product
is very successful in powering a wristwatch, the locations in which *in-vivo*
implantation of this device could occur would be limited due to its size.
Consequently, efforts have been made by researchers to shrink such devices
using microelectromechanical systems (MEMS) technology. MEMS is the
name given to technology which leverages the fabrication processes of integrated circuits to make very small hybrid electrical-mechanical systems. An
example of such a device, fabricated using MEMS technology and designed
to harvest energy from human body motion, is shown in Fig. 13.3.

Unlike larger scale energy generation schemes, which use the electromagnetic force between coils and magnets to generate electrical power, this
generator uses the electrostatic force, i.e. the attractive force between electrical charges of opposite polarities, in order to convert mechanical work
into electrical energy. This is because, as devices are miniaturised, the scal-

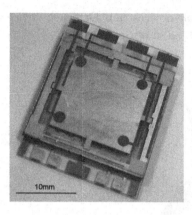

Fig. 13.3   Human body powered generator.

ing effects of different physical effects differ. In the same way that area and volume scale differently with length, so do the electrostatic and electromagnetic forces. The basic principle of operation is as follows: the device is constructed of three plates and the central plate can move up and down between the outer ones, which form a frame for the device as the device is subjected to an external motion. When the moving plate is closest to one of the outer plates during the motion of the device, a charge is placed on the capacitance formed by those plates. As the device frame moves, the distance between the plates increases as the middle plate moves, decreasing the capacitance and increasing the voltage so that electrical power is generated. The device was shown to generate 12 μW from a 40 Hz, 6 mm amplitude motion (Mitcheson *et al.*, 2006). Clearly, 40 Hz is still too high for movement of the human body and, in addition, the reliability of this type of device was not high enough to be capable of producing energy for a critical medical application. An additional problem with this device, and indeed many other moving plate capacitance type generators, is that an initial source of energy is required in order to prime the capacitor. There have been very few, if any, other attempts at prototyping very low frequency energy harvesters using MEMS devices for powering from human body motion, although conventional engineering techniques have been employed (von Büren and Tröster, 2007).

Other devices which have harnessed human motion as a source of power generation have tended to be larger and are not designed to be implantable. However, they are capable of generating orders of magnitude more power

than small implantable devices can. One such device is the knee brace by
Donelan *et al.* (2008), as shown in Fig. 13.4.

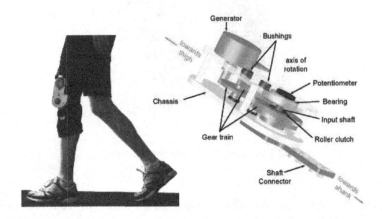

Fig. 13.4   Power generation from human knee (Li *et al.*, 2009) (used with kind permission of the author).

The device generates energy from the bending of the knee during walking
or running. However, the device is designed so that the generator only
engages when the lower leg is falling. Therefore, the wearer does not become
tired whilst wearing the device because the work is effectively performed
by the gravitational force on the leg whilst it falls, rather than by muscle,
and so very little additional work is done by the wearer. Other devices that
have been developed to generate power from human body motion include a
generator mounted in a shoe (Shenck and Paradiso, 2001) and a backpack
which generates energy as you walk (Rome *et al.*, 2005). However, none of
these devices are small enough to be implanted or worn in a way that they
can easily power wireless sensor nodes in or on the body.

Whilst solar is impractical for many body-worn applications and certainly for implantable applications and, as we have discussed, receiving
sufficient RF energy is very challenging, we have not yet considered the
use of thermoelectric devices to convert thermal energy of the body into an
electrical form. A large research effort is underway at IMEC/Holst Centre
in powering body-worn sensors using thermoelectric devices (Leonov *et al.*,
2009), as shown in Fig. 13.5.

Fig. 13.5 Thermoelectric module from IMEC/Holst Centre (Leonov *et al.*, 2009) (used with kind permission of IMEC/Holst Centre and ©2009 IEEE).

Such systems, which make use of the Seebeck effect, generate electrical energy as heat flows through them. Thus, they are often worn on the outside of the body, making contact with the skin on the hot side of the device and with the air on the cold side. Such devices have been shown to generate around 20 μW/cm^2, which is superior to the performance of solar cells in many indoor applications (Leonov *et al.*, 2007).

A final possibility for powering body-implanted sensors is to use what seems like a fuelled system, but in this case one where the supply of fuel is inexhaustible, at least for the required lifetime of the sensor – glucose fuel cells. However, whilst promising in terms of power density, the biocompatibility of such systems still remains a challenge to overcome (Kerzenmacher *et al.*, 2008), and whilst such devices may become feasible in the future they remain impractical at the present time.

Therefore, the two most promising hermetically sealable technologies to power medical sensors seem to be thermal and kinetic energy (Mitcheson, 2010), and so a comparison of the relative performance between the two is important. This comparison can be seen in Fig. 13.6. These graphs have been plotted assuming high efficiency of the thermoelectric devices (70%) and an effectiveness of the kinetic devices of only 1%. This is because whilst thermo devices have been demonstrated as operating quite close to their theoretical limits, kinetic devices have only been shown to operate at around 1% of what they are capable of (Mitcheson *et al.*, 2008). As can be seen, whilst the human subject is running, the performance of kinetic devices and thermal devices is quite similar, but whilst walking the thermoelectric device is superior. Therefore, it is likely that at the moment, thermo devices may be the best choice for powering body-worn sensors, but the potential for kinetic based devices is significant and thus kinetic devices may dominate in the future.

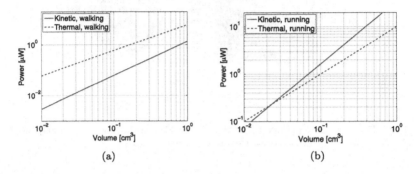

Fig. 13.6 Performance of thermoelectric and kinetic generators on the human body whilst walking (a) and running (b), replotted from Mitcheson (2010).

As discussed previously, another application domain for pervasive sensors is in the monitoring of machines and civil infrastructure, and so we will now discuss a prototype device designed to work from ambient machine vibration. A significant problem with many vibration-driven generators is that they are often tuned to operate at a specific frequency, i.e. the mass and spring structure are tuned to operate at the same frequency as the vibration. This tuning becomes increasingly important for low amplitude vibrations, such as machine motion vibration, and so should the vibration frequency change, such as may happen if the device is fitted to a variable speed motor, the output power will significantly decrease. The device shown in Fig. 13.7 is able to tune its resonant frequency during operation. The generation mechanism uses the electromagnetic force between a magnet and coil to generate power when the cantilever moves. As mentioned earlier, the scaling of forces at the micro scale tends to mean that electromagnetic forces do not perform well at these sizes, and so the generation part of this device could not be substantially miniaturised. The tuning mechanism works by varying the distance between a magnet on a cantilever and a tuning magnet. As the tuning magnet is moved closer to the cantilever, the cantilever is placed into increased tension and thus the resonant frequency increases. The device was shown to be able to tune between 64 and 78 Hz (Ayala *et al.*, 2009) and thus maximise the power density over that range.

Fig. 13.7 Self-tuning energy harvester (Ayala *et al.*, 2009) (used with kind permission of the author and Transducers Research Foundation).

13.2.4 *Energy-harvester powered wireless sensors*

In the discussion above, we have looked at only one part of a self-powered sensor for pervasive use; that of the power generation mechanism. These devices are interesting engineering achievements in their own right, however, and it is worth noting that examples of complete miniature energy harvesting powered wireless sensors have also been demonstrated. One example is a pH sensor powered by an electrostatic energy harvesting device (He *et al.*, 2010), as illustrated in Fig. 13.8. This shows a close up of the generation mechanism and Fig. 13.8(b) shows the complete system.

(a) Rolling rod generator   (b) Complete wireless sensor

Fig. 13.8 Electrostatic self-powered wireless pH sensor (He *et al.*, 2010) (used with kind permission of the author and ©2009 IEEE).

Fig. 13.9   Rotational gravitational torque energy harvester.

Like the electrostatic device shown in Fig. 13.3, this device also requires priming with an initial charge before being able to generate electrical energy. The rod rolls along the curved substrate making and breaking contacts, which allows the rod to be charged and discharged sequentially, generating rapid pulses of current at high voltage into the output circuitry. This device overcomes the problem of electrostatic devices requiring a priming by taking its priming energy directly from a pH sensor. The sensor provides a voltage output (at high impedance) which is proportional to pH. The change in capacitance of the device then amplifies this voltage, which is used to kick a resonant LC tank circuit. The inductor in this tank acts as an antenna for data transmission. The priming voltage, and thus the tank voltage, changes with pH and so, although subject to noise, the system does encode the pH reading from the sensor in the received signal as a function of amplitude. Although this sensor has not been tested for performance when powered from the human body, the fact that the system has a naturally low resonant frequency means that it could be suited for such applications.

Another example of an energy harvesting powered sensor node is a wireless tachometer shown in Fig. 13.9. Unlike the previous device, the wireless tachometer is designed not for body sensor network applications, but for providing a wireless sensing capability on rotating machinery. The device operates using a pendulum attached to a conventional electromagnetic generator. As the frame of the device spins, the gravitational force acting on the pendulum holds it stationary as the rest of the system spins, generating an electromagnetic field across the generator rotor and driving a current through the load.

The device has been demonstrated operating as a wireless tachometer connected to an induction motor, where the speed of the induction machine is wirelessly transmitted to a PC and displayed via a Labview interface. Hundreds of mW can be generated by this system.

Another example of an energy harvesting powered body sensor network is one described by IMEC/Holst Centre as part of their Human++ programme (Gyselinckx *et al.*, 2005). They have demonstrated a working EEG system powered from the heat dissipated from the head of the wearer, supplemented by solar cells, as shown in Fig. 13.10. The system operates on around 0.8 mW average power.

Fig. 13.10   Thermoelectric/solar hybrid powered EEG system from IMEC Holst Centre (used with kind permission of IMEC/Holst Centre).

13.3   Powering the Intelligence

As we have seen, energy harvesting generators are making progress and there have been some examples of working wireless sensors powered by energy harvesting devices. The two main issues which restrict significant deployment of such devices seem to be the need for device miniaturisation and a reduction in manufacturing costs. However, assuming that significant numbers of sensors could be deployed, the data being streamed from these devices would need to be stored and processed by a back end infrastructure, as was discussed earlier in this chapter and by Pitt in Chapter 1.

Whilst Levin's UniComp system might require a vast number of image based data streams to be stored and processed in order to know everything that had happened to every person on the planet, we can start by considering the back end infrastructure required simply to perform what many of us would consider to be a useful task – health monitoring of the population and to alert medical personnel of the need to act if a problem is detected. The first task then is to consider the amount of data that would be created. There are several vital signs that would need to be monitored and possibly stored, which might include blood pressure, blood sugar levels, heart ECG and brain EEG signals. Each of these signals only requires a low sampling-rate, of less than 100 Hz. If we assume an 8-bit resolution for such signals, each one only requires a bandwidth of 0.1 kB/s. We can probably assume therefore that, with a bandwidth per person of 1 kB/s, a significant amount of health monitoring could be achieved. For a world population of 6.7×10^9 people, this is a bandwidth of around 6.7 TB/s. This corresponds to around 2×10^8 TB/year, or 200 EB/year. Given that the total amount of digital content created in 2006 was estimated at 161 EB (Gantz *et al.*, 2007) and that Google processes 20 PB per day in 2008 (Dean and Ghemawat, 2008), equivalent to 7 EB/year, it is reasonable to believe that if some feature extraction was performed within the distributed sensor network, removing some load from the central intelligence, we already have the infrastructure to perform real-time health monitoring of each person on the planet. If we instead simply pass all the data in an unprocessed state to the back end, then after another few iterations of the 18 month Moore's 'law' cycle, Google alone should possess the infrastructure to perform this task by 2015.

A major issue associated with the operation of a large data centre is the large power consumption of the machines and the potentially large power consumption of the equipment required to keep them cool. A typical measure of the efficiency of a data centre is something called 'power usage efficiency', or PUE, which is defined as the total power consumption of a data centre divided by the power consumption of the computer infrastructure inside it. Thus, as the amount of energy required to operate cooling and other ancillary services reduces, the PUE falls towards a value of one. In 2009, Google opened a data centre in Belgium which uses no active cooling mechanism at all, simply relying on relatively low ambient temperatures. In the case that the systems become too hot to continue to operate, Google simply moves workload from that data centre to one which is cooler.

Therefore, if we have the computational power already available to perform much of the status monitoring we may desire, we should answer the question of the power consumption of such a system. It has been estimated that the total power consumption of all IT network and server equipment in use on the planet today is only between 1 and 2% of world electrical energy consumption (Koomey, 2007). Thus, whilst it is important to achieve energy savings to reduce running costs of IT equipment, reducing the power consumption of this equipment alone will not have a profound effect on global energy usage.

13.4   Powering Environmental Controls

In Levin's text, Uni possesses the ability to control the Earth's crust, to dampen the effect of earthquakes and to decide when and where it rains. Here we will discuss the possibility of achieving the tasks of earthquake and weather control and consider the type of equipment that would be required to accomplish these tasks. In some ways, modern day society is already relatively close to being able to control some of these large environmental and weather-related events.

13.4.1   *Earthquakes*

If we wanted to control the movement of the Earth's tectonic plates, we can obtain an idea of how difficult this would be, from an engineering perspective, by considering how much energy would need to be dissipated in such a scheme if we were to dampen out an earthquake. It is estimated that the amount of energy that is released by a severe earthquake is between 10^{15} and 10^{18} J, corresponding to around seven to eight on the Richter scale. To put this in context, this is between 10 and 10,000 times the energy released by the atomic bomb dropped on Hiroshima in 1945. Whilst variable, the main shaking from an earthquake lasts for a period of a few seconds to around one minute. This means that the average power output of such an earthquake is somewhere between 16 TW and 100 PW. If we assume that all of this energy is simply absorbed by an oil shock absorber, heated through 100 degrees Kelvin, then the maximum volume of oil required (assuming a specific heat capacity of oil of 2 kJ/kgK) is around 5×10^{12} kg, or 5 km^3, which is around two thirds of the contents of Loch Ness, the largest (by volume) lake in Scotland.

A more practical approach to earthquake protection has been taken in modern civil engineering practice by trying to protect individual structures, rather than stopping the movement of large land masses. State-of-the-art large actuators and dampers are used in earthquake and wind-induced-vibration reduction systems for large buildings and other structures. The largest passive building-installed damper is currently installed in the 101 story building, Taipei 101. This system essentially comprises a damped resonant system sitting on top of the structure, as shown in Fig. 13.11.

The large pendulum mass is tuned so that when the structure around it moves, the phase difference between the resonating pendulum and the building which houses it means there is a relative motion between them.

Fig. 13.11   Taipei 101 Tuned Mass Damper (used with kind permission of Wei Lei).

This motion can then be damped by large oil filled dampers. This reduces
the sway of the building by up to 40% for wind induced vibrations (Hogg,
2004). It should be noted that such damping technology is not generally
intended to aid the structure if hit by an earthquake, presumably because
shaking of the ground would not necessarily excite the building at its resonant frequency, rendering the damper ineffective. There are many measures
taken to reduce the effect of earthquakes on buildings, but one that is widely
used is to sit the building on a large suspension system (Nawrotzki, 2006).

13.4.2   *Weather*

Although it sounds fanciful, we are already able to control certain aspects
of the weather on our planet. We can consider the earliest example of this
as being a rather basic device, which would not normally be thought of
of as a weather control mechanism, but more of a mechanism for building
protection – the lightning rod. Although simple in concept, we can consider the lightening rod as providing a basic control of localised weather
conditions, by causing lightning strikes to occur at certain chosen points.
However, when we think of what it means to control the weather in the
ways required by Levin, we normally must think on a much larger scale
than just deviating the path of a lightning strike by a few hundred metres.

Currently, it is possible to perform limited control of weather conditions
by causing precipitation, using a technique known as cloud seeding (Dennis,
1980). The usual method involves dispersal of a suitable material, such as

silver iodide, into a cloud. The presence of the seeding material causes ice particles to form in the cloud. These particles then fall either as snow, or if they melt on descent, as rain. Such techniques are presently used to cause precipitation in dry periods, to cause rainfall over one area to keep another dry (often in the case of special events, such as the Beijing Olympics) and to help control other weather conditions such as fog. So, whilst we may not currently be able to completely control rain at will, it is certainly the case that we can already significantly influence it.

However, what about control of temperature? We may be able to modify temperature through the modification of precipitation, but if we wanted to directly heat or cool large masses of the earth, what would be required? One method, previously suggested by von Neumann, was that covering parts of the earth's reflective surface (e.g. glaciers) with dark coloured particles would cause a global temperature rise, due to reduced reflection of the sun's energy from earth. The opposite could be done in order to cool the planet down. However, this technique is not one that could be employed quickly and faster environmental control could be desired. If we consider how much energy would be required to directly heat the environment using some type of infrared heater, comparable to those often used to heat patios, people can be heated outside using around 200 W/m ^{2}. If we consider that a typical city, such as London, has around half of its land area covered with buildings, which are already heated, then we may need to warm around half the land area of a city in the winter if we are to make the outdoor environment more comfortable. Thus, to warm the most central parts of London, say 25 km^2, would require a total power output of 5 GW. Given that the total electrical generation capacity of the UK is around 80 GW, it would be possible to heat a few significant areas in this way, although, obviously, heating more than a few hundred km^2 would prove impossible and the sustainability aspects of such a scheme would be very poor.

13.5 Discussion and Conclusion

As we have seen, there are three main challenges with powering a large pervasive sensing and actuation system which we might call a *human guidance, infrastructure and environment protection system* application provided by Uni. These are: powering the sensors, powering the intelligence and powering the actuation mechanisms. As we have seen, powering the intelligence part of the system, which would probably take the form of a data centre, is not a particularly difficult problem. As discussed, it is probable that the existing computational resource owned by Google would be capable of monitoring the health of every individual on the planet and if not, due to Moore's 'law', such a feature could be achieved in the very near future. The more challenging parts of the system are powering large actuation mechanisms and powering wireless sensors in a reliable sustainable fashion with zero maintenance.

A significant research community exists in the area of power supply for pervasive sensing. To date there has been some commercial success with miniature 'infinite-energy' power generation mechanisms, called energy harvesters, but these devices tend to be tens of cubic cm (Mitcheson *et al.*, 2008). Academic research is focused on smaller devices, often using MEMS technology. Currently, the most promising generation mechanism for powering sensors in a body sensor network is probably thermoelectric generation. These devices can be reliable, as they have no moving parts, work close to their maximum theoretical power density using current materials and achieve higher power densities than solar in many body worn applications. However, whilst kinetic energy based harvesters currently do not outperform thermoelectrics on the human body, existing prototypes only operate at around 1% of their theoretical maximum power density. There is much research focused on this area and a great deal to be gained if the effectiveness of these devices can be improved.

The more speculative aspects of a human guidance and protection system, as discussed by Levin, are the control of the weather and of earthquakes. Whilst present technology does not allow us to stop the movement of the Earth's crust, we have found ways to protect our buildings and infrastructure against such disasters. One of the most impressive things, at least to this author, is that it is possible, and in some parts of the world almost routine, to influence weather through the control of precipitation, and it is possibly more surprising that this technology may indeed precede the first publication of Levin's text.

Bibliography

Aaron, D., Tsouris, C., Hamilton, C. and Borole, A. (2010). Assessment of the effects of flow rate and ionic strength on the performance of an air-cathode microbial fuel cell using electrochemical impedance spectroscopy, *Energies* **3**, pp. 592–606.

Adams, A. and Sasse, A. (1999). Taming the wolf in sheep's clothing: Privacy in multimedia communications, in *Proceedings of ACM Multimedia 1999* (New York: ACM), pp. 101–107.

Ahn, H., Teeters, A., Wang, A., Breazeal, C. and Picard, R. (2007). Stoop to conquer: posture and affect interact to influence computer users' persistence, in Paiva, A., Prade, R. and Picard, R. (eds.), *Proceedings of the Second International Conference on Affective Computing and Intelligent Interaction*, *LNCS*, Vol. 4738 (Berlin: Springer-Verlag), pp. 582–593.

Aiello, L. and Dunbar, R. (1993). Neocortex size, group size and the evolution of language, *Current Anthropology* **34**, pp. 184–193.

Albrecht, K. (2010). Microchip-induced tumors in laboratory rodents and dogs: A review of the literature 1990–2006, in Michael, K. (ed.), *International Symposium on Technology and Society* (Phoenix: IEEE Computer Society Press), pp. 337–349.

Albrecht, K. and McIntyre, L. (2005). *Spychips: How Major Corporations and Government Plan to Track your Every Move with RFID* (Nashville: Thomas Nelson).

Allen, J. and Ferguson, G. (1994). Actions and events in interval temporal logic, *Journal of Logic and Computation* **4**, pp. 531–579.

Allen, S., Colombo, G. and Whitaker, R. (2010a). Cooperation through self-similar social networks, *ACM Transactions on Autonomous Adaptive Systems* **5**, pp. 1–29.

Allen, S., Colombo, G. and Whitaker, R. (2010b). Uttering: Social micro-blogging without the Internet, in *Proceedings of ACM/SIGMOBILE MobiOpp 2010 The Second International Workshop on Mobile Opportunistic Networking* (New York: ACM), pp. 58–64.

Alleyne, R. (2009). The house that twitters, *The Telegraph*, http://www.telegraph.co.uk/science/science-news/6156291/The-house-that-Twitters.html.

Allison, B., McFarland, D., Schalk, G., Zheng, S., Jackson, M. and Wolpaw, J. (2008). Towards an independent brain-computer interface using steady state visual evoked potentials, *Clinical Neurophysiology* **119**, pp. 399–408.

Allwood, J., Laursen, S., Malvido de Rodriguez, C. and Bocken, N. (2006). Well dressed? The present and future sustainability of clothing and textiles in the United Kingdom, Tech. rep., University of Cambridge - Institute for Manufacturing.

Alper, H. and Stephanopoulos, G. (2009). Engineering for biofuels: Exploiting innate microbial capacity or importing biosynthetic potential? *Nature Reviews Microbiology* **7**, pp. 715–723.

Alterovitz, G., Muso, T. and Ramoni, M. (2010). The challenges of informatics in synthetic biology: from biomolecular networks to artificial organisms, *Briefings in Bioinformatics* **11**, pp. 80–95.

Aristotle (1989). *Metaphysics* (Cambridge, MA: Harvard University Press), translated by H. Tredennick and G. Armstrong, 1933 (London: William Heinemann Ltd.).

Asada, M., Hosoda, K., Kuniyoshi, Y., Ishiguro, H., Inui, T., Yoshikawa, Y., Ogino, M. and Yoshida, C. (2009). Cognitive developmental robotics: A survey, *IEEE Transactions on Autonomous Mental Development* **1**, pp. 12–34.

Asimov, I. (1950). Runaround, in *I, Robot* (New York: Gnome Press).

Associated Press (2007). Medical microchip for people may cause cancer, *MSNBC*, http://www.msnbc.msn.com/id/20643620/page/2.

Astor, J. and Adami, C. (2000). A developmental model for the evolution of artificial neural networks, *Artificial Life* **6**, pp. 189–218.

Axelrod, R. (1984). *The evolution of cooperation* (New York: Basic Books).

Ayala, I., Zhu, D., Tudor, M. and Beeby, S. (2009). Autonomous tunable energy harvester, in *Proceedings of PowerMEMS 2009, Washington DC*, pp. 49–52.

Ayer, A. (1987). Mind and body, in Gregory, R. (ed.), *The Oxford Companion to the Mind* (Oxford: Oxford University Press), p. 489.

Babiloni, F., Cincotti, F., Lazzarini, L., Millán, J., Mourino, J., Varsta, M., Heikkonen, J., Bianchi, L. and Marciani, M. (2000). Linear classification of low-resolution EEG patterns produced by imagined hand movements, *IEEE Transactions on Rehabilitation Engineering* **8**, pp. 186–188.

Ballard, J. (1992). Project for a glossary of the twentieth century, in Crary, J. and Kwinter, S. (eds.), *Incorporations, Zone 6* (Cambridge: Zone Books), pp. 268–279.

Balzani, V., Vetturi, M. and Credi, A. (2003). *Molecular Devices and Machines. A Journey into Nanoworld* (Weinheim: Wiley-VCH).

Banbury, C. (1997). *Surviving Technological Innovation in the Pacemaker Industry, 1959-1990* (London: Garland Publishing).

Barabasi, A. (1999). Emergence of scaling in random networks, *Science* **286**, pp. 509–512.

Barad, K. (2003). Posthumanist performativity: Toward an understanding of how matter comes to matter, *Signs: Journal of Women in Culture and Society* **28**, pp. 801–831.

Bartlett, M., Littlewort, G., Fasel, I. and Morvellan, J. (2003). Real time face detection and facial expression recognition: development and application to human-computer interaction, in *Computer Vision and Pattern Recognition Workshop*, Vol. 5 (Los Alamitos: IEEE Computer Society), p. 53.

Bayliss, J. (2003). Use of the evoked potential P3 component for control in a virtual apartment, *IEEE Transactions on Neural Systems and Rehabilitation Engineering* **11**, pp. 113–116.

BBC (2002). US family gets health implants, *BBC News*, http://news.bbc.co.uk/2/hi/health/1981026.stm.

BBC (2009). Residents challenge Google camera, *BBC News*, http://news.bbc.co.uk/1/hi/england/beds/bucks/herts/7980737.stm.

Bensch, M., Karim, A., Mellinger, J., Hinterberger, T., Tangermann, M., Bogda, M., Rosenstiel, W. and Birbaumer, N. (2007). Nessi: an EEG-controlled web browser for severely paralyzed patients, *Computational Intelligence and Neuroscience* **2007**, p. 71863.

Berners-Lee, T., Hendler, J. and Lassila, O. (2001). The semantic web, *Scientific American* **284**, pp. 34–43.

Berry, G. and Boudol, G. (1992). The chemical abstract machine, in *Selected Papers of the Second Workshop on Concurrency and Compositionality* (Essex: Elsevier Science Publishers Ltd.), pp. 217–248.

Best, J. (2004). 44,000 prison inmates to be RFID-chipped, *silicon.com*, http://www.silicon.com/technology/networks/2004/08/02/44000-prison-inmates-to-be-rfid-chipped-39122811/.

Beyer, G., Hammer, M., Kroiss, C. and Schroeder, A. (2009). Component-based approach for realizing pervasive adaptive systems, in *Workshop on User-Centric Pervasive Adaptation UCPA 2009* (unpublished).

Birbaumer, N., Ghanayim, N., Hinterberger, T., Iversen, I., Kotchoubey, B., Kübler, A., Perelmouter, J., Taub, E. and Flor, H. (1999). A spelling device for the paralysed. *Nature* **398**, pp. 297–298.

Boldrini, C., Conti, M. and Passarella, A. (2008). ContentPlace: social-aware data dissemination in opportunistic networks, in *Proceedings of MSWiM 2008* (New York: ACM), pp. 203–210.

Bone, P. and Ellen, P. (1999). Scents in the marketplace: explaining a fraction of olfaction, *Journal of Retailing* **75**, pp. 243–262.

Bonneau, J. (2009). The privacy jungle: on the market for data protection in social networks, in *The Eighth Workshop on the Economics of Information Security (WEIS 2009)*, pp. 1–45.

Bonneau, J., Anderson, J., Anderson, R. and Stajano, F. (2009). Eight friends are enough: social graph approximation via public listings, in *Proceedings of the Second ACM EuroSys Workshop on Social Network Systems (SNS 2009)* (New York: ACM), pp. 13–18.

Boyd, D. and Buckingham, D. (2008). Why youth (heart) social network sites: The role of networked publics in teenage social life, in Buckingham, D. (ed.), *Youth, Identity, and Digital Media* (Cambridge, MA: MIT Press), pp. 119–142.

Boyd, D. and Ellison, N. (2008). Social network sites: Definition, history, and scholarship, *Journal of Computer-Mediated Communication* **13**, pp. 210–230.

Boyd, D. and Hargittai, E. (2010). Facebook privacy settings: Who cares? *First Monday* **15**, http://firstmonday.org/htbin/cgiwrap/bin/ojs/index.php/fm/article/view/3086/2589.

Braddock, S. and O'Mahony, M. (1999). *Techno Textiles: Revolutionary Fabrics for Fashion and Design* (London: Thames & Hudson).

Brant, R. (2010). Birmingham CCTV system leaves police trust in tatters, *BBC News*, http://www.bbc.co.uk/news/uk-10888985.

Braun, S., Beurskens, A., Borm, P., Schack, T. and Wade, D. (2006). The effects of mental practice in stroke rehabilitation: a systematic review, *Archives of Physical Medicine and Rehabilitation* **87**, pp. 842–852.

Braun, S., Kleynen, M., Schols, J., Schack, T., Beurskens, A. and Wade, D. (2008). Using mental practice in stroke rehabilitation: a framework, *Clinical Rehabilitation* **22**, pp. 579–591.

Brauth, S., Hall, W. and Dooling, R. (1991). *Plasticity of development* (Cambridge, MA: MIT Press).

Breazeal, C. (2002). *Designing sociable robots* (Cambridge, MA: MIT Press).

Breyer, J., Ackermann, J. and McCaskill, J. (1997). Evolving reaction-diffusion ecosystems with self-assembling structures in thin films, *Artificial Life* **4**, pp. 25–40.

Brin, D. (1998). *The Transparent Society: Will Technology Force Us to Choose Between Privacy and Freedom?* (New York: Perseus Books).

Broetz, D., Braun, C., Weber, C., Soekadar, S., Caria, A. and Birbaumer, N. (2010). Combination of brain-computer interface training and goal-directed physical therapy in chronic stroke: a case report, *Neurorehabilitation and Neural Repair* **24**, pp. 674–679.

Buratti, C., Ferri, A. and Verdone, R. (2010). An IEEE 802.15.4 wireless sensor network for energy efficient buildings, in Giusto, D., Iera, A., Morabito, G. and Atzori, L. (eds.), *The Internet of Things* (New York, NY: Springer), pp. 329–338.

Business Wire (2003). VeriChip corporation launches first in a planned series of "VeriGuard" secure access control applications; first VeriGuard system now installed and functioning, *BNET*, http://findarticles.com/p/articles/mi_m0EIN/is_2003_Oct_9/ai_108679224/.

Cameron, A., Kolodinski, E., May, H. and Williams, N. (2008). Measuring the effects of video surveillance on crime in Los Angeles, California Research Bureau, CRB-08-007, http://www.library.ca.gov/crb/08/08-007.pdf.

Campbell, A., Choudhury, T., Hu, S., Lu, H., Mukerjee, M., Rabbi, M. and Raizada, R. (2010). NeuroPhone: brain-mobile phone interface using a wireless EEG headset, in *ACM SIGCOMM workshop on Networking, systems, and applications on mobile handhelds* (New York: ACM), pp. 3–8.

Cantrill, S. (2010). Computers in patient care: the promise and the challenge, *Communications of the ACM* **53**, pp. 42–47.

Cao, Y., Fukunaga, A. and Kahng, A. (1997). Cooperative mobile robotics: antecedents and directions, *Autonomous Robots* **4**, pp. 7–27.

Caprari, G., Colot, A., Siegwart, R., Halloy, J. and Deneubourg, J.-L. (2005). Building mixed societies of animals and robots, *IEEE Robotics & Automation Magazine* **12**, pp. 58–65.

Carr, P. and Church, G. (2009). Genome engineering, *Nature biotechnology* **27**, pp. 1151–1162.

Carroll, K. (2009). Employee privacy and physical access control systems, *HID Global*, http://www.hidglobal.com/main/blog/2009/10/employee-privacy-and-physical-access-control-systems.html.

Carson, R. (2002). *Silent Spring* (Boston: Mariner Books).

Cesta, A., Farinelli, A., Iocchi, L., Leone, G., Nardi, D., Pecora, F. and Rasconi, R. (2005). Robotically rich environments for supporting elderly people at home: The RoboCare experience, in *Proceedings of the AISB 2005 Workshop on Robot Companions*, pp. 32–39.

Chavarriaga, R., Biasiucci, A., Förster, K., Roggen, D., Tröster, G. and Millán, J. (2010). Adaptation of hybrid human-computer interaction systems using EEG error-related potentials, in *32nd Annual International Conference of the IEEE Engineering in Medicine and Biology Society (EMBC 2010)*, pp. 4226–4229.

Chavarriaga, R., Ferrez, P. and Millán, J. (2007). To err is human: Learning from error potentials in brain-computer interfaces, in Wang, R., Gu, F. and Shen, E. (eds.), *International Conference on Cognitive Neurodynamics*, pp. 777–782.

Chavarriaga, R. and Millán, J. (2010a). Context-aware brain-computer interfaces, *PerAda Magazine*, doi:10.2417/2201006.003009.

Chavarriaga, R. and Millán, J. (2010b). Learning from EEG error-related potentials in noninvasive brain-computer interfaces, *IEEE Transactions on Neural Systems and Rehabilitation Engineering* **18**, pp. 381–388.

Cho, W. and Choi, H. (2005). Center of pressure (COP) during the postural balance control of high-heeled woman, in *IEEE Engineering in Medicine and Biology 27th Annual Conference*, pp. 2761–2764.

Christensen, C., John, T. and Boyd, J. (2003a). The benefits of fragrances, *Perfumer & Flavorist* **28**, pp. 30–34.

Christensen, C., Warrenburg, S. and Wilson, P. (2003b). Beyond hedonics: Measuring the emotional power of fragrances, in *Fragrance Research* (Esomar Publication), pp. 1–14.

Clark, A. and Grush, R. (1999). Towards a cognitive robotics, *Adaptive Behavior* **7**, pp. 5–16.

Clarke, R. (1994). Human identification in information systems: Management challenges and public policy issues, *Information Technology & People* **7**, pp. 6–37.

Clarke, R. (2010). What is Überveillance? (And what should be done about it?), *IEEE Technology and Society Magazine* **19**, pp. 17–25.

Clausen, J. (2009). Man, machine and in between, *Nature* **457**, pp. 1080–1081.

Collins, W. (1993). *Computer One* (London: No Exit Press).

Constantinescu, C., Kornienko, S., Kornienko, O. and Heinkel, U. (2004). An agent-based approach to support the scalability of change propagation, in *Proceedings of the ISCA 17th International Conference on Parallel and Distributed Computing Systems*, pp. 157–164.

Conti, M. and Kumar, M. (2010). Opportunities in opportunistic computing, *IEEE Computer* **43**, pp. 42–50.

Cooper, R. (1993). *Winning at New Products: Accelerating the Process from Idea to Launch* (Boston: Addison-Wesley).

Coutaz, J., Crowley, J., Dobson, S. and Garlan, D. (2005). Context is key, *Communications of the ACM* **48**, pp. 49–53.

Coutaz, J. and Rey, G. (2002). Foundations for a theory of contextors, in Kolski, C. and Vanderdonckt, J. (eds.), *Computer-aided design of user interfaces*, Vol. 3 (Alphen aan den Rjin: Kluwer), pp. 13–34.

Cozzi, L., D'Angelo, P. and Sanguineti, V. (2006). Encoding of time-varying stimuli in populations of cultured neurons, *Biological Cybernetics* **94**, pp. 335–349.

Craig, J. (2005). *Introduction to Robotics* (Upper Saddle River: Prentice Hall).

Creeger, M. (2006). Better health care through technology, *ACM Queue* **4**, pp. 13–15 [online].

Dale, K. and Husbands, P. (2010). The evolution of reaction-diffusion controllers for minimally cognitive agents, *Artificial Life* **16**, pp. 1–19.

Daly, J. and Wolpaw, J. (2008). Brain-computer interfaces in neurological rehabilitation, *The Lancet Neurology* **7**, pp. 1032–1043.

Dara-Abrams, B. (2008). Toward a model for collaborative gerontechnology: Connecting elders and their caregivers, in *C5 2008: Proceedings of the Sixth International Conference on Creating, Connecting and Collaborating through Computing (c5 2008)* (Washington, DC: IEEE Computer Society), pp. 109–114.

Dautenhahn, K., Woods, S., Kaouri, C., Walters, M., Koay, K. and Werry, I. (2005). What is a robot companion - friend, assistant or butler? in *2005 IEEE/RSJ International Conference on Intelligent Robots and Systems (IROS 2005)*, pp. 1192–1197.

Davies, N. (2009). *Flat Earth News: An Award-winning Reporter Exposes Falsehood, Distortion and Propaganda in the Global Media* (New York: Vintage).

Dean, J. and Ghemawat, S. (2008). MapReduce: simplified data processing on large clusters, *Communications of the ACM - 50th anniversary issue: 1958 - 2008* **51**, pp. 107–113.

DeMarse, T., Wagenaar, D., Blau, A. and Potter, S. (2001). The neurally controlled animat: Biological brains acting with simulated bodies, *Autonomous Robots* **11**, pp. 305–310.

Dennis, A. (1980). *Weather Modification by Cloud Seeding* (New York: Academic Press Inc.).

Dergay, G. and Fiodorov, G. (1996). Odourology serves law and order bodies, in *From Policing in Central and Eastern Europe: Comparing Firsthand Knowledge With Experience From the West* (National Criminal Justice Reference Service (NCJRS)), pp. 355–357.

Di M. Serugendo, G., Foukia, N., Hassas, S., Karageorgos, A., Mostéfaoui, S., Rana, O., Ulieru, M., Valckenaers, P. and van Aart, C. (2003). Self-organisation: Paradigms and applications, in *Engineering Self-Organising Systems*, pp. 1–19.

Dick, P. (1969a). *UBIK* (New York: Double Day).

Dick, P. (1969b). We can remember it for you wholesale, in *The Preserving Machine* (New York: Ace), pp. 134–155.

Directgov (2011). Smoke alarms, http://www.direct.gov.uk/en/HomeAnd Community/InYourHome/FireSafety/DG_071751.

Dishneau, D. (2005). ID chip helps morgue track Katrina victims, *ABC News*, http://www.infowars.com/articles/bb/rfid_no_morgue_track_katrina_victims.htm.

Dittrich, P., Ziegler, J. and Banzhaf, W. (2001). Artificial chemistries – a review, *Artificial Life* **7**, pp. 225–275.

Dobson, J. and Fischer, P. (2003). Geoslavery, *IEEE Technology and Society Magazine* **22**, pp. 47–52.

Donchin, E., Spencer, K. and Wijesinghe, R. (2000). The mental prosthesis: assessing the speed of a P300-based brain-computer interface, *IEEE Transactions on Neural Systems and Rehabilitation Engineering* **8**, pp. 174–179.

Donelan, J., Li, Q., Naing, V., Hoffer, J., Weber, D. and Kuo, A. (2008). Biomechanical energy harvesting: Generating electricity during walking with minimal user effort, *Science* **319**, pp. 807–810.

Dornhege, G., Millán, J., Hinterberger, T., McFarland, D. and Müller, K. (2007). *Towards Brain-Computing Interfacing* (Cambridge, MA: MIT Press).

Dunbar, R. (2003). The social brain: Mind, language, and society in evolutionary perspective, *Annual Review of Anthropology* **32**, pp. 163–181.

Dunbar, R. (2010). *How Many Friends Does One Person Need?: Dunbar's Number and Other Evolutionary Quirks* (London: Faber and Faber).

Durrant-Whyte, H. and Bailey, T. (2006). Simultaneous localization and mapping (SLAM): Part I The essential algorithms, *Robotics and Automation Magazine* **13**, pp. 99–110.

Dutton, W. (2009). The fifth estate emerging through the network of networks, *Prometheus* **27**, pp. 1–15.

Edwards, R. (2010). Complaints about grooming and bullying on Facebook quadruples, The Telegraph. http://www.telegraph.co.uk/news/uknews/crime/7567922/complaints-about-grooming-and-bullying-on-Face book-quadruple.htm/

Eigen, M. (1971). Molekulare Selbstorganisation und Evolution. (Selforganization of matter and the evolution of biological macromolecules), *Naturwissenschaften* **58**, pp. 465–523.

Ellul, J. (1964). *The Technological Society* (New York: Vintage Books).

Ermann, M. D. and Shauf, M. (1997). *Computers, Ethics, and Society* (Oxford: Oxford University Press).

Fairclough, S. (2009). Fundamentals of physiological computing, *Interacting with Computers* **21**, pp. 133–145.

Farrer, J. (2010). Smart dust: Sci-fi applications enabled by synthetic fiber and textiles technology, *Textile: The Journal of Cloth and Culture* **8**, pp. 342–347.

Farrer, J. (2011). Remediation: Discussing fashion textiles sustainability, in Gwilt, A. and Rissanen, T. (eds.), *Shaping Sustainable Fashion: Changing the Way We Make and Use Clothes* (Oxford: Earthscan), pp. 19–33.

Farrer, J. and Fraser, K. (2009). Conscience clothing: Polarisation of the fashion textile market, *Textiles* **36**, pp. 10–13.

Farwell, L. and Donchin, E. (1991). The truth will out: interrogative polygraphy (lie detection) with event-related brain potentials, *Psychophysiology* **28**, pp. 531–547.

FDA (2007). MAUDE adverse event report: VeriChip corporation VeriMed patient identificator VeriChip implant, *US Food and Drug Administration*, http://www.accessdata.fda.gov/scripts/cdrh/cfdocs/cfMAUDE/Detail.CFM?MDRFOI__ID=962453.

Feldman, M. and Chuang, J. (2005). Overcoming free-riding behavior in peer-to-peer systems, *ACM SIGecom Exchanges* **5**, pp. 41–50.

Ferrez, P. and Millán, J. (2008). Error-related EEG potentials generated during simulated brain-computer interaction, *IEEE Transactions on Biomedical Engineering* **55**, pp. 923–929.

Ferscha, A., Hechinger, M., Riener, A., Schmitzberger, H., Franz, M., dos Santos Rocha, M. and Zeidler, A. (2006). Context-aware profiles, in *2nd International Conference on Autonomic and Autonomous Systems* (Phoenix: IEEE Computer Society Press), p. 48.

Fischell, R., Fischell, D. and Fischell, T. (2001). Implantable electronic system with acute myocardial infarction detection and patient warning capabilities, US patent number: 6272379.

Floridi, L. (2007). A look into the future impact of ICT on our lives, *Information Society* **23**, pp. 59–64.

Förster, K., Biasiucci, A., Chavarriaga, R., Millán, J., Roggen, D. and Tröster, G. (2010). On the use of brain decoded signals for online user adaptive gesture recognition systems, in *Pervasive 2010 The Eighth International Conference on Pervasive Computing*, pp. 427–444.

Foster, K. and Jaeger, J. (2007). RFID inside: The murky ethics of implanted chips, *IEEE Spectrum* **44**, pp. 24–29.

Freeman, L. (1996). Some antecedents of social network analysis, *Personality and Individual Differences* **44**, pp. 954–964.

Freeman, L. (2004). *The Development of Social Network Analysis: A Study in the Sociology of Science* (Vancouver: Empirical Press).

Friggieri, A., Michael, K. and Michael, M.G. (2009). The legal ramifications of microchipping people in the United States of America – a state legislative comparison, in *IEEE International Symposium on Technology and Society (ISTAS 2009)* (Phoenix: IEEE Computer Society Press), pp. 1–8.

Fukuda, T., Nakaggawa, S., Kawauchi, Y. and Buss, M. (1989). Structure decision method for self-organizing robots based on cell structure - CEBOT, in *Proceedings of the International Conference on Robotics and Automation* (Phoenix: IEEE Computer Society Press), pp. 695–700.

Futuyma, D. and Slatkin, M. (eds.) (1983). *Coevolution* (Sunderland: Sinauer Associates).

Galán, F., Nuttin, M., Lew, E., Ferrez, P., Vanacker, G., Philips, J. and Millán, J. (2008). A brain-actuated wheelchair: asynchronous and non-invasive brain-computer interfaces for continuous control of robots, *Clinical Neurophysiology* 119, pp. 2159–2169.

Ganguli, I. (2007). Watching the brain lie: Can fMRI replace the polygraph? *The Scientist* 21, p. 40.

Gantt, G. (2004). Implantable radiofrequency transponder system for patient identification and health information, Guidance for industry and FDA staff, Class II special controls guidance document, *US Food and Drug Administration*, http://www.fda.gov/downloads/MedicalDevices/DeviceRegulationandGuidance/GuidanceDocuments/ucm072191.pdf.

Gantz, J., Reinsel, D., Chute, C., Schlichting, W., McArthur, J., Minton, S., Xheneti, I., Toncheva, A. and Manfrediz, A. (2007). The expanding digital universe, IDC white paper.

Gardner, W. (2004). RFID chips implanted in Mexican law-enforcement workers, *Information Week*, http://www.informationweek.com/news/23901004.

Gasson, M. (2010). Human enhancement: Could you become infected with a computer virus? in Michael, K. (ed.), *International Symposium on Technology and Society* (Phoenix: IEEE Computer Society Press), pp. 498–516.

Gerasopoulos, K., McCarthy, M., Royston, E., Culver, J. and Ghodss, R. (2008). Nanostructured nickel electrodes using the tobacco mosaic virus for micro-battery applications, *Journal of Micromechanics and Microengineering* 18, 104003, pp. 1–8.

Gerson, A., Parra, L. and Sajda, P. (2006). Cortically-coupled computer vision for rapid image search, *IEEE Trans Neural Syst Rehabil Eng* 14, pp. 174–179.

Gibson, W. (1984). *Neuromancer* (New York: Ace).

Gilbert, G. and Firestein, S. (2002). Dollars & scents: Commercial opportunities in olfaction, *Nature Neuroscience* 5, pp. 1043–1045.

Glass, T., de Leon, C., Marottoli, R. and Berkman, L. (1999). Population based study of social and productive activities as predictors of survival among elderly Americans, *BMJ* 319, pp. 478–483.

Glotzbach, M. (2009). Google apps is out of beta (yes really), *The Official Google Blog*, http://googleblog.blogspot.com/2009/07/google-apps-is-out-of-beta-yes-really.html.

Goodrich, M., McLain, T., Anderson, J., Sun, J. and Crandall, J. (2007). Managing autonomy in robot teams: observations from four experiments, in *HRI 2007: Proceedings of the ACM/IEEE international conference on Human-robot interaction* (New York: ACM), pp. 25–32.

Graafstra, A. (2006). *RFID Toys: cool projects for home, office, and entertainment* (Indianapolis: Wiley Technology).

Graafstra, A. (2007). Hands on, *IEEE Spectrum* 44, pp. 14–19.

Graafstra, A., Michael, K. and Michael, M.G. (2010). Social-technical issues facing the humancentric RFID implantee sub-culture through the eyes of Amal Graafstra, in Michael, K. (ed.), *International Symposium on Technology and Society* (Phoenix: IEEE Computer Society Press), pp. 498–516.

Granovetter, M. (1973). The strength of weak ties, *American Journal of Sociology* **78**, pp. 1360–1380.

Greely, H. and Illes, J. (2007). Neuroscience-based lie detection: The urgent need for regulation, *American Journal of Law & Medicine* **33**, pp. 377–431.

Greenfield, S. (2008a). *iD: The Quest for Identity in the 21st Century* (London: Sceptre).

Greenfield, S. (2008b). Interviewed by: Malik, K. *Nightwaves* (12 May 2008, 21.15) BBC Radio 3.

Gregory, K. (2010). *The Earth's Land Surface: Landforms and Processes in Geomorphology* (Thousand Oaks: SAGE Publications Ltd).

Gribovskiy, A. and Mondada, F. (2009). Real-time audio-visual calls detection system for a chicken robot, in *Proceedings of the 4th International Conference on Advanced Robotics*, pp. 1–6.

Gwin, J., Gramann, K., Makeig, S. and Ferris, D. (2010). Removal of movement artifact from high-density EEG recorded during walking and running, *Journal of Neurophysiology* **103**, pp. 3526–3534.

Gyselinckx, B., Van Hoof, C., Ryckaert, J., Yazicioglu, R., Fiorini, P. and Leonov, V. (2005). Human++: Autonomous wireless sensors for body area networks, in *Proceedings of the IEEE Custom Integrated Circuits Conference*, pp. 13–20.

Haggerty, K. (2006). One generation is all they need, *The Star*, http://www.thestar.com/printarticle/136744.

Haken, H. (1977). *Synergetics: An introduction* (Berlin: Springer-Verlag).

Haraway, D. (1991). A cyborg manifesto: Science, technology, and socialist-feminism in the late twentieth century, in *Simians, Cyborgs and Women: The Reinvention of Nature* (London: Routledge), pp. 149–181.

Harle, R. and Hopper, A. (2006). Cluster tagging: robust fiducial tracking for smart environments, in Hazae, M., Krumm, J. and Strang, T. (eds.), *Location- and context-awareness*, *LNCS*, Vol. 3987 (Berlin: Springer-Verlag), pp. 14–29.

Harris, M. (2010). Liar! Can brain scans show whether people are telling the truth? *IEEE Spectrum* **47**, pp. 38–43.

Harris, S. (2008). Catwalk goes techno, *Engineering and Technology Magazine*, http://eandt.theiet.org/magazine/2008/18/catwalk-goes-techno-0818.cfm.

Haselager, P., Vlek, R., Hill, J. and Nijboer, F. (2009). A note on ethical aspects of BCI, *Neural Networks* **22**, pp. 1352–1357.

He, C., Kiziroglou, M., Yates, D. and Yeatman, E. (2010). MEMS energy harvester for wireless biosensors, in *Proceedings of the IEEE International Conference on Micro Electro Mechanical Systems*, pp. 172–175.

Heidegger, M. (1954). *The Question Concerning Technology, and Other Essays* (New York: Harper Torchbooks).

Herrmann, K., Muhl, G. and Geihs, K. (2005). Self management: The solution to complexity or just another problem? *IEEE Distributed Systems Online* **6**.

Hettinger, E. (1989). Justifying intellectual property, *Philosophy and Public Affairs* **18**, pp. 31–52.

Hibbert, R. (2006). *Textile Innovation (2nd Edition)* (Manchester: Textiles Institute).

Hinterberger, T., Widman, G., Lal, T., Hill, J., Tangermann, M., Rosenstiel, W., Schölkopf, B., Elger, C. and Birbaumer, N. (2008). Voluntary brain regulation and communication with electrocorticogram signals, *Epilepsy and Behavior* **13**, pp. 300–306.

Hirsch, A. (2006). Effects of ambient odours on slot-machine in Las Vegas casino, *Psychology & Marketing* **12**, pp. 585–594.

Hirsch, A. and Gomez, R. (1995). Weight reduction through inhalation of odourants, *Journal of Neurological and Orthopaedic Medicine and Surgery* **16**, pp. 28–31.

Hochberg, L., Serruya, M., Friehs, G., Mukand, J., Saleh, M., Caplan, A., Branner, A., Chen, D., Penn, R. and Donoghue, J. (2006). Neuronal ensemble control of prosthetic devices by a human with tetraplegia, *Nature* **442**, pp. 164–171.

Hogg, C. (2004). Taipei 101: A view from the top, *BBC News*, http://news.bbc.co.uk/1/hi/world/asia-pacific/4137865.stm.

Hough, A. (2010). Please Rob Me website causes fury for 'telling burglars when Twitter users are not home', *The Telegraph*, http://www.telegraph.co.uk/technology/twitter/7266120/Please-Rob-Me-website-tells-burglars-when-Twitter-users-are-not-home.html.

Huber, N. and Michael, K. (2007). Vendor perceptions of how RFID can minimize product shrinkage in the retail supply chain, in *1st Annual RFID Eurasia 2007*, pp. 1–6.

Hunter, R. (1989). *Foundations of Colloid Science* (Oxford: Oxford University Press).

Hutton, T. (2009). The organic builder: A public experiment in artificial chemistries and self-replication, *Artificial Life* **15**, pp. 21–28.

Huxley, A. (1932). *Brave New World* (London: Chatto & Windus).

Hyyppa, M. and Maki, J. (2003). Social participation and health in a community rich in stock of social capital, *Health Education Research* **18**, pp. 770–779.

ICT Results (2008). Smart clothes: Textiles that track your health, *ScienceDaily*, http://www.sciencedaily.com/releases/2008/03/080329121141.htm.

Illich, I. (1973). *Text: Tools for Conviviality* (New York: HarperCollins).

Indiveri, G., Chicca, E. and Douglas, R. (2009). Artificial cognitive systems: From VLSI networks of spiking neurons to neuromorphic cognition, *Cognitive Computation* **1**, pp. 119–127.

Iossifidis, I., Lawitzky, G., Knoop, S. and Zöllner, R. (2005). Towards benchmarking of domestic robotic assistants, in Prassler, E., Lawitzky, G., Stopp, A., Grunwald, G., Hägele, M., Dillmann, R. and Iossifidis, I. (eds.), *Advances in Human Robot Interaction*, Vol. 14 (Berlin: Springer-Verlag), pp. 403–414.

Ip, R., Michael, K. and Michael, M.G. (2008). The social implications of human-centric chip implants: A scenario – "thy chipdom come, thy will be done", in *Sixth CollECTeR Iberoamérica 2008*, pp. 1–11.

Iturrate, I., Antelis, J., Minguez, J. and Kübler, A. (2009). Non-invasive brain-actuated wheelchair based on a P300 neurophysiological protocol and automated navigation, *IEEE Transactions on Robotics* **25**, pp. 614–627.

Jameson, F. (1991). *Postmodernism, or, The Cultural Logic of Late Capitalism* (London: Verso Press).

Java, A., Song, X., Finin, T. and Tseng, B. (2009). Why we twitter: An analysis of a microblogging community, in Zhang, H., Spiliopoulou, M., Mobasher, B., Giles, C., McCallum, A., Nasraoui, O., Srivastava, J. and Yen, J. (eds.), *Advances in Web Mining and Web Usage Analysis, LNCS*, Vol. 5439 (Berlin: Springer-Verlag), pp. 118–138.

Jelasity, M., Babaoglu, O., Laddaga, R., Nagpal, R., Zambonelli, F., Sirer, E., Chaouchi, H. and Smirnov, M. (2006). Interdisciplinary research: Roles for self-organization, *IEEE Intelligent Systems* **21**, pp. 50–58.

Jellinek, S. (1999). Understanding the psychodynamic effects of odors, *Aroma-Chology Review* **IV**, 2.

Johnson, K., Michael, K. and Michael, M.G. (2007). Consumer awareness in Australia on the prospect of humancentric RFID implants for personalized applications, in *International Conference on Mobile Business* (Phoenix: IEEE Computer Society Press).

Johnson, S. (2005). *Everything that's bad is good for you: How today's popular culture is actually making us smarter* (New York: Riverhead).

Joy, B. (2000). Why the future doesn't need us, *Wired*, http://www.wired.com/wired/archive/8.04/joy_pr.html.

Jung, T.-P., Makeig, S., Humphries, C., Lee, T.-W., McKeown, M., Iragui, V. and Sejnowski, T. (2000). Removing electroencephalographic artifacts by blind source separation, *Psychophysiology* **37**, pp. 163–178.

Kac, E. (1997). Time capsule, http://www.ekac.org/figs.html.

Kahan, L. (2004). Medical devices; general hospital and personal use devices; classification of implantable radiofrequency transponder system for patient identification and health information, *US Food and Drug Administration*, http://www.fda.gov/OHRMS/DOCKETS/98fr/04-27077.htm.

Kapoor, A., Burleson, W. and Picard, R. (2007). Automatic prediction of frustration, *International Journal of Human-Computer Studies* **65**, pp. 724–736.

Kargl, F., Lawrence, E., Fischer, M. and Lim, Y. (2008). Security, privacy and legal issues in pervasive eHealth monitoring systems, in *7th International Conference on Mobile Business*, pp. 296–304.

Karim, A., Hinterberger, T., Richter, J., Mellinger, J., Neumann, N., Flor, H., Kübler, A. and Birbaumer, N. (2006). Neural internet: web surfing with brain potentials for the completely paralyzed, *Neurorehabilitation and Neural Repair* **20**, pp. 508–515.

Kaye, J. (2001). Symbolic olfactory display, Masters Thesis, Boston: MIT Media Lab.

Kephart, J. and Chess, D. (2003). The vision of autonomic computing, *Computer* **36**, pp. 41–50.

Kernbach, S. (2008). *Structural Self-organization in Multi-Agents and Multi-Robotic Systems* (Berlin: Logos Verlag).

Kernbach, S. (ed.) (2011). *Handbook of Collective Robotics: Fundamentals and Challenges* (Singapore: Pan Stanford Publishing).

Kernbach, S., Thenius, R., Kernbach, O. and Schmickl, T. (2009). Re-embodiment of honeybee aggregation behavior in artificial micro-robotic system, *Adaptive Behavior* **17**, pp. 237–259.

Kerzenmacher, S., Ducrée, J., Zengerle, R. and von Stetten, F. (2008). Energy harvesting by implantable abiotically catalyzed glucose fuel cells, *Journal of Power Sources* **182**, pp. 1–17.

Khan, Z. (1998). Attitudes towards intelligent service robots, Tech. Rep. TRITA-NA-P9821, IPLab-154, Nada, KTH Stockholm.

Khornak, L. (1982). *FASHION 2001* (London: Kolumbus Books).

Kim, S., Pakzad, S., Culler, D., Demmel, J., Fenves, G., Glaser, S. and Turon, M. (2007). Health monitoring of civil infrastructure using wireless sensor networks, in *Proceedings of the 6th international conference on Information processing in sensor networks*, pp. 254–263.

Koomey, J. (2007). Estimating the total power consumption by servers in the U.S. and the world, `http://citeseerx.ist.psu.edu/viewdoc/download? doi=10.1.1.87.5562&rep=rep1&type=pdf`.

Kornienko, S., Kornienko, O., Constantinescu, C., Pradier, M. and Levi, P. (2005). Cognitive micro-agents: individual and collective perception in mi-crorobotic swarm, in *Proceedings of the IJCAI-05 Workshop on Agents in real-time and dynamic environments*, pp. 33–42.

Kornienko, S., Kornienko, O. and Levi, P. (2004). Multi-agent repairer of dam-aged process plans in manufacturing environment, in *Proceedings of the 8th Conference on Intelligent Autonomous Systems (IAS-8)*, pp. 485–494.

Krishnamurthy, B. and Wills, C. (2008). Characterizing privacy in online social networks, in *Proceedings of the first workshop on Online social networks (WOSP 2008)* (New York: ACM), pp. 37–42.

Krishnamurthy, B. and Wills, C. (2010a). On the leakage of personally identifiable information via online social networks, *SIGCOMM Computer Communication Review* **40**, pp. 112–117.

Krishnamurthy, B. and Wills, C. (2010b). Privacy leakage in mobile online social networks, in *Proceedings of the 3rd Workshop on Online Social Networks (WOSN 2010)* (New York: ACM), pp. 1–9.

Kübler, A. and Birbaumer, N. (2008). Brain-computer interfaces and commu-nication in paralysis: extinction of goal directed thinking in completely paralysed patients? *Clinical Neurophysiology* **119**, pp. 2658–2666.

Kübler, A., Furdea, A., Halder, S., Hammer, E., Nijboer, F. and Kotchoubey, B. (2009). A brain-computer interface controlled auditory event-related poten-tial (P300) spelling system for locked-in patients, *Annals of the New York Academy of Sciences* **1157**, pp. 90–100.

Kübler, A., Furdea, A., Halder, S. and Hösle, A. (2008). Brain painting – BCI meets art, in *4th International Brain-Computer Interface Workshop and Training Course*, pp. 361–366.

Kübler, A., Nijboer, F., Mellinger, J., Vaughan, T., Pawelzik, H., Schalk, G., Mc-Farland, D., Birbaumer, N. and Wolpaw, J. (2005). Patients with ALS can use sensorimotor rhythms to operate a brain computer interface, *Neurology* **64**, pp. 1775–1777.

Kuhl, B., Dudukovic, N., Kahn, I. and Wagner, A. (2007). Decreased demands on cognitive control reveal the neural processing benefits of forgetting, *Nature Neuroscience* **10**, pp. 908–914.

Kulkarni, P., Ganesan, D. and Shenoy, P. (2005). The case for multi–tier camera sensor networks, in *Proceedings of the international workshop on Network and operating systems support for digital audio and video*, pp. 141–146.

Kumar, V. (2007). Implantable RFID chips: Security versus ethics, in Fischer-Hübner, S., Duquenoy, P., Zuccato, A. and Mariucci, L. (eds.), *The Future of Identity in the Information Society, IFIP International Federation for Information Processing*, Vol. 262 (Berlin: Springer-Verlag), pp. 151–157.

Kurs, A., Karalis, A., Moffatt, R., Joannopoulos, J., Fisher, P. and Soljačić, M. (2007). Wireless power transfer via strongly coupled magnetic resonances, *Science* **317**, pp. 83–86.

Kurzweil, R. (2005). *The Singularity Is Near: When Humans Transcend Biology* (London: Penguin).

Kwak, H., Lee, C., Park, H. and Moon, S. (2010). What is Twitter, a social network or a news media? in *WWW 2010: Proceedings of the 19th international conference on World Wide Web* (New York: ACM), pp. 591–600.

Lacour, S., Wagner, S., Narayan, R., Li, T. and Suo, Z. (2006). Stiff subcircuit islands of diamondlike carbon for stretchable electronics, *Journal of Applied Physics* **100**, pp. 014913-1–014913-6.

Langleben, D., Loughead, J., Bilker, W., Ruparel, K., Childress, A., Busch, S. and Gur, R. (2005). Telling truth from lie in individuals with fast event-related fMRI, *Human Brain Mapping* **26**, pp. 262–272.

Laurance, J. (2010). The pill that reminds you when it's time to take your next dose, *The Independent*, http://www.independent.co.uk/life-style/health-and-families/health-news/the-pill-that-reminds-you-when-its-time-to-take-your-next-dose-2052320.html.

Law, J. (1997). *Puppets of Nostalgia* (Princeton: Princeton University Press).

Lecuyer, A., Lotte, F., Reilly, R., Leeb, R., Hirose, M. and Slater, M. (2008). Brain-computer interfaces, virtual reality, and videogames, *Computer* **41**, pp. 66–72.

Leeb, R., Friedman, D., Müller-Putz, G., Scherer, R., Slater, M. and Pfurtscheller, G. (2007). Self-paced (asynchronous) BCI control of a wheelchair in virtual environments: a case study with a tetraplegics, *Computational Intelligence and Neuroscience* **2007**, p. 79642.

Leeb, R., Gubler, M., Tavella, M., Miller, H. and Millán, J. (2010). On the road to a neuroprosthetic hand: A novel hand grasp orthosis based on functional electrical stimulation, in *International Conference of IEEE Engineering in Medicine and Biology Society (EMBC 2010)*, pp. 146–149.

Lehmann, L., Keller, L., West, S. and Roze, D. (2007). Group selection and kin selection: Two concepts but one process, *Proceedings of the National Academy of Sciences* **104**, pp. 6736–6739.

Leigh, D. (2009). Trafigura drops bid to gag Guardian over MP's question, *The Guardian*, http://www.guardian.co.uk/media/2009/oct/13/trafigura-drops-gag-guardian-oil.

Leonov, V., Torfs, T., Fiorini, P. and Van Hoof, C. (2007). Thermoelectric converters of human warmth for self-powered wireless sensor nodes, *IEEE Sensors Journal* **7**, pp. 650–657.

Leonov, V., Van Hoof, C. and Vullers, R. (2009). Thermoelectric and hybrid generators in wearable devices and clothes, in Lo, B. and Mitcheson, P. (eds.), *Sixth International Workshop on Wearable and Implantable Body Sensor Networks (BSN 2009)*, pp. 195–200.

Levin, I. (1970). *This Perfect Day* (New York: Random House).

Levin, I. (1972). *The Stepford Wives* (New York: Random House).

Lewan, T. (2007). Chips: High-tech aids or tracking devices? Debate rages over proliferation of ever-more-precise tracking, *Security on msnbc.com*, http://www.msnbc.msn.com/id/19904543/.

Lewis, P. (2010). Eye in the sky arrest could land police in the dock, *The Guardian*, http://www.guardian.co.uk/uk/2010/feb/15/police-drone-arrest-backfires.

Li, Q., Naing, V. and Donelan, J. (2009). Development of a biomechanical energy harvester, *Journal of NeuroEngineering and Rehabilitation* **6**, 22.

Lindley, S., Harper, R. and Sellen, A. (2008). Designing for elders: Exploring the complexity of relationships in later life, in *BCS-HCI 2008: Proceedings of the 22nd British HCI Group Annual Conference on People and Computers* (London: British Computer Society), pp. 77–86.

Locher, T., Meier, R., Schmid, S. and Wattenhofer, R. (2007). Push-to-pull peer-to-peer live streaming, in *21st International Symposium on Distributed Computing (DISC), Lemesos, Cyprus, Springer LNCS 4731*, pp. 388–402.

Lu, Y.-E., Roberts, S., Cheng, T., Dunbar, R., Lió, P. and Crowcroft, J. (2009). On optimising personal network size to manage information flow, in *CNIKM 2009: Proceeding of the 1st ACM international workshop on Complex networks meet information & knowledge management* (New York: ACM), pp. 19–26.

Lungarella, M., Metta, G., Pfeifer, R. and Sandini, G. (2003). Developmental robotics: a survey, *Connection Science* **15**, pp. 151–190.

Lyon, D. (ed.) (2003). *Surveillance as Social Sorting: Privacy, Risk and Digital Discrimination* (London: Routledge).

Makeig, S., Gramann, K., Jung, T.-P., Sejnowski, T. and Poizner, H. (2009). Linking brain, mind and behavior, *International Journal of Psychophysiology* **73**, pp. 95–100.

Mamei, M., Menezes, R., Tolksdorf, R. and Zambonelli, F. (2006). Case studies for self-organization in computer science, *Journal of Systems Architecture* **52**, pp. 443–460.

Maney, K. (2004). Get chipped, then charge without plastic – you are the card, *USA Today*, http://www.usatoday.com/money/industries/technology/maney/2004-05-12-chip_x.htm.

Mann, S. (1998). Humanistic intelligence: Wearcomp as a new framework for intelligent signal processing, *Proceedings of the IEEE* **86**, pp. 2123–2151.

Mann, S. (2001). Can humans being clerks make clerks be human? – Exploring the fundamental difference between UbiComp and WearComp, *Informationstechnik und Technische Informatik* **43**, pp. 97–106.

Manz, A., Jenkins, G. and Tillotson, J. (2005). Scent whisper, in *Proceedings of IET Seminar MEMS Sensors & Actuators*, pp. 97–104.

Marcel, S. and Millán, J. (2007). Person authentication using brainwaves (EEG) and maximum a posteriori model adaptation, *IEEE Transactions on Pattern Analysis and Machine Intelligence* **29**, pp. 743–748.

Marcuse, H. (1964). *One-Dimensional Man: Studies in the Ideology of Advanced Industrial Society* (Boston: Beacon Press).

Martel, S., Mohammadi, M., Felfoul, O., Zhao, L. and Pouponneau, P. (2009). Flagellated magnetotactic bacteria as controlled MRI-trackable propulsion and steering systems for medical nanorobots operating in the human microvasculature, *International Journal of Robotics Research* **28**, pp. 571–582.

Martinoia, S., Sanguineti, V., Cozzi, L., Berdondini, L., van Pelt, J., Tomas, J., Le Masson, G. and Davide, F. (2004). Towards an embodied in vitro electrophysiology: the NeuroBIT project, *Neurocomputing* **58-60**, pp. 1065–1072.

Martinoli, A., Ijspeert, A. and Gambardella, L. (1999). A probabilistic model for understanding and comparing collective aggregation mechansims, in *ECAL 1999: Proceedings of the 5th European Conference on Advances in Artificial Life* (Berlin: Springer-Verlag), pp. 575–584.

Maslow, A. (1943). A theory of human motivation, *Psychological Review* **50**, pp. 370–396.

Masters, A. and Michael, K. (2007). Lend me your arms: the use and implications of humancentric RFID, *Electronic Commerce Research and Applications* **6**, pp. 29–39.

Mayer-Schönberger, V. (2009). *Delete: The Virtue of Forgetting in the Digital Age* (Princeton: Princeton University Press).

Mazzolai, B., Mattoli, V., Laschi, C., Salvini, P., Ferri, G., Ciaravella, G. and Dario, P. (2008). Networked and cooperating robots for urban hygiene: the EU funded DustBot project, in *The 5th International Conference on Ubiquitous Robots and Ambient Intelligence (URAI 2008)*.

McClintock, M. (1971). Menstrual synchrony and suppression, *Nature* **229**, pp. 244–245.

McClintock, M. and Stern, K. (1998). Regulation of ovulation by human pheromones, Department of Psychology, The University of Chicago.

McCulloch, M., Jezierski, T., Broffman, M., Hubbard, A., Turner, K. and Janecki, T. (2006). Interdiagnostic accuracy of canine scent detection in early stage and late stage lung and breast cancers, *Integrated Cancer Therapy* **5**, pp. 30–39.

McDonough, W. and Braungart, M. (2002). *Cradle to Cradle: Remaking the Way We Make Things* (New York: North Point Press).

McGee, E. and Maguire, G. (2007). Becoming a borg to become immortal: Regulating brain implant technologies, *Cambridge Quarterly of Healthcare Ethics* **16**, pp. 291–302.

McLuhan, M. (1964). *Understanding Media: The Extensions of Man* (New York: McGraw-Hill).

Mead, M. (1978). *Culture and Commitment: The New Relationships Between the Generations in the 1970s* (Garden City: Anchor Books/Doubleday).

Mejia, E. and Casey, S. (2007). Passive integrated transponder tag with unitary antenna core, US patent number : 7176846.

Mellinger, J., Schalk, G., Braun, C., Preissl, H., Rosenstiel, W., Birbaumer, N. and Kübler, A. (2007). An MEG-based brain-computer interface (BCI). *Neuroimage* **36**, pp. 581–593.

Menon, C., de Negueruela, C., Millán, J., Tonet, O., Carpi, F., Broschart, M., Ferrez, P., Buttfield, A., Tecchio, F., Sepulveda, F., Citi, L., Laschi, C., Tombini, M., Dario, P., Rossini, P. and de Rossi, D. (2009). Prospects of brain-machine interfaces for space system control, *Acta Astronautica* **64**, pp. 448–456.

Michael, K. (2003a). The technological trajectory of the automatic identification industry: the application of the systems of innovation (SI) framework for the characterisation and prediction of the auto-ID industry, Ph.D. thesis, University of Wollongong.

Michael, K. (2003b). Trends in the selection of automatic identification technology in electronic commerce applications, in Cerpa, N. and Bro, P. (eds.), *Building Society Through E-Commerce: e-Government, e-Business and e-Learning* (Talca: University of Talca), pp. 135–152.

Michael, K. and Masters, A. (2004). Applications of human transponder implants in mobile commerce, in Callaos, N., Lesso, W., Kurogi, S., Tanaka, A. and Castillo, O. (eds.), *The 8th World Multi-Conference on Systemics, Cybernetics and Informatics*, Vol. V (Orlando: International Institute of Informatics and Systemics), pp. 505–512.

Michael, K. and Masters, A. (2006). Realised applications of positioning technologies in defense intelligence, in Essam, D. and Abbass, H. (eds.), *Applications of Information Systems to Homeland Security and Defense* (Boston: IDG Press), pp. 164–192.

Michael, K. and McCathie, L. (2005). The pros and cons of RFID in supply chain management, in Brookes, W., Lawrence, E., Steele, R. and Chang, E. (eds.), *International Conference on Mobile Business (ICMB 2005)*, pp. 623–629.

Michael, K. and Michael, M.G. (2005). Microchipping people: The rise of the electrophorus, *Quadrant* **414**, pp. 22–33.

Michael, K. and Michael, M.G. (2007). *From Dataveillance to Überveillance and the Realpolitik of the Transparent Society* (Wollongong: University of Wollongong Press).

Michael, K. and Michael, M.G. (2008). Homo electricus and the continued speciation of humans, in Quigley, M. (ed.), *The Encyclopedia of Information Ethics and Security* (Hershey: IDG Press), pp. 312–318.

Michael, K. and Michael, M.G. (2009). *Innovative Automatic Identification and Location Based Services: from Bar Codes to Chip Implants* (Hershey: IGI Global).

Michael, K., Michael, M.G. and Abbas, R. (2009). The dilemmas of using wearable computing to monitor people: An extended metaphor on the tracking of prison inmates and parolees, in *Australia and New Zealand Society of Criminology Conference: Crime and Justice Challenges in the 21st Century: Victims, Offenders and Communities (Perth, Western Australia)*.

Michael, K., Roussos, G., Huang, G., Chattopadhyay, A., Gadh, R., Prabhu, B. and Chu, P. (2010). Planetary-scale RFID services in an age of Überveillance, *Proceedings of the IEEE* **98**, pp. 1663–1671.

Michael, M.G. (2010). Demystifying the number of the beast in the book of revelation: Examples of ancient cryptology and the interpretation of the 666 conundrum, in Michael, K. (ed.), *IEEE Symposium on Technology and Society* (Wollongong: IEEE Computer Society), pp. 23–41.

Michael, M.G., Fusco, S. and Michael, K. (2008). A research note on ethics in the emerging age of Überveillance, *Computer Communications* **31**, pp. 1192–1199.

Michael, M.G.. and Michael, K. (2006). National security: The social implications of the politics of transparency, *Prometheus* **24**, pp. 359–364.

Michael, M.G. and Michael, K. (2009). Microchipping people and the assault on privacy, *Quadrant* **LIII**, pp. 85–89.

Michael, M.G. and Michael, K. (2010). Towards a state of Überveillance, *IEEE Technology and Society Magazine* **29**, pp. 9–16.

Middendorf, M., McMillan, G., Calhoun, G. and Jones, K. (2000). Brain-computer interfaces based on the steady-state visual-evoked response, *IEEE Transactions on Rehabilitation Engineering* **8**, pp. 211–214.

Millán, J. and Carmena, J. (2010). Invasive or noninvasive: Understanding brain-machine interface technology, *Engineering in Medicine and Biology Magazine, IEEE* **29**, pp. 16–22.

Millán, J., Ferrez, P., Galán, F., Lew, E. and Chavarriaga, R. (2008). Non-invasive brain-machine interaction, *International Journal of Pattern Recognition and Artificial Intelligence* **22**, pp. 959–972.

Millán, J., Renkens, F., Mouriño, J. and Gerstner, W. (2004). Noninvasive brain-actuated control of a mobile robot by human EEG, *IEEE Transactions on Biomedical Engineering* **51**, pp. 1026–1033.

Millán, J., Rupp, R., Müller-Putz, G., Murray-Smith, R., Giugliemma, C., Tangermann, M., Vidaurre, C., Cincotti, F., Kübler, A., Leeb, R., Neuper, C., Müller, K. and Mattia, D. (2010). Combining brain-computer interfaces and assistive technologies: State-of-the-art and challenges, *Frontiers in Neuroscience* **4**, p. 161.

Millikan, A. (2010). I am a cyborg and I want my Google implant already, *The Atlantic*, http://www.theatlantic.com/technology/archive/2010/09/i-am-a-cyborg-and-i-want-my-google-implant-already/63806/.

Miranda, E., Bull, L., Gueguen, F. and Uroukov, I. (2009). Computer music meets unconventional computing: Towards sound synthesis with in vitro neuronal networks, *Computer Music Journal* **33**, pp. 9–18.

Mitcheson, P. (2010). Energy harvesting for human wearable and implantable bio-sensors, in *Proceedings of 32nd IEEE Engineering in Medicine and Biology Conference, EMBC 2010, Argentina*, pp. 3432–3436.

Mitcheson, P., Miao, P., Stark, B., Yeatman, E., Holmes, A. and Green, T. (2006). MEMS electrostatic micropower generator for low frequency operation, *Sensors and Actuators A: Physical* **115**, pp. 523–529.

Mitcheson, P., Yeatman, E., Rao, G., Holmes, A. and Green, T. (2008). Energy harvesting from human and machine motion for wireless electronic devices, *Proceedings of the IEEE* **96**, pp. 1457–1486.

Moreno, J. (1934). *Who shall survive?* : *a new approach to the problem of human interrelations* (Washington, DC: Nervous and Mental Disease Publishing Company).

Morozov, E. (2011). *The Net Delusion* (London: Allen Lane).

Motani, M., Srinivasan, V. and Nuggehalli, P. (2005). PeopleNet: engineering a wireless virtual social network, in *Proceedings of MobiCom 2005* (New York: ACM), pp. 243–257.

Mugler, E., Bensch, M., Halder, S., Rosenstiel, W., Bogdan, M., Birbaumer, N. and Kübler, A. (2008). Control of an internet browser using the P300 event-related potential, *International Journal of Bioelectromagnetism* **10**, pp. 56–63.

Müller-Putz, G. and Pfurtscheller, G. (2008). Control of an electrical prosthesis with an SSVEP-based BCI, *IEEE Transactions on Biomedical Engineering* **55**, pp. 361–364.

Müller-Putz, G., Scherer, R. and Pfurtscheller, G. (2007). Control of a two-axis artificial limb by means of a pulse width modulated brain-switch, in *European Conference for the Advancement of Assistive Technology*, pp. 888–892.

Müller-Putz, G., Scherer, R., Pfurtscheller, G. and Rupp, R. (2006). Brain-computer interfaces for control of neuroprostheses: from synchronous to asynchronous mode of operation, *Biomedizinische Technik* **51**, pp. 57–63.

Nawrotzki, P. (2006). Earthquake protection for buildings and other structures, Presented at the International Forum – Earthquake Prognostics, http://www.gerb.com/en/bibliothek/downloads/dokumente/06Berlin EPI-Center.pdf.

Newman, M. (2002). Spread of epidemic disease on networks, *Physical Review E* **66**, p. 016128.

Newman, M., Barabási, A. and Duncan, W. (2006). *The Structure and Dynamics of Networks* (Princeton: Princeton University Press).

Nicolelis, M. (2001). Actions from thoughts, *Nature* **409**, pp. 403–407.

Nijboer, F., Sellers, E., Mellinger, J., Jordan, M., Matuz, T., Furdea, A., Halder, S., Mochty, U., Krusienski, D., Vaughan, T., Wolpaw, J., Birbaumer, N. and Kübler, A. (2008). A P300-based brain-computer interface for people with amyotrophic lateral sclerosis, *Clinical Neurophysiology* **119**, pp. 1909–1916.

Nijholt, A., Tan, D., Allison, B., Millán, J., Graimann, B. and Jackson, M. (2008a). Brain-computer interfaces for HCI and games, in *Proceedings ACM CHI 2008*, pp. 3925–3928.

Nijholt, A., Tan, D., Pfurtscheller, G., Brunner, C., Millán, J., Allison, B., Graimann, B., Popescu, F., Blankertz, B. and Müller, K. (2008b). Brain-computer interfacing for intelligent systems, *IEEE Intelligent Systems* **23**, pp. 72–79.

Nonami, K. (2007). Prospect and recent research and development for civil use autonomous unmanned aircraft as UAV and MAV, *Journal of System Design and Dynamics* **1**, pp. 120–128.

Norman, D. (2007). *The Design of Future Things* (New York: Basic Books).

Novellino, A., D'Angelo, P., Cozzi, L., Chiappalone, M., Sanguineti, V. and Martinoia, S. (2007). Connecting neurons to a mobile robot: an in vitro bidirectional neural interface, *Computational Intelligence and Neuroscience* **2007**, pp. 1–13.

Oestreicher, L. and Severinson Eklundh, K. (2006). User expectations on human-robot co-operation, in *The 15th IEEE International Symposium on Robot and Human Interactive Communication, 2006. ROMAN 2006*, pp. 91–96.

Orbell, J. and Dawes, R. (1993). Social welfare, cooperators' advantage, and the option of not playing the game, *Journal of Economic Behavior and Organization* **12**, pp. 87–106.

Oreskes, N. and Conway, E. (2010). *Merchants of Doubt: How a Handful of Scientists Obscured the Truth on Issues from Tobacco Smoke to Global Warming* (London: Bloomsbury Press).

Orwell, G. (1949). *Nineteen Eighty-Four* (London: Secker & Warburg).

Pantic, M. and Rothcrantz, J. (2000). Automatic analysis of facial expressions: State of the art, *IEEE Transactions on Pattern Analysis and Machine Intelligence* **22**, pp. 1424—1445.

Pantic, M. and Rothcrantz, J. (2003). Towards an affect-sensitive multimodal human-computer interaction, *Proceedings of the IEEE* **919**, pp. 1370–1390.

Pasparakis, G., Krasnogor, N., Cronin, L., Davis, B. and Alexander, C. (2010). Controlled polymer synthesis – from biomimicry towards synthetic biology, *Chemical Society Reviews* **39**, pp. 286–300.

Passant, A., Hastrup, T., Bojars, U. and Breslin, J. (2008). Microblogging: A semantic and distributed approach, in *Proceedings of the 4th Workshop on Scripting for the Semantic Web (SFSW2008)*, pp. 1–12.

Patil, A., Dubois, T., Sifer, N., Bostic, E., Gardner, K., Quah, M. and Bolton, C. (2004). Portable fuel cell systems for America's army: technology transition to the field, *Journal of Power Sources* **136**, pp. 220–225.

Perakslis, C. and Wolk, R. (2006). Social acceptance of RFID as a biometric security method, *IEEE Technology and Society Magazine* **25**, pp. 32–42.

Perrin, X., Chavarriaga, R., Colas, F., Siegwart, R. and Millán, J. (2010). Brain-coupled interaction for semi-autonomous navigation of an assistive robot. *Robotics and Autonomous Systems* **58**, pp. 1246–1255.

Pfurtscheller, G., Müller, G., Pfurtscheller, J., Gerner, H. and Rupp, R. (2003). "Thought"-control of functional electrical stimulation to restore handgrasp in a patient with tetraplegia, *Neuroscience Letters* **351**, pp. 33–36.

Pfurtscheller, G. and Neuper, C. (1994). Event-related synchronization of mu rhythm in the EEG over the cortical hand area in man, *Neuroscience Letters* **174**, pp. 93–96.

Pfurtscheller, G. and Neuper, C. (2001). Motor imagery and direct brain-computer communication, *Proceedings of the IEEE* **89**, pp. 1123–1134.

Picard, R. (1997). *Affective Computing* (Cambridge, MA: MIT Press).

Pilato, F. (2003). Human 'chipping' on its way with VeriChip, *mobile magazine*, http://www.mobilemag.com/2003/11/27/human-chipping-on-its-way-with-verichip/.

Pinker, S. (1994). *The Language Instinct* (New York: William Morrow).

Pitt, J. and Bhusate, A. (2010). Privacy in pervasive and affective computing environments, in Portela, I. and Cruz-Cunha, M. (eds.), *Information Communication Technology Law, Protection and Access Rights, Global Approaches and Issues* (Hershey: IGI Global), pp. 168–187.

Platzer, M., Jones, K., Young, J. and Lai, J. (2008). Flapping-wing aerodynamics: Progress and challenges, *AIAA Journal* **46**, pp. 2136–2149.

Poole, S. (2005). What Zelda did, *The Guardian*, http://www.guardian.co.uk/books/2005/jul/02/highereducation.news.

Pope, A., Bogart, E. and Bartolome, D. (1995). Biocybernetic system evaluates indices of operator engagement in automated task, *Biological Psychology* **40**, pp. 187–195.

Popescu, F., Fazli, S., Badower, Y., Blankertz, B. and Müller, K. (2007). Single trial classification of motor imagination using 6 dry EEG electrodes. *PLoS ONE* **2**, p. e637.

Preti, G., Charles, J., Wysocki, J., Kurt, T., Sondheimer, J. and Leyden, J. (2003). Male axillary extracts contain pheromones that affect pulsatile secretion of luteininizing and mood in women recipients, *Biology of Reproduction* **68**, pp. 2107–2113.

Prinzel, L. (2002). Research on hazardous states of awareness and physiological factors in aerospace operations, NASA/TM-2002-211444.

Priya, S. and Inman, D. (2008). *Energy Harvesting Technologies* (Berlin: Springer-Verlag).

Queisser, H. (1990). *The Conquest of the Microchip: Science and Business in the Silicon Age* (Harvard: Harvard University Press).

Quinn, B. (2002). Hussein Chalayan, fashion and technology, *Fashion Theory* **6**, 4.

Rani, P., Sarkar, N. and Liu, C. (2005). Maintaining optimal challenge in computer games through real-time physiological feedback, in *11th International Conference on Human-Computer Interaction*, pp. 184–192.

Rasch, B., Buchel, C., Gais, S. and Born, J. (2007). Odour cues during slow-wave sleep prompt declarative memory consolidation, *Science* **315**, pp. 1426–1429.

Rebsamen, B., Burdet, E., Guan, C., Zhang, H., Teo, C., Zeng, Q., Ang, M. and Laugier, C. (2006). A brain-controlled wheelchair based on P300 and path guidance, in *IEEE International Conference on Biomedical Robotics and Biomechatronics (BioRob 2006)*, pp. 1101–1106.

Reger, B., Fleming, K., Sanguineti, V., Alford, S. and Mussa-Ivaldi, F. (2000). Connecting brains to robots: an artificial body for studying the computational properties of neural tissues, *Artificial Life* **6**, pp. 307–324.

Remarque, E. (1929). *Im Westen nichts Neues (All Quiet on the Western Front)* (Berlin: Ullstein).

Renegar, B. and Michael, K. (2009). The privacy-value-control harmonization for RFID adoption in retail, *IBM Systems Journal* **48**, pp. 8.1.1–8.1.14.

Reynolds, C. and Picard, R. (2004). Affective sensors, privacy, and ethical contracts, in *CHI 2004 extended abstracts on Human factors in computing systems* (New York: ACM), pp. 1103–1106.

Reynolds, M. (2004). Despite the hype, microchip implants won't deliver security, Tech. rep., Gartner.

Richter, K. and Frappaolo, P. (2002). Enforcement Actions/Warning Letters: Applied Digital Solutions, Inc. 08-Nov-02, *US Food and Drug Administration*, http://www.fda.gov/ICECI/EnforcementActions/WarningLetters/2002/ucm145298.htm.

Roberts, S., Dunbar, R., Pollet, T. and Kuppens, T. (2009). Exploring variation in active network size: Constraints and ego characteristics, *Social Networks* **31**, pp. 138–146.

Robinson, L., Brittain, K., Lindsay, S., Jackson, D. and Oliver, P. (2009). Keeping in touch everyday (KITE) project: developing assistive technologies with people with dementia and their carers to promote independence, *International Psychogeriatrics* **21**, pp. 494–502.

Robinson, L., Olivier, P., Monk, A. and Wherton, J. (2008). The Ambient Kitchen; how technology can provide helpful hints, *Journal of Dementia Care* **16**, pp. 38–39.

Rodota, S. and Capurro, R. (2005). Ethical aspects of ICT implants in the human body, *EGE*, http://ec.europa.eu/european_group_ethics/docs/avis20_en.pdf.

Rogers, E. (1995). *Diffusion of Innovations* (New York: The Free Press).

Rome, L., Flynn, L., Goldman, E. and Yoo, T. (2005). Generating electricity while walking with loads, *Science* **309**, pp. 1725–1728.

Rose, S. (2008). In search of the God neuron, *The Guardian*, http://www.guardian.co.uk/books/2008/dec/27/books-about-the-brain.

Rouhi, A. (2002). Exploring the chemical senses, *Chemical and Engineering News* **80**, pp. 24–29.

Ruffini, G., Dunne, S., Farrés, E., Cester, I., Watts, P., Silva, S., Grau, C., Fuentemilla, L., Marco-Pallarés, J. and Vandecasteele, B. (2007). ENOBIO dry electrophysiology electrode; first human trial plus wireless electrode system, in *29th International Conference of the IEEE Engineering Medicine and Biology Society*, pp. 6689–6693.

Rulon, M. (2006). New technology raises privacy concerns, *USA Today*, http://www.usatoday.com/tech/news/surveillance/2006-08-31-rfid-privacy_x.htm.

Russell, J., Bachorowski, J. and Fernandez-Dols, J. (2003). Facial and vocal expressions of emotion, *Annual Review of Psychology* **54**, 329–349.

Saini, A. (2009). The brain police: Judging murder with an MRI, *Wired Magazine*, http://www.wired.co.uk/magazine/archive/2009/06/features/guilty?page=all.

Sarma Mallela, V., Ilankumaran, V. and Srinivasa Rao, N. (2006). Trends in cardiac pacemaker batteries, *Indian Pacing and Electrophysiology Journal* **4**, pp. 201–212.

Sayama, H. (2009). Swarm chemistry, *Artificial Life* **15**, pp. 105–114.

Schauer, F. (2010). Neuroscience, lie-detection, and the law: contrary to the prevailing view, the suitability of brain-based lie-detection for courtroom or forensic use should be determined according to legal and not scientific standards. *Trends in Cognitive Sciences* **14**, pp. 101–103.

Scheeres, J. (2002). Why, Hello, Mr. Chips, *Wired,* http://www.wired.com/science/discoveries/news/2002/04/51575.

Scherer, R., Lee, F., Schlögl, A., Leeb, R., Bischof, H. and Pfurtscheller, G. (2008). Toward self-paced brain-computer communication: navigation through virtual worlds, *IEEE Transactions on Biomedical Engineering* **55**, pp. 675–682.

Schlögl, A., Keinrath, C., Zimmermann, D., Scherer, R., Leeb, R. and Pfurtscheller, G. (2007). A fully automated correction method of EOG artifacts in EEG recordings, *Clinical Neurophysiolgy* **118**, pp. 98–104.

Schmickl, T. and Crailsheim, K. (2008). Trophallaxis within a robotic swarm: bio-inspired communication among robots in a swarm, *Autonomous Robots* **25**, pp. 171–188.

Schmidt, A. (1999). Implicit human-computer interaction through context, in *2nd Workshop on Human Computer Interaction with Mobile Devices,* pp. 191–199.

Schroeder, A., Zwaag, M. and Hammer, M. (2008). A middleware architecture for human-centred pervasive adaptive applications, in *1st PerAda Workshop (SASO 2008)* (unpublished).

Schwager, M., Detweiler, C., Vasilescu, I., Anderson, D. and Rus, D. (2008). Data-driven identification of group dynamics for motion prediction and control, *Journal of Field Robotics* **25**, pp. 305–324.

Schwarz, A., Van Langenhove, L., Guermonprez, P. and Deguillemont, D. (2010). A roadmap on smart textiles, *Textile Progress* **42**, pp. 99–180.

Sellers, E. and Donchin, E. (2006). A P300-based brain-computer interface: initial tests by ALS patients, *Clinical Neurophysiology* **117**, pp. 538–48.

Sellers, E., Turner, P., Sarnacki, W., Mcmanus, T., Vaughan, T. and Matthews, B. (2009). A novel dry electrode for brain-computer interface, in *13th International Conference on Human-Computer Interaction,* pp. 623–631.

Serbedzija, N. (2010). Reflective assistance for eldercare environments, in *Second Workshop on Software Engineering in Health Care* (New York: ACM), pp. 104–110.

Serbedzija, N., Calvosa, A. and Ragnoni, A. (2008). Vehicle as a co-driver, in *Proceedings of the First Annual International Symposium on Vehicular Computing Systems.*

Serbedzija, N. and Fairclough, S. (2009). Biocybernetic loop: from awareness to evolution, in *IEEE Congress on Evolutionary Computation,* pp. 2063–2069.

Seymour, S. (2008). *Fashioning Technology* (Berlin: Springer-Verlag).

Sheckley, R. (1967). Watchbird, in *Untouched by Human Hands* (London: Four Square Books), pp. 72–90.

Shenck, N. and Paradiso, J. (2001). Energy scavenging with shoe-mounted piezoelectrics, *IEEE Micro* **21**, pp. 30–42.

Shikfa, A., Önen, M. and Molva, R. (2010). Privacy and confidentiality in context-based and epidemic forwarding, *Computer Communications* **33**, pp. 1493–1504.

Siciliano, B. and Khatib, O. (eds.) (2008). *Springer Handbook of Robotics* (Berlin: Springer-Verlag).

Sidener, J. (2006). Implant ID chips called big advance, Big Brother, *Union-Tribune*, http://tribes.tribenetwork.com/time_4_hemp/thread/d03f0a0b-cc04-4fc0-9966-2ae28c01aa60.

Sieberg, D. (2006). Is RFID tracking you? *CNN News*, http://edition.cnn.com/2006/TECH/07/10/rfid/.

Simmons, L., Sharma, N., Baron, J.-C. and Pomeroy, V. (2008). Motor imagery to enhance recovery after subcortical stroke: who might benefit, daily dose, and potential effects. *Neurorehabilitation and Neural Repair* **22**, pp. 458–467.

Sitaram, R., Zhang, H., Guan, C., Thulasidas, M., Hoshi, Y., Ishikawa, A., Shimizu, K. and Birbaumer, N. (2006). Temporal classification of multichannel near-infrared spectroscopy signals of motor imagery for developing a brain-computer interface, *Neuroimage* **34**, pp. 1416–1427.

Solove, D. (2004). *The Digital Person: Technology and Privacy in the Information Age* (New York: New York University Press).

Solove, D. (2007). 'I've got nothing to hide' and other misunderstandings of privacy, *San Diego Law Review* **44**, pp. 745–772.

Spence, S. (2008). Devil's advocate: the case against fMRI lie detection, *Legal and Criminological Psychology* **13**, pp. 11–25.

Spencer, J., Thomas, M. and McClelland, J. (2008). *Toward a Unified Theory of Development: Connectionism and Dynamic Systems Theory Re-Considered* (Oxford: Oxford University Press).

Srinivasan, S., Moghadam, A., Gi, S. and Hen, H. (2007). Schulzrinne 7DS - node cooperation and information exchange in mostly disconnected network, in *Proceedings of IEEE International Conference on Communication*, pp. 3921–3927.

Starner, T. (1993). Lizzy: MIT's wearable computer design, http://www.media.mit.edu/wearables/lizzy/lizzy/.

Strangman, G., Culver, J., Thompson, J. and Boas, D. (2002). A quantitative comparison of simultaneous BOLD fMRI and NIRS recordings during functional brain activation, *NeuroImage* **17**, pp. 719–731.

Strogatz, S. (2001). Exploring complex networks, *Nature* **410**, pp. 268–276.

Suchman, L. (2007). *Human-Machine Reconfigurations: Plans and Situated Actions* (Cambridge: Cambridge University Press).

Sullivan, T., Deiss, S., Jung, T. and Cauwenberghs, G. (2008). A brain-machine interface using dry-contact, low-noise EEG sensors, in *2008 IEEE Int Symposium on Circuits and Systems*, pp. 1986–1989.

Swartz, L. (2001). Overwhelmed by technology: How did user interface failures on board the USS Vincennes lead to 290 dead? http://xenon.stanford.edu/~lswartz/vincennes.pdf.

Tamburrini, G. (2009). Brain to computer communication: Ethical perspectives on interaction models, *Neuroethics* **2**, pp. 137–149.

Tangermann, M., Krauledat, M., Grzeska, K., Sagebaum, M., Vidaurre, C., Blankertz, B. and Müller, K. (2008). Playing pinball with non-invasive BCI, in *Proceedings of NIPS*, pp. 1641–1648.

Thrun, S. and Others (2006). Stanley: The robot that won the DARPA Grand Challenge, *Journal of Field Robotics* **23**, pp. 661–692.

Tilton, J. and Lagos, G. (2007). Assessing the long-run availability of copper, *Resources Policy* **32**, pp. 19–23.

Tonin, L., Leeb, R., Tavella, M., Perdikis, S. and Millán, J. (2010). The role of shared-control in BCI-based telepresence, in *IEEE International Conference on Systems, Man and Cybernetics*, pp. 1462–1466.

Traulsen, A. and Nowak, M. (2006). Evolution of cooperation by multilevel selection, *Proceedings of the National Academy of Sciences USA* **103**, pp. 10952–10955.

Travers, J. and Milgram, S. (1969). An experimental study of the small world problem, *Sociometry* **32**, pp. 425–443.

Trevarthen, A. and Michael, K. (2007). Beyond mere compliance of RFID regulations by the farming community: A case study of the Cochrane dairy farm, in *The Sixth International Conference on Mobile Business* (Los Alamitos: IEEE Computer Society), pp. 1–8.

Trevarthen, A. and Michael, K. (2008). The RFID dairy farm: Towards total farm management, in *7th International Conference on Mobile Business* (Los Alamitos: IEEE Computer Society), pp. 1–10.

Trivers, R. (1971). The evolution or reciprocal altruism, *Quarterly Review of Biology* **46**, pp. 35–57.

Trocchia, P. and Ainscough, T. (2006). Characterizing consumer concerns about identification technology, *International Journal of Retail & Distribution Management* **34**, pp. 609–620.

Turkle, S. (2011). *Alone Together: Why We Expect More from Technology and Less from Each Other* (New York: Basic Books).

Vaerenberg, B., Govaerts, P., De Ceulaer, G., Daemers, K. and Schwauwers, K. (2011). Experiences of the use of FOX, an intelligent agent, for programming cochlear implant sound processors in new users, *International Journal of Audiology* **50**, pp. 50–58.

Vallina-Rodriguez, N., Hui, P. and Crowcroft, J. (2009). Has anyone seen my goose? Social network services in developing regions, in *CSE 2009: Proceedings of the 2009 International Conference on Computational Science and Engineering* (Phoenix: IEEE Computer Society Press), pp. 1048–1053.

Vasilash, G. (2006). "Safe" & cooperative robots, *Automotive Design & Production* (June 2006).

Verbunt, J., Seelen, H., Ramos, F., Michielsen, B., Wetzelaer, W. and Moennekens, M. (2008). Mental practice-based rehabilitation training to improve arm function and daily activity performance in stroke patients: a randomized clinical trial, *BMC Neurology* **8**, doi:10.1186/1471-2377-8-7.

von Büren, T. and Tröster, G. (2007). Design and optimization of a linear vibration-driven electromagnetic micro-power generator, *Sensors and Actuators A: Physical* **135**, pp. 765–775.

Wang, J. and Loui, M. (2009). Privacy and ethical issues in location-based tracking systems, in *Proceedings of the 2009 IEEE International Symposium on Technology and Society (ISTAS 2009)* (Phoenix: IEEE Computer Society Press), pp. 1–4.

Wang, J., Pohlmeyer, E., Hanna, B., Jiang, Y.-G., Sajda, P. and Chang, S.-F. (2009). Brain state decoding for rapid image retrieval, in *Proceedings of the 17th ACM International Conference on Multimedia* (New York: ACM), pp. 945–954.

Warwick, K. (2002). *I, Cyborg* (Salt Lake City: Century).

Watanabe, M., Furukawa, M., and Kakazu, Y. (2001). Intelligent AGV driving toward an autonomous decentralized manufacturing system, *Robotics and Computer Integrated Manufacturing* **17**, pp. 57–64.

Watts, D., Dodds, P. and Newman, M. (2002). Identity and search in social networks, *Science* **296**, pp. 1302–1305.

Weckert, J. and Moor, J. (2006). The precautionary principle in nanotechnology, *Nanoethics* **20**, pp. 191–204.

Weiser, M. (1991). The computer for the 21st century, *Scientific American (Special Issue: Communications, Computers, and Networks)* **265**, pp. 94–104.

West, D., Quigley, A. and Kay, J. (2007). MEMENTO: a digital-physical scrapbook for memory sharing, *Personal Ubiquitous Comp* **11**, pp. 313–328.

Wheelwright, S. and Clark, K. (1992). *Revolutionizing product development: quantum leaps in speed, efficiency, and quality* (New York: Free Press).

Wilkes, D., Alford, A., Pack, R., Rogers, T., Peters II, R. and Kawamura, K. (1998). Toward socially intelligent service robots, *Applied Artificial Intelligence* **12**, pp. 729–766.

Williamson, J., Murray-Smith, R., Blankertz, B., Krauledat, M. and Müller, K. (2009). Designing for uncertain, asymmetric control: Interaction design for brain-computer interfaces, *International Journal of Human Computer Studies* **67**, pp. 827–841.

Winfield, A. and Griffiths., F. (2010). Towards the emergence of artificial culture in collective robotic systems, in Levi, P. and Kernbach, S. (eds.), *Symbiotic Multi-Robot Organisms Reliability, Adaptability, Evolution* (Berlin: Springer-Verlag), pp. 425–433.

Wolfson, O., Xu, B. and Sistla, A. (2004). An economic model for resource exchange in mobile peer to peer networks, in *Proceedings of the 16th International Conference on Scientific and Statistical Database Management (SSDBM 2004)* (Los Alamitos: IEEE Computer Society), pp. 235–244.

Wolpaw, J., Birbaumer, N., McFarland, D., Pfurtscheller, G. and Vaughan, T. (2002). Brain-computer interfaces for communication and control, *Clinical Neurophysiology* **113**, pp. 767–791.

Wood, J. (1999). Osmosensing by bacteria: Signals and membrane-based sensors, *Microbiology and Molecular Biology Reviews* **63**, pp. 230–262.

World Commission on Environment and Development (1987). *Our common future* (Oxford: Oxford University Press).

World Net Daily (2006). Employees get microchip implants: Company requires controversial device for certain workers, *World Net Daily*, http://www.wnd.com/?pageId=34751.

Yarney, S. (2010). *The Banjo Player* (Cambridge: Story Bay Press).

Ye, J., Coyle, L., Dobson, S. and Nixon, P. (2009). Using situation lattices in sensor analysis, in *Proceedings of the 7th IEEE International Conference on Pervasive Computing and Communications (Percom 2009)*, pp. 1–11.

Ye, J. and Dobson, S. (2009). Human-behaviour study with situation lattices, in *Proceedings of the IEEE International Conference on Systems, Man and Cybernetics* (Phoenix: IEEE Computer Society Press), pp. 343–348.

Yeatman, E. (2004). Advances in power sources for wireless sensor nodes, in *Proceedings of the first International Workshop on Wearable and Implantable Body Sensor Networks*, pp. 6–7.

Zambonelli, F. and Mamei, M. (2004). Spatial computing: An emerging paradigm for autonomic computing and communication, in *International Workshop on Autonomic Communication*, pp. 44–57.

Zander, T. and Jatzev, S. (2009). Detecting affective covert user states with passive brain-computer interfaces, in *Proceedings of the International Conference on Affective Computing and Intelligent Interaction*, pp. 1–9.

Zhao, D. and Rosson, M. (2009). How and why people twitter: the role that micro-blogging plays in informal communication at work, in *GROUP 2009: Proceedings of the ACM 2009 international conference on Supporting group work* (New York: ACM), pp. 243–252.

All URLs were accessed May 11, 2011.

Index